VISUALLY SPEAKING:
ART THERAPY AND THE DEAF

Photo by N. Bachrach.

ABOUT THE EDITOR

Ellen G. Horovitz, Ph.D., LCAT, ATR-BC is Professor, Chair of Creative Arts Therapy, and Director of the Art Therapy Clinic at Nazareth College of Rochester. She has had over 30 years of experience with myriad patient populations and specializes in family art therapy with the Deaf. Dr. Horovitz currently is in private practice. She is the author of numerous articles, book chapters and the following books: *Spiritual Art Therapy: An Alternate Path, A Leap of Faith: The Call to Art* and *Art Therapy As Witness: A Sacred Guide.* As well, Dr. Horovitz has directed and produced over ten films available in DVD format (Dr. Horovitz's films are available though www.arttxfilms.com). Dr. Horovitz is past President-Elect of the American Art Therapy Association (AATA). For additional information contact: Dr. Ellen G. Horovitz, ATR-BC / Director of Graduate Art Therapy / Nazareth College / 4245 East Avenue Rochester, N.Y. 14618 / e-mail: ehorovi4@naz.edu or ehorovit@rochester.rr.com

VISUALLY SPEAKING

Art Therapy and the Deaf

Edited by

ELLEN G. HOROVITZ, Ph.D., LCAT, ATR-BC

CHARLES C THOMAS • PUBLISHER, LTD.
Springfield • Illinois • U.S.A.

Published and Distributed Throughout the World by

CHARLES C THOMAS • PUBLISHER, LTD.
2600 South First Street
Springfield, Illinois 62704

© 2007 by CHARLES C THOMAS • PUBLISHER, LTD.

ISBN 978-0-398-07715-0 (hard)
ISBN 978-0-398-07716-7 (paper)

Library of Congress Catalog Card Number: 2006051120

With THOMAS BOOKS *careful attention is given to all details of manufacturing
and design. It is the Publisher's desire to present books that are satisfactory as to their
physical qualities and artistic possibilities and appropriate for their particular use.*
THOMAS BOOKS *will be true to those laws of quality that assure a good name
and good will.*

Printed in the United States of America
SM-R-3

Library of Congress Cataloging-in-Publication Data

Visually speaking : art therapy and the deaf / edited by Ellen G. Horovitz.
  p. cm.
  Includes bibliographical references and index.
  ISBN 0-398-07715-0 -- ISBN 0-398-07716-9 (pbk.)
  1. Art therapy. 2. Deaf. I. Horovitz, Ellen G.

RC489.A7V574 2007
616.89'1656--dc22

2006051120

*Dedicated to my wonderful, albeit complicated children,
Kaitlyn Leah Darby and Bryan James Darby,
whose language I have yet to speak.*

CONTRIBUTORS

Jacob M. Atkinson has completed his Masters in Creative Art Therapies (MCAT) at Nazareth College in Rochester, New York. His collegiate career began at Snow College, were he studied printmaking, ceramics, and sculpture. Upon completing his Associate of Science degree from Snow College, he attended Utah State University where he received his Bachelors of Fine Art with an emphasis in printmaking. During his time at school, Jacob had the opportunity to study art in Switzerland, tour parts of Western Europe and live in Alaska, Hawaii, Florida, Utah and New York. Although his degree is in printmaking, Jacob also works in clay, wood, paint, glass, paper, and photographic mediums. Additionally, he has exhibited his art in the United States and Canada. Jacob believes the healing power of art comes from the creating and sharing of one's experiences and emotions through an individual's art. Jacob hopes to be more equipped and able to help others discover the healing power of art, as a practicing Art Therapist.

Sally Brucker, M.A., MSW., ATR received her masters in Early Childhood Special Education (1973) and in Art Therapy from George Washington University in 1978. Ms. Brucker has been practicing art therapy for over 20 years, has taught introductory courses in art therapy at Gallaudet University and has taught art therapy at Art Therapy Italiana (in Italy) for the last two years. Ms. Brucker has presented many workshops both throughout the United States and internationally on the Use of Art Therapy with the Deaf. She has also worked at St. Elizabeth's Deaf Program (Washington, D.C.) since 1980 and currently works in spearheading a special studio for disabled adults at www.studiodownstairs.org.

Sharon M. Duchesneau, M.A., received her masters in mental health counseling from Gallaudet University. She has over 12 years of experience working as a deaf psychotherapist in the Washington, D.C. metropolitan community mental health settings. She has led weekly group psychotherapy sessions for seriously mentally ill deaf individuals at a psychiatric day program, contracts with Deaf Abused Women's Network (DAWN), and teaches graduate-level courses at local colleges. Ms. Duchesneau works at the Alternative Solutions Center along with Dr. McCullough, providing therapy to deaf and hard of hearing individuals and their hearing family members.

David R. Henley, Ph.D., ATR has been an art therapist and art educator with exceptional children for over 15 years. He has authored many journal articles and has written *Exceptional Children: Exceptional Art: Teaching Art to Special Needs* and *Clayworks in Art Therapy: Plying the Sacred Circle.* Henley has worked with a variety of populations including emotionally disturbed, mentally retarded, autistic, visually impaired, and most recently was an art therapist at the New Jersey School for the Deaf. He has consulted to a Very Special Arts in New Jersey, New York City, and Illinois, and has lectured widely at universities in the United States and abroad. Henley is currently chair of the Long Island University Art Therapy department; he is a practicing artist in bas-relief, paper canvas, plaster, and clay. This chapter on the multiply handicapped deaf child is one of a series of writings by Henley on the use of Art Therapy Education with children with special needs.

Ellen G. Horovitz, Ph.D., LCAT, ATR-BC, is a Professor and Director of Graduate Art Therapy at Nazareth College of Rochester. She has had over 30 years of experience with myriad patient populations and specializes in family art therapy with the deaf. Dr. Horovitz currently is in private practice. She conducts two art therapy clinics at Nazareth College: the Aphasia Clinic at Nazareth College for adults who have sustained a stroke as well as the Finger Lakes Regional Burn Association Clinic for children who have been burned. Dr. Horovitz is the author of numerous articles, book chapters and the following books: *Spiritual Art Therapy: An Alternate Path, A Leap of Faith: The Call to Art* and *Art Therapy As Witness: A Sacred Guide.* Dr. Horovitz has also directed and produced ten films. Her most recent 2-set DVD, *A Guide to Phototherapy: Artistic Methods,* is formatted for the deaf. Dr. Horovitz is past President-Elect of the American Art Therapy Association (AATA).

Carole Kunkle-Miller, Ph.D., ATR, is a registered art therapist, licensed psychologist and personal coach residing in Pittsburgh, Pennsylvania. She directed the art therapy program at Carlow College and guest lectured at Vermont College of Norwich University, Naropa

Institute and the University of Pittsburgh, among others. Dr. Kunkle-Miller worked as an art therapist at Western Psychiatric Institute and Clinic, University of Pittsburgh Medical Center and served as art therapist and family art therapist at the Western Pennsylvania School for the Deaf. Dr. Kunkle-Miller was consultant for the Arts in Special Education Project of Pennsylvania, on the Editorial Board of the *American Journal of Art Therapy*, and was honored as American Art Therapy Association Clinician of the Year in 1999. She has been published in numerous books and journals, including a chapter in *Approaches to Art Therapy* edited by Judith Aron Rubin, and *Portrait of the Artist as a Poet*, edited by Carol Thayer Cox and Peggy Osna Heller.

Candace A. McCullough, Ph.D., is a deaf psychotherapist at the Alternative Solutions Center in Bethesda and Frederick, Maryland. Dr. McCullough received her doctorate in clinical psychology and her masters in mental health counseling from Gallaudet University. She completed her post-doctoral fellowship training at Springfield Hospital Center in Sykesville, Maryland, and her doctoral internship at the Veterans Affairs Medical Center in Baltimore, Maryland. Dr. McCullough has worked for over 15 years in the mental health field, in private practice, community mental health, university, judicial, and psychiatric hospital settings. She is an Adjunct Faculty in the Department of Counseling at Gallaudet University and also teaches at McDaniel College in Westminster, Maryland.

Rawley Silver, Ed.D., HLM, ATR, is author of *Developing Cognitive and Creative Skills Through Art, The Silver Drawing Test of Cognitive and Creative Abilities,* and many articles in professional journals. She has received grants from the U.S. Department of Education, the National Institute of Education and the New York State Department of education. In the field of art therapy, she has served as teacher, supervisor, consultant and lecturer and is an Honorary Life Member of the American Art Therapy Association.

Amy A. Szarkowski, Ph.D., received her degree in Clinical Psychology from Gallaudet University in Washington, D.C. She currently serves as member of the Faculty of Comparative Culture at Miyazaki International College (MIC) in Japan. Her interests include Deafness and Deaf Culture, Positive Psychology, and Peace Studies. Dr. Szarkowski serves as the advisor to a Peace Studies Group and is involved in student development. She most recently published a book chapter on Sign Language and Service Learning. Dr. Szarkowski thoroughly enjoys traveling, exploring, and continuing to learn. Her latest endeavor is learning Japanese Sign Language and becoming involved in the Japanese Deaf Community.

FOREWORD

In my first job as an art therapist, I worked on an inpatient unit for youngsters who had been diagnosed with "childhood schizophrenia." Four-year-old Johnny was a sweet little boy who, like the others, seemed to be living in his own private world. He loved his individual art sessions, and quickly became attached to working at the easel with tempera paints on the largest size of paper available. Although he clearly enjoyed the process, he was rigidly stuck on using all of the jars in the easel tray, going from left to right, and moving the brush up and down to make a blob of each color. As this ritual was repeated week after week with no variations, I began to wonder how I could help him to give up such a compulsive way of working. So one day I suggested that he use the paper vertically instead of horizontally, showing him by placing it that way myself.

Because the paper was not wide enough for him to use each color above its jar in the tray, he was forced to work differently. For the first time, his brush moved in many directions, sweeping freely in horizontal, vertical, and diagonal arcs. And the colors, which had thus far been used straight out of the jar, began to mingle. Initially, the color mixing was involuntary, but as Johnny responded with pleasure to the new tones, he began to blend colors intentionally. The paintings became more interesting, and more attractive as well. Although Johnny did not talk, he was clearly happy with the results.

When Johnny—whose silent withdrawal had been attributed to schizophrenia—moved to Chicago, his parents took him to another medical center to be evaluated. Much to their surprise (and the embarrassment of the staff in Pittsburgh), it was found that he had a profound hearing loss. Instead of being treated as a youngster with a severe psychotic illness, he was then treated appropriately as a Deaf child, and given the kind of help he really needed to be able to relate to others. This kind of tragic misdiagnosis was not uncommon in 1963; alas, it even happens at times today.

It was a powerful lesson for me, as I was just beginning my work as a therapist, about the power of expert opinions and resultant expectations. Four years later, I was invited to start an art program at a place then called the "Home for Crippled Children." Because of my previous experience, when the administrators told me that only about ten percent of the residents would be capable of participating, I suggested that each of them be assessed for possible inclusion. Although it is no surprise now, in 1967 the staff was amazed that everyone could do something in art, given creative adaptations.

But the biggest surprise for the teachers and therapists was that the art assessments revealed talents and potentials they had not known about in a number of children. One was a girl named Claire. At age ten, she had been withdrawn from both school and speech therapy, since the staff was sure from her behavior that she must be profoundly retarded—unteachable and unreachable.

Claire's art evaluation was scheduled right after a visit to the dentist. She wheeled herself up to the table, grabbed a marker and paper, and drew a picture that—more eloquently than any words—told what it feels like to be invaded by the dentist's tools, to be open and vulnerable and terrified. Though helpless, like any patient in a dentist's chair, Claire could master the traumatic event by expressing her feelings in art, effectively turning passive into active (see figure P–1).

Figure P–1.

More important for her future, the age-appropriate drawing revealed that Claire's intelligence was much higher than anyone had imagined. As a result, she was put back in a classroom and resumed speech/language therapy. In both settings, she used a "talking book" to communicate with others (see figure P–2). The pictures were drawn by Claire and then labeled by the teacher or speech therapist, as in this drawing of the doctor and the nurse.

Figure P–2.

Unlike Johnny, Claire's Deafness was already known and her mute behavior was evident. But her drawings revealed an intellect, which had not been visible in any of the assessments then available. Thanks to her articulate art, Claire gained a new lease on growing, eventually learning gestures and sign language, through which she entered into the community of her peers (see figure P–3).

There are lessons to be learned from both of these stories. From Johnny, that a child who neither speaks nor understands may not be able to hear, an obvious but overlooked diagnosis. It was also clear that his defensive maneuvers were not psychotic, but that like many youngsters under stress, he had developed a compulsive ritual. He needed to find ways to create order, albeit rigidly, in a confusing and chaotic world in which he could not yet participate fully.

From Claire, we learn that Deaf is not "dumb," although it is all too easy

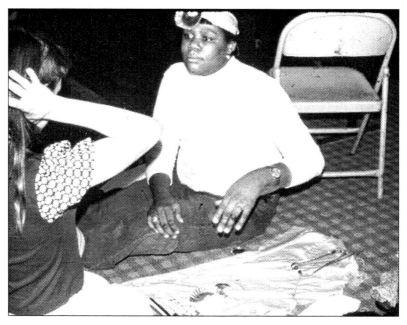

Figure P–3.

to assume that someone who doesn't respond can't process information. That fate had befallen Claire, who had been labeled as "profoundly retarded." Art that reveals potentials as often as it reflects problems gave her another way to speak. She was also fortunate that the director of speech therapy at the Home was creative enough to conceptualize the "talking book" idea, which worked amazingly well as Claire began the process of learning to communicate.

One more story . . . In 1983, I was invited to conduct a pilot art therapy program at a school for the deaf. The 16 children referred for diagnostic interviews quickly told me that what they most needed was a chance to express and cope with powerful feelings for which they had no words. Since an art education program was already available for cognitive and creative growth, I was free to encourage the children to use art and drama to express and deal with confused and conflicted feelings and fantasies (see figure P–4).

The intensity of their need for this kind of help was reflected in their ability to relate to me, despite my total lack of signing skills. I could understand some of the speech of the few who talked, and could use writing and drawing with some of the others, but I came away convinced of the need for an art therapist of the deaf to know sign language and, when appropriate, to use an interpreter. It was clear that I could have helped them much more had I been better able to understand their communications.

Figure P–4.

Sixteen-year-old Eleanor, whose suicidal impulses had been known to the staff for some time, had tried to cut her wrist the night before our fourth art therapy session. Realizing, after describing to me what had occurred, that she had hurt herself rather than the real target of her rage, she drew—with much excitement—a picture of what she would like to do to the grown-up, who had angered her (see figure P–5)

In the drawing a many-toothed, monstrous creature is holding a huge knife over a small, fearful person. She first said that she was the big one and the adult was the small one; then she reversed herself, explaining that in reality she felt helpless to deal with the power of those in charge of her. I suggested that she might also feel frightened of the extent of her own rage, of what she would really like to do to the grown-up in the picture. I wondered if she had turned the anger on herself as a punishment, as well as a way to protect the adult, who she then said cared a lot about her.

She spent the remaining time in the session drawing a volleyball net, perhaps to screen out the fearful imagery of her first picture, and then made four balloons tied together with colorful finger-paints. Eleanor was thus able to use the art therapy session first to express the feared impulse, and then to defend against it. Both were helpful to her in the ongoing task of self-awareness and self-control.

On the basis of the pilot study, which involved Eleanor and several others seen weekly for a term, a part-time art therapist who knew sign language

Figure P–5.

was hired and worked at the school for a number of years, seeing both individuals and group. Carole Kunkle-Miller's chapter about that work is one of the many valuable contributions in this book–a volume which was unthinkable when I first met Johnny and Claire in the sixties, and even when I met Eleanor in the early eighties. As many of the contributors note, there was a prejudice against Deaf culture and a reluctance to treat those who are Deaf in an appropriate fashion.

In addition to the mistaken conviction that Deaf individuals could not be creative or intelligent, noted by many authors in this volume, there was an equally insidious but widely-held notion that they were incapable of being helped through psychotherapy. As with those labeled retarded, the low expectations of the experts led to dreadful practices in the arts and in mental health. Either these were absent or, if available, were offered in such a way that the Deaf individual could not be creative and could not grow.

One of the most wonderful things about this book is that finally the Deaf are being recognized as the full human beings they have always been, who deserve full access to all of our resources. A recognition of their uniqueness rather than their deficits is found throughout the pages of this book, which presents an attitude that is both optimistic and realistic. And best of all, there are chapters, which will sensitize, inform, and inspire. Ellen Horovitz has done a service to anyone who offers art therapy to the Deaf. Through promoting better art therapy for the hearing impaired, those who are served will be able to live fuller, more rewarding, and more creative lives.

Judith A. Rubin, Ph.D., ATR–BC, HLM

PREFACE

For ages it has been thought that deaf children are nonverbal and are not capable of having any language. While this belief may still be widespread, a quiet revolution is taking place and changing these concepts. This revolution seems to be spreading.

Some of the insights behind this new thinking has come through the field of creative arts therapy. The creative arts therapists recognize that deaf children can image as well as anyone and perhaps better. There has been an increased awareness developing from the research conducted by Joe Khatena (1984) and others that the ability to image is a critical key to learning and thinking and probably as valuable as that of using words. Deaf children have also excelled in the visual arts where the skills involved are as available to them as to anyone else. Many deaf children have received recognition for the excellence of their work in the visual arts.

Recent developments in the area of kinesthetic learning have also brought a change in attitude about the teaching and learning styles of deaf children. Some children have learned these skills and have gone into creative dance and ballet and have excelled. Here and again the skills are as available to the deaf as well as to the hearing.

However, not all deaf children receive training in movement. Studies with deaf preschool children illustrate that children who have not had much experience with movement do not do as well as on tests of movement. This has been demonstrated using the test of Thinking Creatively in Action and Movement (Torrance, 1981). However, when these children are given training in creative movement, they make significant gains.

The tests that have been typically given to deaf children for placement in school programs have generally shown them to be deficient. This is because the tests do not make a demand on the abilities in which the deaf excel. Through the work of Rawley A. Silver (1978), Bill Kalstounis (1970), and others who have experimented with the Torrance Tests of Creative Thinking (Torrance, 1984), it has been shown that deaf children succeed just as well as hearing children on tests of creative thinking skills. They perform best when they are permitted to respond and express their thoughts in a modality, which is more compatible with their abilities.

People like Walter B. Barbe (1985) are not looking at learning through the perspective of the visual, kinesthetic, and auditory modalities. Unfortunately, schools have tended to place almost exclusive emphasis on the auditory modality. The recognition of the importance of other styles of teaching and learning may lead to better learning experiences not only for the deaf but for all children.

A book such as this on creative arts therapy and language for the deaf gives emphasis to these neglected modalities of expression. As educators gain insights into the language of the deaf, increased understanding and opportunities for the deaf should take place.

E. Paul Torrance
Alumni Foundation Distinguished Professor Emeritus

REFERENCES

Barbe, W. B. (1985). *Growing up learning: The key to your child's potential.* Washington, D.C.: Acropolis.

Khatena, J. (1984). *Imagery and creative imagination.* Buffalo, N.Y.: Bearly Limited.

Kalstounis, B. (1970). Comparative Study of Creativity in Deaf and Hearing Children. *Child Study Journal, 1*(1), 11–19.

Silver, R. A. (1978). *Developing cognitive and creative skills through art: Programs for children with communication disorders or learning disabilities.* Baltimore: University Park Press.

Torrance, E. P. (1981). *Thinking creatively in action and movement.* Bensenville, IL: Scholastic Testing Service, Inc.

Torrance, E. P. (1984). *Torrance Tests of Creative Thinking: Streamlined Manual.* Bensenville, IL: Scholastic Testing Service, Inc.

ACKNOWLEDGMENTS

Generally I start off by thanking family, friends, colleagues, contributors and previous patients, (and of course I wish to acknowledge all), but in this instance, rather than be redundant and naming the contributors and aforementioned, the real thanks goes to three of my students, past and present: First, Christie Linn, who discovered a portion of the manuscript covered in dust on my bookshelf and inquired as to why it had not seen the light of day. Thus, began her role as taskmaster. Secondly, was Elizabeth (Lizzie) Brandt. She tirelessly digitized past files and notes of my clients, wading through my hand-scrawled notes—referring to this tedious experience as "accessing gold." (Indeed, even upon graduating, she offered to continue this work, just to have a window inside the recesses of my head and private wanderings. Imagine that—such dedication and loyalty to a project.) Thirdly, was Sarah Eksten, who in good faith, picked up the reins after Christie and Lizzie graduated and helped me pump this manuscript into fruition by doing the most arduous task, the subject/author index and galley proofing.

Yet, categorically, I need to thank two very important people: Dr. Robert Pollard, of the Deaf Wellness Program, Strong Memorial Hospital at the University of Rochester, who linked me to many of the contributors herein; as well, my dear friend and colleague from Cornell University, Dr. William D. Schulze, who not only read a good deal of this manuscript, but also offered thoughtful suggestions and corrections to the work; his support has been unparallel.

CONTENTS

VISUALLY SPEAKING:
ART THERAPY AND THE DEAF

INTRODUCTION

ELLEN G. HOROVITZ

BACKGROUND

As in all of my books, there is generally a story, a tale that leads me to its beginning. In this case, it is deeply personal and had lifelong ramifications. At the age of six, I developed a very high fever, which consequently left me deaf for close to a week. Discussion was light around the house; my parents carefully tiptoed around the fact that I might indeed be deaf, if the illness had not lifted.

But most discordant for me was not so much the lack of sound, but the inability to hear my brother play the piano. "Close" pales as a descriptor when categorizing my relationship with my brother, Len. As a child, I spent hours listening to his talented fingers lilt across the ebony and white piano keys. What bothered me the most during this small sashay into deafness was my incapacity to hear the purity of this sound.

So one day, when feeling particularly sorry for myself, I leaned against the upright Baldwin piano so I could *feel* the sound since I was unable to hear it. And I cried. But in one miraculous moment, my ears popped, my head spun from the onslaught and I was once again in the hearing world. My pediatrician, Dr. Feinberg, never understood why this happened since he had just informed my mother two days earlier, to expect the worst (possibly an operation). And while my ears have remained ultrasensitive to sound, (sometimes picking up more than I wish) I find it fascinating that perhaps because of this, I oftentimes experience what I would coin auditory recall. So fascinated am I by sound that I have become adept at languages and relish when challenged to learn a new language system.

Ironically, I landed in Rochester, New York shortly after graduate school and secured a job in the metropolis that had invented finger spelling. Because Rochester was home to the Rochester School for the Deaf as well as

3

National Technical Institute for the Deaf (NTID), it was fairly common to rub elbows with deaf people.

By 1981, I was working at PS 29 (then touted as the largest public school for orthopedically and perceptually challenged children). As a result, I began working with one child who relied principally on bliss boards and sign language for exchange. In order to communicate with him, I had to learn his language system. I signed up at Monroe County Association for the Hearing Impaired (MCAHI) in Rochester, NY in order to facilitate my communication with him.

Soon after, I continued my training at NTID and immersed myself in deaf culture–probably most memorable was a "silent retreat" coupled with a two-day experience of wearing "white-noise" hearing aids and attempting to function in a hearing world without the aid of sound. Most numbing was how difficult it was to not only be understood but also translate the mouthed words of hearing people. I relied on pencil and paper and the occasional word or two that I was able to decipher from reading a person's lips.

Thereafter, I worked with emotionally disturbed deaf children in a residential treatment facility and in time began to work with the Deaf in private practice. While I could never fully be accepted in the Deaf or hard-of-hearing world since I was not Deaf, I forged many friendships with Deaf clinicians and professionals. I found myself immersed in a world view that seemed incredibly fit for Art Therapy, a profession whose hallmark is indeed nonverbal communication.

A Word about Deaf versus deaf

Before discussing the contents of this book, I want to explain the reason behind capitalization of the word "Deaf." In order for the reader to understand this, I will quote from the chapter written by Dr. Amy Szarkowski:

> The use of *'Deaf'* in this chapter, consistent with the form often used by academics and researchers in the area, refers to individuals who identify with Deaf culture. The use of *'deaf'* is also used, in to the context of referring to those with hearing loss, who do not define themselves as members of Deaf communities. For some, Deafness is a social construction of identity involving the use of Sign Language, understanding the Deaf Culture of one's country or place of origin, and being involved in the Deaf community. Deaf people who adopt this identity are likely to be against the inclusion of Deafness in this discourse about disabilities. . . . [clarification of] the situation of persons who consider themselves *Deaf*, as well as those who call themselves *deaf*, and identify themselves as persons with a disability [is up for discussion]. Both realities are important and justified in the world as it is today.

In sum, Deafness may or may not be considered a "disability" by those afflicted with auditory loss. But, it is indeed a physical difference that has resulted in a language system. From language springs culture and Deaf language is indeed a cultivation that celebrates such ethnology. As a result, most of the authors in this book, will be capitalizing "Deaf" when referring to this culture.

Contents

In short order, sign language, (clearly a visual language) made abundant sense to me. This silent language of the Deaf vibrates through space as a three-dimensional language system, which arcs in past, present, and future just by mere body positioning and facial expression. It is a magical language, which crosses culture and is indeed classified, codified, and uniquely its own system.

Because of the complexity of this system, (from a developmental, cognitive, and emotional standpoint), I have invited contributions from some of the foremost authorities on Deafness. It is my intent to inspire other art therapists and mental health professionals through these readings. Coupling the exquisite complexity of this beautiful language system with the inner workings of Deaf culture is the bridge to transliteration, understanding and elucidation.

In chapter 1, McCullough and Duchesneau review the historical trends of the mental health Deaf person–who is a Deaf person, what kinds of treatment are available and have been readily accessible in the past, the psychology of the Deaf person, use of interpreters and finally implications of utilizing art therapy with this population. In chapter 2, pioneer art therapist, Silver reviews the use of SDT (Silver Drawing Test) with the Deaf population, vis a vis case studies and cross cultural analysis. Having been one of the first art therapists to work with the Deaf, Silver's contributions are both historical and scientific in nature. In chapter 3, Horovitz reviews family art therapy in the long-term treatment of a talented child and discusses the use of interpreters in this complex familial art therapy anecdote. In chapter 4, Brucker describes the use of art therapy as a treatment modality with Deaf/hearing-impaired adults who suffer from varied forms of mental illness. The majority of the persons described here were patients in a special mental health program for the Deaf at a psychiatric inpatient facility. The focus of this chapter is on the process and content of one art therapy group and the themes of the artwork of another over the course of a four-year period described in terms of the patient population, group characteristics, goals, and treatment effectiveness. In chapter 5, Atkinson and Horovitz describe working with a medically ill KODA ({Hearing} Kids Of Deaf Adults, very young children) who existed in a rather convoluted culture and world. This case was complicated by the child's serious, ongoing medical condition of Eosinophilic Gastroenteritis (EG), which currently prohibited from eating anything other than a few selected fruits and vegetables; as well, this disorder resulted in multiple surgeries and hospitalizations. In chapter 6, Henley articulates his work at a residential school for the Deaf during the 1980s, where he worked with Deaf children who, for various reasons, could not benefit from verbal or language-based therapy. The fascinating case of a Deaf/legally blind boy (age 9) is described in rich detail. In chapter 7, Szarkowski explored the meaning of "Deaf Culture" in several locales, and reflected upon differences found in the definitions of both *Deafness* and *disability* worldwide. Current paradigms in Disability Studies are addressed, as well as the application of Disability Studies to the field of Deafness. In chapter 8, Horovitz examines the possibilities and advantages of computers and culture coupled with hypermedia and computer animation as a specific educational tool in which these resources are applied to the teaching-learning process when working with emotionally disturbed Deaf/hearing-impaired clients. Moreover, Horovitz reviews the methodology of fostering improved spoken and written communication skills of the hearing-impaired via examining language systems (speech, linguistic structure, writing, etc.) and the different communication codes employed when working with this population. In chapter 9, Kunkle–Miller reviews both the theoretical and the practical aspects of establishing an art therapy program within a residential school setting. She offers numerous therapeutic modalities to lead the therapist treating hearing-impaired children in designing an effective treatment program. In the final chapter, Horovitz summarizes her work with two emotionally disturbed adolescents using both individual and family art therapy modalities in the recovery of these amazingly artistic individuals.

Chapter 1

MENTAL HEALTH AND DEAF PEOPLE

CANDACE A. MCCULLOUGH AND SHARON M. DUCHESNEAU

In order to place art therapy with Deaf people into a meaningful context, it is essential to have a clear understanding of Deaf people as a unique and highly diversified minority group. Equally important is an awareness of the historic and complex relationship between Deaf people and the American mental health system. Even today, entering the twenty-first century, long-entrenched paternalistic and oppressive attitudes toward Deaf people continue to have ramifications on the quality of mental health services they receive. Not only do some clinicians, knowingly or not, persist in misunderstanding or overlooking the needs of Deaf clients, but also so do some Deaf clients lack a sense of entitlement and knowledge of how to obtain adequate and effective mental health services. Accessibility of mental health services for this population remains an ongoing issue. In spite of these obstacles, hopeful signs point to a brightening tableau in the field of mental health and Deaf people. One such sign is the increasing number of graduates of specialized training programs designed to teach students how to work effectively with Deaf clients (Leigh, 1991; Sussman & Brauer, 1999). Another is the growing body of literature on mental health and Deaf people, this book included. An appreciation of the great potential of utilizing art therapy with the Deaf population, thus, begins with an understanding of who Deaf people are, what their experiences have been as marginal members of a hearing society, and how they have fared to date as clients in the mental health system.

Who are Deaf People?

Deaf people are a vibrant community of individuals who share a rich cultural, linguistic, and historical heritage. Contrary to what many hearing people may believe, being Deaf entails far more than simply being without the sense of hearing; defining and interpreting Deaf people's lives in terms of their hearing status is a limiting approach that overlooks just how diverse and remarkable Deaf people are (Padden & Humphries, 1988). Within their community, Deaf people represent a wide spectrum of humanity, shaped by a variety of factors, including family history of Deafness, race, ethnicity, socioeconomic and educational background, and self-perception. One can no more assume that all Deaf people are fundamentally alike than one can assume all shades of green are the same.

A positive definition of Deaf people describes them as primarily visually-oriented people (Bahan, 2004). Beyond this, a definition of Deaf people defies generalization, in the same way that no one definition of African Americans will suffice to define all African Americans, nor will one characterization of women define all women. Deaf people can be descended from families with six or more generations of Deaf relatives or they may be the only Deaf member of their family. They may be native users of American Sign Language (ASL), or if they come from hearing families, they may have learned to sign when they entered school or college, or even afterwards. Everyone in the family may sign, making communication a nonissue; or there may be no signing family members at all, resulting in the Deaf person experiencing a sense of isolation. Deaf people may have been born Deaf or they may have become Deaf later in life. Some Deaf people may opt to use hearing aids or cochlear implants; others choose not to use amplification devices. There are Deaf people with professional degrees and Deaf people with less than eighth grade educations; Deaf people who exhibit healthy self-esteem and confidence and Deaf people who harbor feelings of inferiority likely borne out of years of oppression.

Population data and etiological information on deafness have long been the province of hearing researchers, reflecting their relative lack of importance for Deaf people, who are typically less concerned with pathological aspects of deafness and more concerned with cultural and community issues. For those who are interested, accurate demographic information about the Deaf population is difficult to come by, given the wide range of definitions of deafness employed in different studies. The 1990 and 1991 Health Interview Studies identified around 20 million Americans aged three or older as having "significant hearing loss," a figure that represents 8.6 percent of the population (National Center for Health Statistics, 1994). Approximately 550,000 Americans, or 0.23 percent of the population, do not hear or understand any speech (National Center for Health Statistics, 1994). In gender distribution, males tend to be Deaf or hard-of-hearing more often than females, although this is much more apparent after age 18 (National Center for Health Statistics, 1994). Across racial and ethnic groups, 9.4 percent of Caucasians are Deaf or hard-of-hearing, compared to 4.2 percent of African Americans and 4.2 percent of Hispanics (National Center for Health Statistics, 1994).

The most common causes of deafness in infants and young children are genetics, meningitis, and pregnancy/birth complications, including Rh incompatibility, prematurity, and birth trauma (Annual Survey, 1992–93). Approximately 50 percent of these etiologies are considered genetic (Marazita, Ploughman, Rawlings, Remington, Arnos & Nance, 1993). It has been suggested that deafness may often be attributed to genetics when there is no other obvious cause, hence the actual percentage of genetic deafness may be lower (Moores, 2001).

Views of Deaf People

Hearing professionals and lay people, as well as some Deaf people themselves, generally perceive Deaf people in one of two ways. The largely prevailing pathological perspective considers Deaf people to have an impairment that is in need of correction. The social minority perspective, on the other hand, considers Deaf people to be members of a unique cultural and linguistic minority (Padden, 1980; Padden & Humphries, 1988; Lane, Hoffmeister, & Bahan, 1996).

The pathological, or medical, perspective presumes that deafness is a disabling condition that can and should be corrected by the use of hearing aids, surgical implantation of cochlear implants, or other medical intervention. Adherents of this view believe that it is in the Deaf person's best interest to assimilate as much as possible into the larger hearing culture by learning to speak the majority language and by maximizing hearing ability through amplification devices and surgical intervention. The closer to the hearing norm that Deaf people can mold themselves, the better their lives will be, it is presumed. There are people with hearing loss, whose primary mode of communication is oral, who do live their lives determined to fit into the hearing world.

The implications of the pathological view of deafness, however, can be far-reaching and oppressive. Amplification is not an exact science and does not turn a Deaf person into a hearing person. Deaf children learning to speak may spend countless hours in speech therapy each year, sacrificing not only learning time in the classroom, but socialization opportunities as well. It is not a given that clear speech will be the outcome of all of this effort. It is not uncommon for a Deaf person to be encouraged and praised by teachers and family members for achieving "good speech skills," only to discover when trying to order dinner in a restaurant, that the waiter comprehends nothing of the Deaf person's speech. One Deaf woman, for example, recalled trying to order a glass of milk as a child. She tried several times to enunciate the order to the best of her ability, all the while gauging from the bewildered looks on the waiter's face that she was getting nowhere. Frustrated and humiliated, she gave up and asked instead for a root beer.

The physical and emotional toll of constantly striving to lip-read and voice soundless words can be exhausting and ego-deflating. The typical Deaf person lip-reads about 30 percent of what is being said, filling in the remaining 70 percent of the conversation with guesswork. A common experience of many Deaf people is to rely on the "Deaf nod," acknowledging the hearing person's remarks, even if they did not fully comprehend what was said. After asking the hearing person to repeat the remarks several times and still not understanding, the awkwardness and embarrassment usually lead to the "Deaf nod" as a last resort, hoping that will suffice and end the conversation. Hearing educators, audiologists, and speech therapists, as well as hearing family members, constantly tell the Deaf person to try harder to pronounce words more clearly, to pay closer attention when lip-reading. For some Deaf people, the reality of being Deaf may be pushed aside in favor of making them as "un-Deaf" as possible. With the emphasis on assimilation into the hearing world, people who view Deafness as a pathological condition may interpret using sign language or sign language interpreters as a sign of weakness or a failure to succeed in the hearing world. Little attention is paid to the psychological implications of the ongoing effort to deny or minimize the fact that the person is Deaf.

In contrast to the pathological view of Deaf people, those who view Deaf people as part of a social minority place language and culture, not hearing status, at the center of Deaf people's identity. As Padden and Humphries (1988) note, rather than defining Deaf people according to a central reference point of the hearing world, a more affirmative definition relies instead on a "different center," that of American Sign Language and Deaf culture. The Deaf person is seen as whole, as having the complete ability to function and communicate with others, albeit in a different way than hearing people.

From a historical vantage point, the social minority view of Deaf people is a relatively recent one. Deaf people have recognized for many years the kinship they share, evident in their status as visual people, in the close bonds formed in Deaf residential schools, clubs, and organizations, and in their shared history of oppression (Lane, Hoffmeister, & Bahan, 1996). Even so, it was not until the research of William C. Stokoe and colleagues in the 1960s, that American Sign Language first began to be recognized as formal language (Stokoe, Casterline, & Croneberg, 1965). In the decades that followed, recognition of ASL Deaf culture grew. With this came an emerging sense of Deaf pride, culminating in the 1988 Deaf President Now (DPN) movement at Gallaudet University in Washington, D.C., the premier institution of higher learning for Deaf students from all over the world. Rallying together for a politically charged week of protests and demonstrations, Deaf people and their hearing allies were successful in their quest to see the installment of the University's first Deaf president. The media attention garnered by DPN also brought to light to the larger hearing community, the idea of the social minority perspective of Deaf people. In the years following DPN, the establishment of Deaf studies and linguistics and interpreting graduate programs at universities across the country lent further credibility to Deaf people's vision of themselves as a social minority group.

Early and Current Mental Health Treatment

From a historical standpoint, the American mental health system has woefully neglected to meet the needs of its Deaf clients (Pollard, 1994; Steinberg, Sullivan, & Loew, 1998). Prior to the 1960s, Deaf people in need of serious psychological treatment were often warehoused, or relegated to the back wards of psychiatric hospitals, where they received little more than what can be described as maintenance or custodial care. It was not unheard of for Deaf clients to be misdiagnosed as mentally retarded and confined in psychiatric wards for the large part of their lives. Even today, on occasion, a report will surface about a long-institutionalized client suddenly being found to be Deaf and not mentally retarded or autistic as had previously been thought.

Throughout the mental health system, Deaf clients faced paternalistic and oppressive attitudes from the hearing professionals who directed their treatment. Clinicians were usually unfamiliar with Deaf culture, unable to communicate in sign language, and typically believed their Deaf clients incapable of responding to treatment. Reflective of societal views of Deaf people at the time, these professionals perceived Deaf people as lacking in cognitive and intellectual abilities and incapable of thinking or reasoning abstractly. Treatment, when given, was mostly directive and simplistic in scope and nature, with little expectation for improvement. Psychotherapies oriented toward insight or psychoanalysis, as well as those of cognitive or affective natures, were thought inappropriate for use with Deaf clients (Sussman & Brauer, 1999). Specialized outpatient services for Deaf clients did not develop until the 1960s. Among the first such programs available were St. Elizabeth's Hospital in Washington, D.C., and a New York State Psychiatric Institute clinic (Robinson, 1978; Altshuler, Baroff, & Rainer, 1963).

The growth of the American mental health deinstitutionalization movement in the 1970s, the subsequent shift in focus to community-based mental health services, and the burgeoning political empowerment of Deaf people inspired further changes in the treatment of Deaf people in the mental health system. Emboldened by recognition of ASL as a formal language, the aforementioned history-making and empowering DPN movement at Gallaudet University in 1988, and the signing of the Americans with Disabilities Act in 1992, Deaf people and their hearing allies began speaking up about the gross injustices the mental health system was doing to its Deaf clients. Their demands, along with the emergence of the first graduates of Gallaudet University's counseling and social work programs, led to the establishment of growing numbers of pioneering Deaf day and residential programs in the 1970s and 1980s.

The 1982 case of Nancy Doe (*Doe v. Buck*, 1983) in Maryland illustrates one of first precedents for improving Deaf people's access to inpatient psychiatric services. Sued by the Maryland Disability Law Center and the National Association of the Deaf Legal Defense Fund, the state of Maryland faced charges of confining Doe to 20 years of "antitherapeutic custodial isolation." During Doe's hospitalization for schizophrenia, she was provided with very little, if any, access to interpreters, forced to reside in a housing unit apart from other Deaf clients, and her case given no consultation with mental health professionals with specific training and experience in working with Deaf clients (Raifman & Vernon, 1996, New Rights). The case was settled in 1986 with a Consent Decree mandating that the state of Maryland create an inpatient unit to serve "as a model for treating hearing impaired mentally ill persons using appropriate communication methods" (Raifman & Vernon, 1996, New Rights). In addition to delineating staffing levels for the inpatient treatment team, the Decree also required that a certified interpreter or fluent signing staff member be present in the unit 24 hours a day.

On paper, the mandate reflects a new trend toward recognizing the need for improved quality of services to Deaf clients; in reality, there was, and still remains, a long way to go to ensure this. The presence of an interpreter or signing staff member 24 hours a day does not necessarily mean that Deaf clients have full access to all communication occurring in the unit. It is not a given that every spoken conversation between nonsigning staff will be interpreted for the Deaf clients' benefit. Already stressed by communication issues in the world outside the hospital, Deaf clients may find themselves retraumatized when observing two nurses at the front desk conversing in spoken English, gesturing, and laughing, oblivious to the fact that most of the people in the room have no idea what they find so funny. For clients experiencing paranoia, when the treatment environment presents situations such as the one just described, their level of paranoia may be elevated and their treatment made more complicated as a result of clinicians minimizing the potential impact of language issues.

It is not surprising then, that when one of the authors worked in a Deaf inpatient unit of a psychiatric hospital, she observed a higher rate of seclusions during the periods when there were no Deaf staff members on the floor. In addition to reflecting the critical need for fluent-signing staff in mental health settings, this may also reflect the need for Deaf clients to receive treatment from Deaf professionals in inpatient settings. A situation precipitating seclusion is likely to be stressful and overwhelming for the client and staff. In many cases, the Deaf client facing seclusion may be more receptive to redirection and de-escalating interventions made by a Deaf professional than by a hearing one. This can be likened to a situation in which an African American person involved in an emotional confrontation may find it easier to accept feedback from another African American person than from a Caucasian one. In both cases, it is easier for the distraught person to listen to someone who is perceived as being on one's side, as opposed to someone who may represent an historically oppressive group.

Today, approximately 123 specialized outpatient and 24 specialized inpatient mental health service programs for Deaf people exist in the United States (Kendall, 2002; Morton & Kendall, 2003). As late as 1994, however, research continued to indicate a lack of accessibility of services for Deaf people, as well as a significantly high percentage of mental health professionals who lacked sufficient experience in working with Deaf clients that they did not have enough knowledge to complete a full diagnostic report for their Deaf clients (Pollard, 1994). The same study showed that compared to treatment provided to hearing consumers, the treatment given to Deaf consumers was more likely to consist of case management and follow-up and less likely to include assessment and therapy. As is true for many minority consumers, the closer they live to a major metropolitan area, the greater the possibility that accessible and adequate treatment options will be available.

In recent years, technology has played an influential role in expanding Deaf people's access to mental health services. Since the early 1990s, Deaf people living in rural or underserved areas increasingly have been able to utilize videophone and video relay services for psychiatric evaluations and therapy appointments. Therapists have begun using videophones and webcams to conduct therapy sessions with Deaf clients who may live in geographic areas where no qualified therapists work or who may be unable to travel to an office for an appointment. For geographically isolated clients who live in regions where there are no interpreters, as a last resort, video relay services (VRS) allow interpreters to be present in the communication between Deaf clients and nonsigning psychiatrists or therapists. The Deaf client places a videophone call to the VRS center, where an interpreter appears onscreen. The interpreter then dials the telephone number of the nonsigning, hearing person, and proceeds to facilitate the conversation by voicing what the Deaf client signs onscreen and signing what the hearing person says.

Videophone and webcam technology, however, are very much in the development stage. Highly dependent on the reliability and consistency of broadband and cable services, this technology may at times result in fuzzy or unclear pictures onscreen. For therapists and even interpreters who are nonnative ASL signers, understanding and grasping the nuances of a Deaf client's signing and nonverbal expressions such as tearfilled eyes can be difficult in these situations. When the internet is down or equipment malfunctioning, appointments may need be to be cancelled at the last minute or even cut off abruptly in the middle. This can be disadvantageous to both the therapeutic relationship and treatment. For these reasons, the use of this technology is best limited to situations in which the benefits of the client being able to work with a native ASL signing therapist outweigh other alternatives to therapy. Likewise, for the Deaf client residing in a region where there are no interpreters available and no other feasible options for communicating with a hearing psychiatrist, VRS may be the only option.

Psychology and Deaf People

Although it is not always feasible to make direct comparisons of the rates of mental illness and impairment between Deaf and hearing people, research in general indicates that the prevalence of mental illness in the Deaf population is comparable to that in the hearing population (Altshuler & Rainer, 1966; Pollard, 1994). Misdiagnosis, unfortunately, remains common, more so when the assessing clinician is a professional with little or no understanding of Deaf people. In the majority of cases, these professionals are unaware that they even lack the qualifications to diagnose Deaf people. Paranoid personality disorder, for instance, is one diagnosis that has been disproportionately, and inappropriately, assigned to Deaf patients over the years, despite research that shows no greater incidence of paranoia or paranoid schizophrenia among Deaf patients than among hearing patients (Robinson, 1978). While some Deaf people may react to experiences of being taken advantage of by hearing people by developing a certain level of distrust, this behavior represents more of an adaptive defense mechanism than it does pure paranoia. This is true as well for members of other racial and ethnic minority groups.

Deafness alone does not cause psychopathology; instead a combination of genetics, neural functioning, environmental stressors, and resilience do so (Leigh & Pollard, 2003). Keeping in mind this distinction, research has shown that certain etiologies of hearing loss do appear to be correlated with specific psychiatric conditions. Cytomegalovirus infection, meningitis, and rubella, all well-documented causes of Deafness, have been associated with learning disability, attention difficulties, cognitive dysfunction or mental retardation, impulsive behaviors, and affective instability (Gulati, 2003). Each of these infections can, but may not necessarily, impact the developing brain in ways other than causing Deafness.

A much-debated issue among professionals working with Deaf clients is whether or not to make a note of the client's hearing status in the Axis III line of the diagnostic report. Axis III is reserved for coding medical issues that may impact on the client's mental health. A client with chronic fatigue syndrome, for instance, may experience depressive symptoms that are recognized as outcomes of the limitations that the physical illness places on the client. Traditionally, psychiatrists and other mental health professionals, many operating from a pathological perspective of deafness, have automatically coded Deaf clients' hearing status on Axis III without considering whether or not it actually has any impact on the clients' mental health. A case in point is the psychiatrist who recorded a Deaf client's hearing status on Axis III, when the client's presenting problem involved anxiety related to an impending divorce. In this situation, where the client has no neurological impairment, there is no reason to attribute the anxiety to a medical condition. For a case in which a client's deafness is a result of an extreme bout of meningitis, which also caused organic damage with clear symptoms, however, the coding of the client's hearing status on Axis III may be justified. In other circumstances, the Axis III recording of hearing status may be mandated by an agency as a means of maintaining statistical information on the number of Deaf clients it serves, for its own internal statistics or in order to receive grants. Since Axis III refers to medical conditions, when deafness is not related to the mental health issues being treated, documentation of the client's hearing status is more appropriately recorded elsewhere.

Ongoing Issues

For Deaf people seeking mental health services, finding a qualified therapist who is fluent in ASL, knowledgeable about Deaf culture, and formally trained in working with Deaf clients can be a difficult and sometimes daunting task. There is currently no standardized credentialing process in use in the mental health field for determining who is qualified to work with Deaf clients. Many insurance companies, for example, give their Deaf consumers a list of in-network providers whose names were added to the company's provider list after they self-identified as "fluent in ASL" on a form indicating their credentials. This process of identifying competent therapists essentially leaves the door open for any number of clinicians to claim expertise in working with Deaf clients, no matter their actual qualifications. To demonstrate how ineffective this process is, one of the authors was told by her client that her insurance company sent her to a doctor who had checked off the box marked "fluent in ASL." When the client arrived for her appointment, she discovered to her annoyance that the doctor only knew four signs. Just as it is understood that someone who has studied a foreign language for two years is not qualified to interpret a formal test in that language (Rogers, 2005), it should also be a given understanding that someone who has studied ASL and Deaf culture for two years or even more may not be qualified to provide therapy to Deaf clients.

If Deaf clients are dissatisfied with a therapist's signing skills and request authorization to work with another out-of-network therapist with whom they know they can communicate easily, insurance companies may not always be sensitive to the Deaf person's needs. Some companies even go so far as to require the Deaf person to obtain a letter from a self-identified "fluent" signing therapist on their provider list. The Deaf client must ask the therapist to attest that the therapist's signing skills are not satisfactory to the client, before the client can obtain the insurance company's approval to see a more qualified out-of-network provider. One can imagine the awkwardness involved in making this request, for the Deaf person who must critique the therapist's so-called signing ability and qualifications, and for the therapist, who may or may not have realized how the Deaf person felt about their communication in the first place. There is a surprisingly high number of hearing professionals who overestimate their signing abilities and knowledge of Deaf culture, as well as an equal number of Deaf clients who are reluctant to tell them directly that their signing is not up to par. Due to the small size of the Deaf community and the likelihood that the Deaf client will run into the hearing therapist sometime in the future, Deaf clients may be even more hesitant about the prospect of burning their bridges by criticizing an unqualified therapist.

It is vital that therapists working with Deaf clients possess a thorough understanding of Deaf culture, fluency in ASL, and specific training in working with this population. At the very least, hearing therapists who do not sign should have access to qualified ASL interpreters who can serve as linguistic and cultural liaisons in the therapeutic process. Clear communication is an essential component in ensuring that the Deaf client feels validated and connected (Leigh et al., 1996). A therapist who has little knowledge of or familiarity with Deaf culture and community and no means of communicating directly with the Deaf client, is comparable to an English-speaking American therapist attempting to conduct therapy with a Hindi-speaking Indian client. Without any concept of what the client's life experience may have been like, without a sense of the norms and values of the client's culture, without any way of knowing what may be typical or atypical within that cultural group, a therapist cannot ascertain meaning from the client's narrative, nor put it into any meaningful framework of understanding.

Mental health interpreters should have specialized training to ensure they are familiar with the concepts of mental health and illness and the vocabulary that is unique to the field. Such training can also help interpreters understand how the therapeutic process works and their role as interpreters in such settings. To illustrate, take the situation in which an interpreter observes a sobbing client during a therapy session. An interpreter with specialized training in mental health interpreting would realize the inappropriateness of offering the client a box of tissues and refrain from doing so. Such a seemingly harmless gesture could undermine the therapist's goal of encouraging the client's self-assertiveness. Another example would be an untrained interpreter's acquiescence to a client's request for change for bus fare, unaware that one of the therapeutic issues involves the client developing appropriate social skills.

Any hearing therapist who is working with a Deaf client needs to be aware of cross-cultural issues that may arise in the therapeutic relationship. Not surprisingly, Deaf people's experiences of oppression or discrimination can sometimes lead to feelings of distrust or resentment toward hearing professionals. Some Deaf people question hearing professionals' motives for working with Deaf people, often because they have encountered far too many misguided hearing people who look at Deaf people as unfortunate beings in need of rescuing or assistance from hearing people. Such distrust or suspicion can be contradictory to the therapeutic relationship. Another example of a cross-cultural issue that may come up involves eye contact. For Deaf people, maintaining eye contact when communicating is virtually non-negotiable. Looking away while someone is talking is seen as rude. If a hearing clinician is hunched over writing notes while the Deaf client is talking, chances are that the Deaf client will come away from the encounter feeling that the clinician was not very attentive or interested. Even worse are situations in which the clinician directs the interpreter to "ask her" or "tell him" something, instead of addressing the client directly. Without a sense of rapport and connectedness, achieving any therapeutic progress will be difficult.

The presence of interpreters in the mental health setting can bring up a number of issues. Foremost among these is the reality that using an interpreter does not automatically resolve all communication issues between the clinician and the Deaf client. A widespread misconception among hearing people is that ASL merely substitutes signs for words. In reality, English and ASL are two completely different languages, with their own grammatical structures and syntax. Interpreting is an intricate process that requires great skill and judgment from the interpreter; it is not a black and white process of signing word for word what the clinician is saying or voicing aloud the Deaf person's signs in the same order they are produced. In the process of translation, meaning can sometimes be misrepresented or misunderstood. Interpreters who are nonnative ASL users may not always sign fluently enough for Deaf native ASL users, which means some Deaf clients can be left struggling to understand what the interpreter is actually signing. As a result, their responses to the therapist's questions or comments may be inappropriate. In such a situation, one hearing clinician may be left confused and uncertain as to whether or not a breakdown in communication with either of the three parties has occurred, if something else is happening. Another clinician may incorrectly assume that the Deaf client has cognitive or intellectual limitations, instead of recognizing the client's puzzling answers as the outcome of an interpreting error.

In the same vein, interpreters may not always understand what the Deaf client is signing, resulting in an inaccurate interpretation for the hearing clinician, and ultimately, an inaccurate diagnosis and treatment plan. On one occasion, an interpreter misread a Deaf client's signing the word "miscarriage," interpreting it instead as "abortion." One can begin to imagine the repercussions of such a misinterpretation in a therapy setting. Clearly then, the simple act of placing an interpreter in the room does not always suffice to level the playing field between the hearing clinician and the Deaf client.

Another illustration of this can be found in the misconstruing of a "word salad," a rambling string of meaningless, incoherent words and phrases caused by disorganized thought processes, typically seen in certain forms of schizophrenia (Corsini, 1999). Interpreters well-trained in mental health issues will likely recognize what is happening and translate accordingly, taking care to inform the clinician of the situation. Interpreters unfamiliar with word salads, in contrast, may attempt to "clean up" the signing and translate it into something that makes more sense, thereby failing to communicate a critical symptom to the clinician. Or in a reverse situation, an unqualified interpreter who misunderstands a client's ASL, may go ahead and voice the client's signing word for word, following the ASL structure, resulting in the hearing clinician being given the impression that the client is speaking in a word salad, when in fact that is not true at all.

Other issues relating to interpreting may be logistical in nature, such as scheduling interpreters, verifying skills, or ensuring that all parties involved know how to work with an interpreter. Issues of transference and countertransference can arise between the different parties involved. In some situations, Deaf people may not trust the interpreter to maintain confidentiality, particularly if they share mutual friends or if they meet often in other settings. They may not want an interpreter to know their personal issues. Although it can be an effective and empowering solution, rarely are Deaf clients given the freedom to choose whom they would like to interpret a mental health appointment.

Also essential is an awareness of the impact that interpreters may have on the therapeutic process, both positive and negative. In spite of their best efforts, interpreters may not always be neutral. Consider the following example related to the generally accepted practice of an interpreter conversing briefly with a Deaf client in the waiting room, prior to the scheduled meeting or interaction with the hearing professional. This is done in order for interpreters to assess clients' signing styles and to make adjustments in their own signing in order to accommodate the clients' needs. In a mental health setting, however, it is particularly important that this "getting acquainted" conversation focus on innocuous topics and that the interpreter remain impartial. If, while sitting in the waiting room, for instance, an interpreter shares with the client a recent experience going snow-tubing with a church group, this may have unintended consequences, however innocent the context in which the remark was thought to be made. Aware that the interpreter has an affiliation with a church group and may possibly hold certain religious beliefs, the client may later be self-conscious or wary about disclosing to the therapist her dilemma about whether or not to have an abortion, thereby hindering the therapeutic process.

Clinicians who use assessment instruments with Deaf people need to consider the appropriateness of their use with this population. Instruments that require written or verbal English can be administered to Deaf clients only after careful consideration. Since English is often a second language for Deaf people, it is crucial that reading level be ascertained before administering the person an instrument in English. Even when English happens to be a Deaf person's first language due to an oral or Signed Exact English background, the person's access to English is not comparable to that of a normal hearing person. When English is learned solely through the eyes or through limited hearing skills, there is the absence of learning subtle nuances of the language that are commonly reinforced through auditory reception, via radios and conversations, for example. Because tests measuring verbal aptitude also indirectly measure education, these tests may not be reliable indicators of Deaf people's verbal performance, due to the fact that not all Deaf people have been fortunate enough to receive accessible education. It is also important to keep in mind that many assessment tools assume knowledge of American culture, as seen from a hearing perspective. Test items related to music, for example, may be unfamiliar to a Deaf test-taker.

The fact that many instruments lack validity norms for the Deaf population poses a challenge in interpreting scores. Additionally, the process of administering certain assessments to Deaf people warrants special attention. A measure of memory, for example, may involve the client listening to a string of numbers and then reiterating them in reverse order. If the examiner is not a native ASL signer, the "accented" rhythm and fingerspelling during the recitation may jar the Deaf client's perceptual sense, negatively impacting the client's ability to hold the numbers accurately in memory. A comparable example for a hearing client might be listening to a heavily accented examiner recite a string of numbers; the unfamiliarity of the voice may inadvertently affect the client's memory, thereby impacting the assessment results. Since visual and auditory memory may be measured differently, as well, the validity of translating an auditory memory task into a visual memory task may be questionable.

Mental status exams present another potential area of misunderstanding. When working with Deaf clients, the clinician must be able to ascertain the difference between affect and ASL, taking care not to confuse ASL modifiers, which are often shown on the face, with expressions of emotions. More than one inexperienced hearing clinician has described a Deaf client as "overly emotional," not realizing that the client's behavior fell well within the linguistic and cultural norms of the Deaf community. So too, must behavior such as stomping a foot loudly to get someone's attention from across the room, be placed into the cultural context, and not misinterpreted as overt aggression. Idioms and colloquial language that are commonly part of mental status exams are often inappropriate when working with Deaf clients. A clinician who asks a nonnative English user for an explanation of "a rolling stone gathers no moss" will probably be met with a blank stare, not reflecting a lack of intelligence or ability to think abstractly, but rather a cultural barrier. The same goes for asking a Deaf client to memorize the expression "no ifs, ands, or buts" and repeat it 15 minutes later. Hearing people may have heard that expression in song lyrics and on the radio, making it not altogether that difficult to retrieve it from memory. For the Deaf person, however, the expression carries no meaning nor does it have any sense of familiarity, making it nearly impossible to recall. Likewise, the expression "feeling blue" may not be one that is understood by a Deaf person with minimal exposure to English.

Use of Art Therapy with Deaf Clients

Art therapy, by virtue of being a visual and tactile treatment modality, lends itself especially well to working with Deaf people. As a creative outlet for self-expression and communication, it offers a safe and accessible way for clients to explore and give meaning to their innermost thoughts and feelings. Where words and signs sometimes fail us, colors and shapes created on paper, molded in clay, or constructed into three-dimensional forms can often convey previously unexpressed thoughts or feelings.

While art therapy should neither be used as a substitute for communication using ASL nor as a compensation for the clinician's lack of signing skills, it can be used effectively with Deaf clients in certain situations where communication may be an issue. Both Deaf adult and child clients with minimal language skills may also find new freedom of expression using the tools of art therapy, which serve to bridge communication gaps. In the same way that hearing children enjoy and flourish through art therapy, so, too, do Deaf children, regardless of their communication abilities or fluency in ASL, benefit from art therapy.

When interpreting or discussing artwork, the therapist should be aware of special issues or themes that may surface with Deaf clients. Trauma issues specific to Deaf clients, for instance, can include experiences at oral schools where signing was forbidden and punished in cruel and abusive ways. In some families where communication barriers between hearing parents and a Deaf child may have led to frustration, the child may have been subjected to abusive treatment. Certain themes such as isolation, inferiority, or self-hatred may come up when a Deaf person has experienced negativity related to being Deaf. Likewise, oppression may be another theme. The therapist will want to take care to avoid generalizations in processing Deaf clients' artwork. To illustrate, the meaning of missing or present ears in a drawing may differ from one Deaf client to another. Missing ears could suggest loss for one client, a preoccupation with hearing status for another, or they may simply reflect the lack of importance of ears to the client. Likewise, proportionally oversized ears may indicate great concern with hearing status or they may just be representative of a lack of artistic skill.

An art therapist working with Deaf clients should be attentive to communication and its presence in art therapy. Therapists should be able to recognize ASL signs that clients may incorporate into their artwork, including, but certainly not limited to, "ILY," the handshape for "I love you," and the sign for "love." Writing that is characterized with grammatical errors should be placed into the context of the Deaf client's educational background and status as a nonnative English user, and not necessarily interpreted as a reflection of the client's intelligence level. Some Deaf people may write English in ASL word order on purpose, as a means of creative expression.

When utilized with families in which the Deaf member is a minority, family art therapy can reveal patterns of interaction and communication that might otherwise have gone unnoticed. The impact of directly experiencing or observing Deaf-hearing family dynamics can be powerful and enlightening, leading to insight and change within family members' relationships. The aquarium building activity, for example, provides families with an opportunity to design their own two-dimensional aquarium, complete with fish constructed individually by each family member, in addition to other adornments such as seaweed, caves, or rocks. The design and placement of each person's fish relative to the others, as well as the interactions during and after the construction phase can reveal much about family relationship patterns.

As a unique assessment and treatment modality, art therapy has much to offer Deaf clients and the mental health professionals who work with them. Visual and tactile in nature, this particular type of therapy is especially well-suited for use with Deaf people. The clinicians who can establish the most effective rapport with this population are those who possess an awareness and understanding of the diversity of Deaf people, their culture and language, as well as sensitivity to the historic patterns of oppression and paternalism they have endured within the American mental health system. Within this therapeutic framework, art therapy offers great potential for inspiring positive change.

REFERENCES

Altshuler K. Z. (1971). Studies of the Deaf: Relevance to psychiatric theory. *American Journal of Psychiatry, 127*(11), 1521–1526.

Altshuler, K. Z., & Rainer, J. D. (1966). *Comprehensive mental health services for the Deaf.* New York: Department of Medical Genetics, New York State Psychiatric Institute, Columbia University.

Altshuler, K. Z., Baroff, G. S., & Rainer, J. D. (1963). Operational description of pilot clinic. In J. D. Rainer, K. Z. Altshuler, & F. J. Kallmann (Eds.), *Family and mental health problems in a deaf population* (pp. 155–166). New York: Department of Medical Genetics, New York State Psychiatric Institute.

Annual Survey of Hearing Impaired Children and Youth (1992–93), Center for Assessment and Demographic Studies, Gallaudet University.

Bahan, B. (2004, April 14). Memoir upon the formation of a visual variety of the human race. Deaf Studies Today 2004 Conference Proceedings, 17–35.

Corsini, R. (1999). *The dictionary of psychology.* Braun-Brumfield: Ann Arbor, MI.

Gulati, S. (2003). Psychiatric care. In N. Glickman, & S. Gulati (Eds.), *Mental health care of Deaf people: A culturally affirmative approach.* Mahwah, NJ: Lawrence Erlbaum Associates.

Kendall, C. J. (2002). Unpublished predissertation. Psychiatric hospitals and residential facilities in the United States specifically serving Deaf adults with mental illnesses. Gallaudet University.

Lane, H., Hoffmeister, R., & Bahan, B. (1996). *A Journey into the Deaf world.* San Diego, CA: DawnSignPress.

Leigh, I. W. (1991). Deaf therapists: Impact on treatment. In Proceedings of the Eleventh World Congress of the World Federation of the Deaf: Equality and Self-reliance (pp. 290–297). Tokyo.

Leigh, I. W., Corbett, C. A., Gutman, V., & Morere, D. A. (1996). Providing Psychological Services to Deaf individuals: A response to new perceptions of diversity. *Professional Psychology: Research and Practice, 27*(4), 364–371.

Leigh, I. W., & Pollard, R. Q. (2003). Mental health and deaf adults. In M. Marschark & P. Spencer (Eds.). *Oxford handbook of deaf studies and deaf education* (pp. 203–215). New York: Oxford University Press.

Marazita, M. L., Ploughman, L. M., Rawlings, B., Remington, E., Arnos, K. S., & Nance, W. E. (1993). Genetic epidemiological studies of early-onset Deafness in the U. S. school-age population. *American Journal of Medical Genetics, 46,* 286–491.

Moores, D. (2001). *Educating the Deaf: Psychology, principles, and practices* (5th Ed.). Boston: Houghton Mifflin.

Morton, D., & Kendall, C. J. (2003). *Mental health services for Deaf people: A resource directory,* 2003 edition. Washington, DC: Gallaudet.

Nancy Doe V. Charles Buck, Case #N-82-2409 (d. Md.).

National Center for Health Statistics (1994). *Data from the National Health Interview Survey* (Series 10, Number 188, Tables 1, B, C, 2). Washington, D.C.

Padden, C. (1980). The Deaf community and the culture of Deaf people. In C. Baker & R. Battison (Eds.), *Sign language and the Deaf community* (pp. 89–103). Washington, D.C.: National Association of the Deaf.

Padden, C., & Humphries, T. (1988). *Deaf in America: Voices from a culture.* Cambridge, MA: Harvard University Press.

Pollard, R. Q. (1994). Public mental health services and diagnostic trends regarding individuals who are Deaf or hard of hearing. *Rehabilitation Psychology, 39*(3), 147–160.

Raifman, L. J., & Vernon, M. (1996), Important implications for psychologists of the Americans with Disabilities Act: Case in point, the patient who is Deaf. *Professional Psychology: Research and Practice, 27*(4), 372–377.

Raifman, L. J., & Vernon, M. (1996). New rights for Deaf patients; New responsibilities for mental hospitals. *Psychiatric Quarterly, 67*(3), 209–220.

Robinson, L. (1978). Sound minds in a soundless world (DHEW Publication No. ADM 77-560). Washington, D.C.: U.S. Government Printing Office.

Rogers, P. (2005). Sign language interpretation in testing environments. In J. L. Monty & D. S. Martin (Eds.), *Assessing deaf adults* (pp. 109–122). Washington D.C.: Gallaudet University.

Steinberg, A. G., Sullivan, V. J., & Loew, R. C. (1998). Cultural and linguistic barriers to mental health service access: The Deaf consumer's perspective. *American Journal of Psychiatry, 155*(7), 982–984.

Stokoe, W. C., Jr., Casterline, D., & Croneberg, C. (1965). *A dictionary of American sign language on linguistic principles.* Washington, D.C.: Gallaudet College Press.

Sussman, A. E., & Brauer, B. A. On being a psychotherapist with Deaf clients. In Leigh, I. W. (1999), *Psychotherapy with Deaf clients from diverse groups,* (pp. 3–22). Washington, D.C.: Gallaudet University Press.

Chapter 2

USING ART TO ASSESS AND DEVELOP THE COGNITIVE SKILLS OF DEAF CHILDREN AND ADOLESCENTS

RAWLEY SILVER

When I began working with Deaf students in 1961, manual communication was prohibited in most of their schools. It seemed to be generally agreed that the students must learn to lip-read and speak or else remain isolated from the hearing world. Consequently, most of the school day was devoted to lip-reading and speech, and manual languages were banned because they were easier to learn. Even so, the children signed to one another furtively, and it was said that each school developed a secret sign language of its own.

I became interested in Deaf children when I was deafened accidentally in mid-life. Although most of my hearing gradually returned, being Deaf for a while made a profound impression. I wondered what my life would have been like had I been Deafened as a child. I also wondered if the visual arts were important in their lives because they were very important in mine. Painting was my vocation and I had been given several one-person shows before the accident.

I visited art classes in several schools for Deaf students. In one, adolescents were taking turns with a single brush, dipping it into green paint, and filling in outlines of an abstract design. In another school, ten-year-olds were copying their teacher's model of a Christmas tree ornament, step-by-step, and even adolescents were not allowed to model clay, only pour it into molds. A third school posted a list of names, identifying students who had broken a crayon or wasted a sheet of paper.

In a school that did not have an art teacher, I asked if I might teach art as a volunteer. The answer was yes, but only if I were a graduate student doing approved research. I enrolled in Teachers College, Columbia University, and since the Department of Special Education had no interest in my ideas, enrolled for a Masters Degree in Fine Arts and Fine Arts Education, taking additional courses in Special Education. The year was 1961 and I had not heard of art therapy. My proposal to the New York City Board of Education was accepted, and I began to work with children who could neither lip-read nor speak. Since I could not sign, we communicated through gestures at first; then I tried drawing to convey ideas. I would make a quick sketch; they would sketch in reply, and so on, stopping as soon as a message was perceived. Gradually, the messages became more personal, about particular individuals and relationships between them.

As new children joined the class, I would start with a quick sketch of my family (two children, husband, and myself) then ask the children to draw those who lived with them. Later meetings were devoted to drawing and painting from imagination. If a child needed help in getting started, I would sketch an animal or some other subject. The most popular sketches were presented again to other children, and eventually became the 56 cards in the *Stimulus Drawing* assessment (Silver, 1982–2002).

Some of the children's responses were so expressive that I prepared a manuscript on the potentials of art in the education of children with hearing impairments, and submitted it to the *Volta Review* journal. After waiting three months for a reply, I asked for its return, and then sent it off to *American Annals of the Deaf* whose editor returned it promptly. When I submitted it to *Eastern Arts Quarterly*, however, it was accepted (Silver, 1962). In addition, it was abstracted in *Rehabilitation Literature*, and then reprinted in a book edited by a former editor of the *Annals* and Vice President of Gallaudet University, among his other titles (Fusfeld, 1967).

Although my views received some support, they also aroused opposition, which seemed to grow as additional journal articles appeared. Some educators of Deaf students saw my approach as a threat to oral methods of instruction. Others saw art as a vaguely enriching kind of busy work. A 1967 survey found that only 54 percent of schools for Deaf students employed art teachers, and 20 percent had no art classes at all (Howell, 1967).

Art educators found my approach harmful to art education. Some objected to using art "as a psychological tool," and warned that standards could not be maintained if students found easy and unjustified success. Others objected to using art for communication. I became aware of unrealistically low expectations of ability when conducting a demonstration project, supported by a grant from the U.S. Office of Education (Silver, 1967). The aim of the project was to obtain information about aptitudes, interests, and vocational opportunities in the visual arts, and to identify effective methods of teaching

Deaf children and adults. Although the Board of Directors of the sponsoring organization had approved the project, its administrators had doubts. One told me that anyone who came to my art class would expect to be paid. Another advised that I would have difficulty finding any students. They were mistaken. After announcing that art classes were available, so many applications arrived that we had to add a second term.

Since the second term was planned for new students, it was necessary for first-term students to find art classes elsewhere if they wanted to continue. To help them find instruction, I approached 23 art schools, settlement houses, YMCAs, and adult education programs. Although some welcomed Deaf students, many did not, and no classes were found for five of the eight children who had attended the first term. For example, the director of a "Y" after-school program said she had no experience with Deaf children but might consider a child who had "intense interest in art and could function well with normal children." She said she would interview the children recommended but would not consider their portfolios or observe the Project art classes.

In addition, I wrote to the Director of an art program for children provided by the Museum of Modern Art, asking if it would be possible for one of my (Deaf) students to attend. I wrote that he was fourteen years old and seemed exceptionally talented. Although he had few words, he was quick to understand and had an attractive personality.

The director was not interested because the Museum program was "not equipped" to handle handicapped students. If he were younger, it might have been possible with his mother in attendance, but at age 14, he was too old.

As the Project continued, I invited eleven educators to observe the art classes and then respond to questionnaires. Two taught academic subjects to Deaf student, three taught art to hearing students, and six had taught both Deaf and hearing students (two taught art and four taught academic subjects).

The only educators who found the Deaf students inferior were the two who taught Deaf children exclusively. The other educators found the Deaf students superior or equal to hearing students in originality, independence, expressiveness, and sensitivity.

One of the students in the Project art class, a boy who will be called, "Charlie," seemed particularly intelligent as well as talented, even though he could not lip-read or speak. Unable to interest psychologists in testing him, I wrote to three prominent specialists for assistance. One did not respond, another suggested that Charlie be tested, and the third, E. Paul Torrance, replied as follows:

> It might be interesting and worthwhile to give him the tests of creative think-ing without a time limit but with a record of time consumed. . . If he does show a high level of performance, such information along with his other

performances might be useful in obtaining support for the kind of training and opportunities he needs to develop his possibilities. I am enclosing herewith a set of the tests, in case you and he are interested. If you will return it to me, I shall be glad to evaluate his performance.

The Torrance Test of Creative Thinking (TTCT) is a measure of creative thinking in general rather than creativity in art and is published in two forms, verbal and figurative. I gave Charlie the figurative test, and sent his response to Dr. Torrance who replied that Charlie had scored in the upper third percentile in Fluency, in the upper tenth percentile in Flexibility, in the upper one-half percentile in Originality, and in Elaboration his score was "almost unexcelled." In addition, Torrance wrote that Charlie's performance was "truly outstanding. His is a record that one does not need to score in order to recognize that it is the production of a creative mind of considerable power . . . (and) reflected a high order of ability to acquire information, form relationships, and, in general, to think."

Dr. Torrance sent additional copies of the test to be administered to other Deaf children in the project art classes, and offered to evaluate the results. The 12 students tested had a very high level of performance. Eight scored in the ninety-ninth percentile (including Charlie). The lowest of the 12 scored in the ninety-third percentile.

I sent copies of the scoring worksheets as well as information about the test to the schools the children attended. Receiving no replies, I made an appointment with the psychologist in Charlie's school who was not impressed. As she wrote, Charlie's performance on the Torrance test "changes nothing because language comes first and there is a limit to what you can do without language" (Silver, 1978, p. 72). One of the observations that concluded the Project report stated that people who work with Deaf students tend to underestimate their abilities, aptitudes, interests, and vocational opportunities.

Even parents of the students who participated in the Project had low expectations. One mother told me that I was wasting my time, and I overheard another tell her son when he showed her his work, "Don't tell me you did that. You couldn't do that. Your teacher must have done it for you." (My suggestions were always made on scrap paper; never on the student's own work).

On the other hand, I heard from teachers of Deaf students elsewhere who shared my expectations and views. One wrote:

> I was fortunate to have a uniquely gifted child and was so excited about his work that I took it to Corcoran Gallery in Washington, D.C. The director of education there was equally enthusiastic. Unfortunately, little can be done now because of almost total disinterest of the parents and relatively little encouragement at school. . . .

We corresponded during the next six years, and then met in 1971 at the Los Angeles conference on Art for the Deaf, which she had arranged.

A teacher in Delaware wrote as follows:

> . . . I have seen teachers give their students stencils to fill in and pictures to copy–and sincerely believing that these are art activities. . . . I have worked very closely with one very sensitive, creative and bright teenager and have seen him able to understand and apply any art concept presented–concepts often not formally verbalized with the hearing until college level courses.

From a teacher in England:

> I am intensely interested in the art of Deaf children but I can find no work on this subject . . . the art of the Deaf has been severely ignored. . . . I have tried every source of information and can find no previous work done, and I am told over and over again this is a field where Deafness makes no difference–how can this be?

And from a teacher in Tennessee:

> . . . I could not agree with you more. My experiences with educators of the Deaf has been mostly negative to my ideas . . . I am now teaching people with normal hearing because nothing has opened in the Nashville area with the Deaf. My heart still belongs with the Deaf and I still dream that I will make a small breakthrough.

Subsequent Studies

During the next 12 years, I wrote 13 journal articles and a book about developing and assessing the cognitive skills of Deaf and language-impaired children and adults (Silver, 1968–1977). In addition, I received a grant from the New York State Department of Education to develop cognitive skills through studio art experiences (Silver, 1973), and the Smithsonian Institution circulated two exhibitions of drawings and paintings by my Deaf students (Silver, 1976, 1979). The letters, drawings, and other materials that were collected have been donated to the archives of Gallaudet University.

Charlie and the Silver Drawing Test of Cognition and Emotion (SDT)

When the Demonstration Project ended, Charlie remained in the class for slow learners. When he graduated, he found employment in a greenhouse, and then built a greenhouse of his own. He also continued to draw. For example, he drew Figure 2–1 almost a year after visiting me at home and walking in the woods nearby. The three large oak trees did exist as he portrayed them, and a maple seedling did grow from the base of the oak in the foreground. Charlie had remembered the spatial relationships between the oak trees seen in one brief visit, then after learning that a hurricane had come our way, drew the devastation he imagined. At the time of his visit, I was trying to develop a test to tap cognitive skills nonverbally, and asked Charlie to respond to drawing tasks, which were subsequently standardized and published as the SDT.

Figure 2-1.

The SDT is based on the theory that cognitive skills evident in verbal conventions also can be evident in visual conventions, and that drawing can bypass verbal weaknesses and capitalize on visual strengths. It presents conceptual problems visually as well as verbally, and asks respondents to respond through drawings (Silver, 1983–2002). It is designed to assess ability to solve problems through Predictive Drawing, Drawing from Observation, and Drawing from Imagination. Scores are based, in part, on observations by Piaget (1970), who noted that the three most fundamental concepts in reading and mathematics are concepts of space, sequential order, and class inclusion.

Charlie's response to the Predictive Drawing subtest is shown in Figure 2–2. The task asks respondents to predict changes in appearance by drawing lines on outline drawings. Their responses are scored for level of ability to represent concepts of horizontality, verticality, and sequential order. In horizontality, his drawing received the maximum score because his line in the tilted bottle parallels the table surface within five degrees. In verticality, his drawing received the highest score because the house on the mountain slope is vertical with adequate support (more than adequate!).

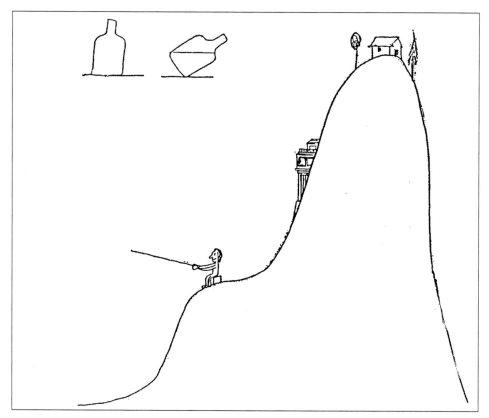

Figure 2–2.

Charlie's response to the Drawing from Observation subtest is shown in Figure 2–3. The task asks respondents to draw an arrangement of three cylinders and a stone. Responses are scored for level of ability to represent spatial relationships in three dimensions horizontally, vertically, and in depth. In horizontality, Charlie's drawing received the maximum score, because all adjacent objects are in the correct left-right positions, and his discriminations are fine rather than crude. In verticality, his drawing received the maximum score because all four objects are correctly related in height, with fine discriminations. In depth, his drawing received the maximum score because all four objects are correctly related, again with fine discriminations.

Charlie's response to the Drawing from Imagination subtest is shown in

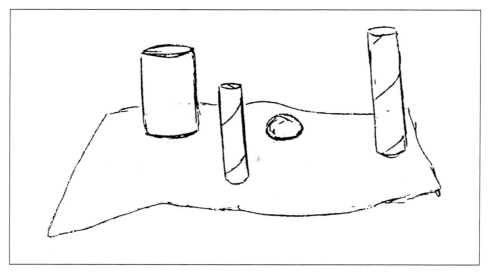

Figure 2–3.

Figure 2–4. This task is to select two subjects from an array of stimulus drawings, imagine something happening between the subjects selected, and then draw what is happening. Responses are scored for ability to select (content of the drawing), ability to combine (form of the drawing), and ability to represent (the creativity or originality of the drawing). Charlie's response drawing also receives the maximum possible scores. It represents an imaginative, well-organized idea at the level of abstraction (implying more than is visible). It shows overall coordination, and in creativity, it goes beyond restructuring the stimulus drawings he chose, and is both original and playful.

Comparing the SDT Scores of Hearing-Impaired and Hearing Children

It is often assumed that children with language and hearing impairments lag behind unimpaired children. To test the assumption, a recent study compared the SDT performances of 27 Deaf and 28 hearing children, ages 9 to 11 (Silver, 2001).

The hearing-impaired subjects included 13 girls and 14 boys in an urban nonresidential school for Deaf children in New York. They included all the children in the fourth grade who previously had responded to the SDT. Their scores on the WISC Performance Scale ranged from 72 to 130. One girl and one boy had "multiple handicaps."

The hearing subjects included 14 girls and 14 boys attending two public elementary schools, matched in age and selected at random by a classroom

Figure 2–4.

teacher in New Jersey and an art therapist in Pennsylvania, and scored by teachers and art therapists.

In vertical orientation, the group of Deaf children received significantly higher scores than the group of hearing children ($F_{(1.51)} = 14.34$, $p < .001$). Their mean scores were 3.13 and 2.00 respectively. In horizontal orientation and ability to sequence, no significant differences between groups were found.

In Drawing from Observation, no significant differences between groups emerged in ability to represent spatial relationships in height, width, and depth.

In Drawing from Imagination, however, the hearing children received higher scores than the Deaf children in each of the three cognitive skills under consideration: ability to select ($F_{(1.51)} = 12.85$, $p < .001$; ability to combine ($F_{(1,51)} = 57.66$, $p < .000001$); and ability to represent ($F_{(1,51)} = 30.99$, $p < .000001$). The mean scores were 3.68 versus 2.90 for selecting, 3.93 versus 1.98 for combining, and 3.89 versus 2.27 for representing. (See Tables 2–1, 2–2, 2–3.)

It was surprising to find the Deaf children superior to the hearing children in vertical orientation. Only four of the 55 children drew vertical houses on the slope, and three of the four were Deaf. Perhaps they were more observant and had discovered that houses remain vertical even on steep slopes, but must be cantilevered or supported by posts. Several psychologists who responded to the drawing task drew houses perpendicular to the slope, perhaps because they have not yet made this discovery.

Why did the Deaf children lag behind the hearing children in the Drawing from Imagination subtest? Perhaps because they lagged behind in ability to select, combine, and represent their thoughts and feelings through words. If so, additional experiences in Drawing from Imagination may lead to gains in language skills. On the other hand, it may be that selecting images and combining them in drawings involves mental operations that differ from selecting words and combining them in sentences.

Comparing the Scores of Deaf, Learning Disabled, and Unimpaired Children

In a subsequent study, 28 learning–impaired children were added, bringing the total number of subjects to 83 children ages 9 to 11. The additional students included 22 boys and six girls who attended three special schools in Connecticut and New York. The SDT was administered and scored by teachers and art therapists, and the findings were analyzed by a psychologist (Madeline Altabe, Ph.D).

An overall ANOVA was conducted and an effect group found (Rao's R = 4.21, p < .000001). Subsequent ANOVA's and LSD tests were used to determine which group differed on what measures. For ability to predict verticality, the Deaf children (3.13) scored higher than either learning disabled (2.23) or unimpaired children (2.00), ($F_{(2,77)}$ = 6.17 , p < .05). For ability to represent horizontal relationships, the Deaf (3.93) and unimpaired children (3.54) scored higher than the learning disabled (2.80). For ability to select, combine, and represent, the unimpaired children scored higher than either Deaf or learning disabled children.

A Cross-Cultural Study

Investigators in Russia have translated the SDT, developed normative data, and compared age, gender, and national differences (Kopytin et al., 2002). They also administered the SDT to students with and without disabilities. They found no significant differences in the scores of children and adolescents with normal language skills and those with language-impairments, and concluded that the cognitive skills assessed by the SDT were independent of verbal skills.

Concluding Observations

In 1995 as in 1962, I submitted a manuscript to a journal for educators of hearing–impaired students, did not receive a reply, withdrew the manuscript, and submitted it elsewhere. The manuscript had reported the study that compared the SDT performances of Deaf, learning disabled, and unimpaired students, and found the Deaf students superior in ability to represent verticality; inferior in ability to select, combine, and represent; and equal in the other abilities under consideration, as reviewed above.

This chapter concludes with one of the concluding observations of the 1967 Demonstration Project: that some educators and others who work with Deaf students seem to have unrealistically low expectations of what these students are able to do; and low expectations tend to be self-fulfilling.

Table 2–1. Verticality Scores.

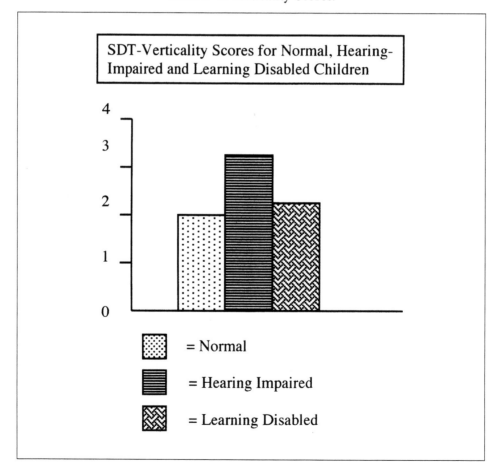

Table 2–2. Horizontality Scores.

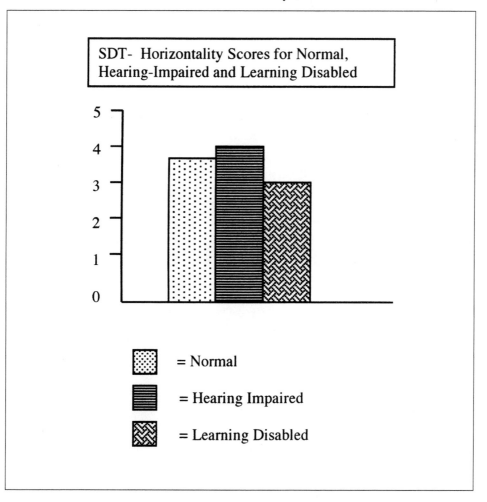

Table 2–3. Select Scores.

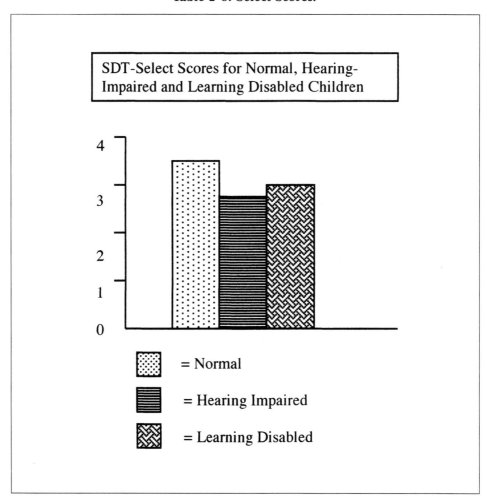

Table 2–4. Represent Scores.

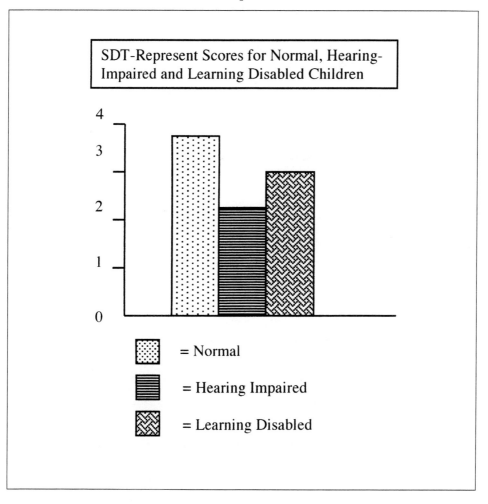

Table 2–5. Combined Scores.

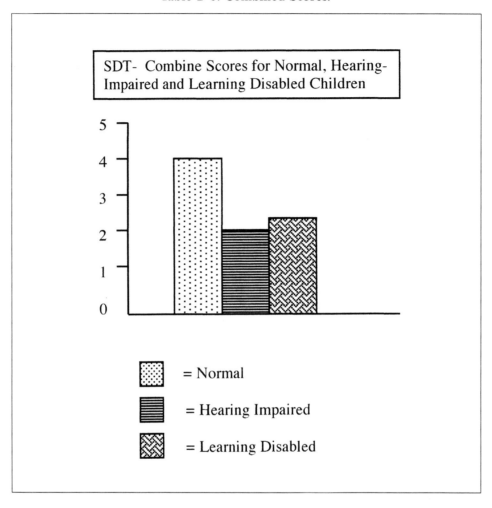

REFERENCES

Fusfeld, I. S. (1967). *A handbook of readings in education of the deaf and postschool implications.* Springfield, IL: Charles C Thomas.

Howell, S. S. (1967). *An Evaluation of the Art and Crafts Programs Available for Students Sixteen and Above in the Public Residential and Day School for the Deaf in the U.S.*, Unpublished Master of Science thesis, University of Tennessee.

Kopytin, A. (2002). The Silver Drawing test of Cognition and Emotion: Standardization in Russia. *American Journal of Art Therapy, 40* (4), 223–237.

Piaget, J. (1970). *Science of Education and the Psychology of the Child.* New York: The Viking Press.

Silver, R. (1962). Potentials in Art for the Deaf. *Eastern Arts Quarterly, 1* (2).

____ (1966). The role of Art in the Conceptual Thinking, Adjustment, and Aptitudes of Deaf and Aphasic Children. *Doctoral Project Report.* Teachers College, Columbia University.

____ (1967). A Demonstration Project in Art Education for Deaf and Hard of Hearing Children and Adults. *U.S. Office of Education Bureau of Research.* Project # 6-8598

____ (1968). Art education and the education of Deaf students, Co-author John Harrington, *The Volta Review, 70* (60), 475–478. Reprinted in Curriculum, Cognition, and Content, Washington, D.C.: A. G. Bell Association.

____ (1970a). Art and the Deaf. *Bulletin of Art Therapy, 9* (2), 63–67.

____ (1970b). Art breaks the silence. *Children's House, 4* (4), 10–13.

____ (1971). The role of art in the cognition, adjustment, transfer, and aptitudes of Deaf children. In Claire Deussen (Ed.), *Proceedings of the Conference on Art for the Deaf,* (pp. 15–26). Junior Arts Center of the City of Los Angeles.

____ (1972). The transfer of cognition and attitudes of Deaf and aphasic children through art. *State of Illinois Instructional Materials Center.* No. 62706.

____ (1973). A study of cognitive skills development through art experiences. *NY State Urban Education Project* No. 147 232 10. ERIC ED No. 084 745.

____ (1975a). Using art to evaluate and develop cognitive skills: Children with communication disorders and children with learning disabilities. Paper presented at the 1975 *AATA Conference.* ERIC ED No. 116 401.

____ (1975b). Children with communication disorders: Cognitive and artistic development. *American Journal of Art Therapy, 14* (2), 39–47.

____ (1975c). Clues to cognitive functioning in the drawings of stroke patients. *American Journal of Art Therapy, 15* (1), 3–8.

____ (1976a). *Shout in silence: Visual arts and the Deaf.* Exhibition circulated by the Smithsonian Institution, 1969–1976. Catalogue published by the Metropolitan Museum of Art.

____ (1976b). Using art to develop cognitive skills. *American Journal of Art Therapy, 16* (1), 11–19.

____ (1976c). Objectives and methods of teaching art to Deaf students. *Viewpoints: Dialogues in Art Education, 3* (1), 26–28.

____ (1977a). The question of Imagination, originality, and abstract thinking by Deaf children. *American Annals of the Deaf, 122* (3), 349–354.

____ (1978–2000). *Developing Cognitive and Creative Skills Through Art.* Baltimore, University Park Press, and Lincoln, NE, iUniverse.com, and Author's Guild Backinprint edition.

____ (1979a). *Art as language for the handicapped.* Exhibition circulated by the Smithsonian Institution, ERIC ED No. 185 774.

____ (1979b). Teaching handicapped children. *Arts & Activities, 85* (3), 41.

____ (1982–2002). *Stimulus drawings and techniques in therapy development.* New York: Trillium Press and Brunner-Routledge.

_____ (1983–2002). *Silver Drawing Test of Cognitive and Creative Skills.* Seattle: Special Child Publications, and New York, Brunner-Routledge.

_____ (2001). *Art as language.* New York, Brunner-Routledge.

Torrance, E. P. (1966). *Torrance Test of Creative Thinking, Figural Form A.* Princeton: Personnel Press, Inc.

Chapter 3

FAMILY ART THERAPY WITH THE DEAF: INTERPRETATIONS

ELLEN G. HOROVITZ

INTRODUCTION

In this chapter, I will explore the research, which I found relevant in working with family systems and the Deaf population. Although I might have spent an extraordinary amount of time discussing family therapy theories—that is structural, paradoxical, strategic and/or other family system modalities, this chapter was not intended to color the reader's perspective in that arena. While my work is embedded in Bowenian theory with a structural systems approach, my intention was not to focus on family systems theories but rather to illuminate the considerations that one needs to explore when working within the Deaf culture.

Three areas of concern are relevant in understanding family dynamics with the Deaf population: language systems, the mourning process, and the role of an interpreter. This paper investigates these three factors and also highlights the family art therapy process with two quite different clinical cases.

Initially, my formulation of family art therapy with Deaf people seemed relatively simple. Armed with such experiences of previous family therapy texts by such pioneers as Haley (1963) and Minuchin (1974), and Bowen (1963), my expectations were undauntingly hopeful, not to mention dangerously naive. Soon it became all too clear that methods for engaging a Deaf child and his/her family in art therapy treatment had not heretofore been explored. Several reasons accounted for this omission including parental resistance to treatment, geographical distance (when children were institutionalized), communication difficulties, and denial of the Deafness issue, just to mention a few.

Nevertheless, I contended that treating the child within the confines of the family configuration was important–especially if a child resided in a residential treatment facility for emotionally disturbed, Deaf children. Distance problems, and compartmentalized communication often undercut family treatment possibilities. This raised a significant barrier when working with a family and the Deaf child where two language systems had to be integrated.

Language Systems

Analyzing a family's system via its communication style is fundamental to family therapy. With the Deaf population, this becomes crucial. For example, modes of communication employed by family members vary and the range of language systems may be expansive, circumscribed, bimodal or virtually absent. For the Deaf child, visual information constitutes inner language. Without expression or a way to communicate this language, the Deaf child becomes trapped, isolated from his family.

Meadow (1980) reviewed language acquisition for three categories of Deaf children whose linguistic environments and socialization inputs differed according to the communication modes of their parents. The first group included Deaf children of Deaf parents who used only Ameslan (American Sign Language). The second group was composed of those whose hearing or Deaf parents used a simultaneous combination of spoken and/or signed English. Finally, the third group's hearing parents spoke English as their sole means of communication.

While Deaf children whose parents exposed them to a simultaneous combination of signed and spoken English developed bimodal expressive language, the children whose parents used the strict oral English approach acquired language at a "painfully slower" rate. Furthermore, Meadow (1980) noted that children who were "exposed to early simultaneous manual/oral input appeared to develop more adequate inner language, with no reduction in their abilities to use speech and speech reading for communication than those children who weren't so exposed" (p. 42–43).

Moores (1982) reports consistent research findings, which consistently indicate that Deaf children of Deaf parents were superior in academic achievement and English language abilities when compared to Deaf children of hearing parents.

According to the research of Rainer et al. (1969), Rawlings (1973), Schein (1974) and Delk (1974), 90 percent of the United States Deaf population has hearing parents of which 88 percent do ***not*** know sign language. Although this is shocking to learn, given the educational changes which have moved from an oral/aural approach to total communication (e.g., sign language, gesture, mime, writing, fingerspelling, etc.), it is somewhat understandable, although certainly not palatable, in this writer's opinion.

In 1980, Padden and Trybus noted the primary language of the Deaf to be American Sign Language. Harvey (1982) found most Deaf children and their hearing parents unable to communicate in this primary language system, i.e., Ameslan. (This language is linguistically distinct from signed English even though both are considered manual communication.) Ameslan has its own syntax and is not derived from English grammatical structure, whereas Signed English follows the same syntax as spoken English (Harvey, 1984). Ameslan, the primary language of the Deaf, seemed to be central to perpetuating the very heart of the Deaf culture.

When both parents and child are Deaf, then the child is more fully accepted and subject to less emotional tensions than in families where Deafness is an unprecedented occurrence (Levine, 1960). Yet, according to the aforementioned research, this situation is not the prevalent one. Therefore, what the family therapist commonly faces are families whose members don't speak the same language at all.

This finding should not be underestimated in treatment. Generally, a prototypical family includes at least one Deaf child, hearing parents, and at least one hearing sibling. Two distinct cultures and languages are represented. Harvey (1984) states that a hearing family therapist becomes a "cross cultural and bilingual phenomenon." Consequently, in facilitating communication, the clinician first needs an understanding of the mourning process, which unfolds in reaction to the reality of Deafness.

Mourning Process

Stein and Jabaley (1981) discussed reactions of parents following the initial diagnosis of Deafness. These reactions include shock, denial, anger, depression and eventually acceptance. Although these mourning stages characterize parental reaction to any severe disability, Harvey (1984) concluded that the stage of denial is prolonged for parents of Deaf children. Earlier, Mindel and Vernon (1971) had observed denial to be among the most common of defense mechanisms in families in which there are Deaf children.

Shapiro and Harris (1976), Stein and Jabaley (1981) and Harvey (1984) found in families with one Deaf child that the mother is often overinvolved with the handicapped child, that the father usually retreats into excessive work or alcoholic consumption, and that the hearing children often become the parental children. The sibling supervises the Deaf child while the mother investigates educational and/or treatment programs because the father is "busy."

Distribution of labor and power sustains the family myth of the Deaf child as relatively helpless and unintelligent. However, the fact of that matter is that the child has poor communication skills. This isolates and causes passive anger in the Deaf child who acts inept and incompetent. Haley (1963) recognized this "sick" stance as disguised anger relatively common in all families with an identical member in the patient role.

Yet, threatening this established "balance of power" (Harvey, 1984) is paramount to recasting a family communication system. The interactions and interdependence of family members governs the functioning system. Although the therapist can usually mediate a shift in this family arrangement, the decision to introduce an outside party in the person of an interpreter can dramatically alter the way family members relate in therapy.

Role of the Interpreter

Utilizing interpreter services has been a controversial and much debated topic. Harvey (1984) insists that the presence of an interpreter immediately restructures this "balance of power." Moreover, the interpreter offers the child a vehicle of communication for articulating in English what the child has signed in ASL. Thus the family is forced to realize that the child is not helpless. Yet there is resistance to changing the status quo. In Harvey's words, "logic does not always dictate action." Moreover, the parents experience comparable feelings to the time when their child was diagnosed as Deaf, disbelief in the impairment and in their ability to cope with it. In the family session, the interpreter, by default, symbolizes the crises presented by the Deaf child and is often viewed as the symbolic, Deaf child.

This symbolic identity can be incorporated into treatment. The interpreter perforce becomes the child's voice and augments it. Harvey (1984) proposes that the Deaf child and interpreter appear to meld, allowing the family members to project, displace and transfer their feelings and attitudes onto the interpreter. In this context, the interpreter can serve a twofold purpose: to facilitate communication and to aid the transference process.

As with all hypotheses, there are other ideas to refute them. The research findings of Maher and Waters (1984) presented both sides of the argument–the interpreter as a third party detrimental to counseling and the converse, nothing that an interpreter provided fast, accurate communication which "might not otherwise be (available)."

Scott (1984) attacked the writings of Harvey (1984) and questioned the wisdom of an interpreter's functioning as a "tabula rasa" (blank slate). He cautioned that the interpreter's presence implied that communication would be impossible without him (or her) and that this compounded the family's isolation by driving a deeper wedge between the members.

In a rejoinder to Scott (1984), Harvey (1984) pointed out his rationale for using an interpreter: (1) Effective therapy requires intense concentration and that conducting therapy combined with transliteration of two different languages systems is impossible; (2) It is the therapist's responsibility to respect the Deaf person's modus operandi and provide him with the best possible vehicle of communication.

Therein lies the heart of the argument in working with the Deaf population and family systems. A family practitioner faces essentially three alternatives: (1) To use an interpreter; (2) Not to use an interpreter and; (3) To try both and discover stylistically which approach works best for the family and clinician. I found it necessary to experiment with all three methods.

When working with smaller family systems (e.g., a mother/child dyad), I have found that working without the interpreter is possible because there are few interacting members and concentration on both transliterating and effective therapy can be achieved. Moreover, the therapist's direct involvement in the transactions expedites intimacy and communication between family members. However, when working with the kinds of families previously described (hearing parents and hearing siblings who don't sign), and one Deaf child, the use of an interpreter is an essential ingredient in enhancing the communication and transference process. Furthermore, in my experience, the interpreter's presence not only aids the family in connecting with the child but also aids the Deaf child, in viewing the parents' helplessness. While the interpreter becomes the symbolic stand-in for the Deaf child for the parents, he/she often also serves as the symbolic stand-in parent for the Deaf child. For these reasons, the interpreter needs to be well-versed in mental health principles.

This transferential shift from therapist to interpreter is quite complex. The therapist needs to clearly define the interpreter's role and his expectations for functioning in the context of family therapy. By definition an interpreter is a person who conveys one person's message to another and this may involve (1) "a change in the mode of communication used by the sender; (2) a change in the language used by the sender; and (3) a change in the mode of communication and the language" (Dirst & Caccamise, 1980). Thus, by intent, the interpreter can function as a co-therapist. Apparently, many clinicians' sole objection to an interpreter is based on this premise and do not see a therapeutic devise, namely the interpreter coupled with the (art) therapist (and art materials) facilitating the transference process.

The Use of Art Therapy

Because art therapy can be a nonverbal intervention, it is a particularly valuable approach when working with Deaf/hearing-impaired population.

The language of Deaf people, made up of fingerspelling, manual signs, gestures, mime, facial expression, and body language, is primarily visual. Utilizing visual media when working with this population can offer another avenue for communication. Both the art process and product have meaning and form which take on the structure of conceptual, visual language.

Art Therapy has the unique power of reaching even the most regressed clients who have been unsuccessful in resolving their inner conflicts through traditional psychotherapeutic intervention. Children who have difficulty bridging the gap between their hearing parents and themselves often need an alternative mode of expression. (N.B. Editor's Note: The same is true when hearing children are in treatment with Deaf parents, as will be reviewed in chapter 5.)

As cited earlier, the role of the interpreter can be paramount in facilitating communication within the family context. Hence, it is not only important to offer the family another avenue for communication (e.g., art therapy) but often a necessity for some children's survival within that environment.

When working with families in an art therapy milieu, the art process becomes integrated into the family system's functioning. With the Deaf child, the interaction in the group process reflects the family's communication patterns, its networking aspects, and the parameters of the family constellation.

Whether the family works separately or as a group, the interaction or lack of interaction is reflected not only in the graphic process but also in the family's verbal interaction. Aspects of isolation, integration, and individuation surface both through the art symbols, the signed work, and in the unsigned (e.g., oral) communication. The therapist's role is to recognize these strata and mediate appropriate family interaction among the various communications. Because this is often a painful process, the art therapist must proceed in a cautious manner, offering interpretation when appropriate while gently nudging the family towards self-interpretation and actualization.

The specific art materials chosen can expedite this process. As with any population, the art therapist must choose these materials geared for the task at hand. Whether the need be regression or integration, the art materials can help foster change both in communication and family systems functioning. Specifically, the graphic components of the art mirror the visual aspects of sign language and pictorially aid the Deaf client's ability to bridge the gap between the Deaf culture and the hearing world.

Since art therapy treatment is based on a complete diagnostic work-up of the individual Deaf child, much consideration must be given to the child's basic presenting problems and to family history. Some of the instruments used in an art therapy diagnosis (Horovitz-Darby, 1987, 1988), includes administration of the following tests: Cognitive Art Therapy Assessment (exploration in three media–drawing, painting, and clay scored according to

Lowenfeld and Brittain, 1975); the Silver Drawing Test of Cognitive and Creative Skills, (Silver, 1983, revised 2002); the House Tree Person Test (both chromatic and achromatic), Buck (1950); the Kinetic Family Drawing Test, (Burns & Kaufman 1972); and the Bender-Gestalt Visual Motor Test II, (Koppitz, 1968, revised Brannigan & Decker, 2003). The results of these tests on a pretest/post-test administration have been consistently uniform and valid in prediction. Administration of these tests, both pre-treatment and annually, allows the practitioner to chart cognitive progress, emotional growth, and reassess family-related issues. In addition, the family members are often administered the Kinetic Family Drawing in order to assess the family's perspective of the members' roles and that of the Deaf child in a global, interactional context.

Case Illustrations

Case one, John, is a patient who was in long-term, individual art therapy treatment for three years. Family art therapy sessions, interspersed through-out this patient's treatment, aided his ability to communicate with his family and thus expedited discharge from his residential placement. Later, he continued in weekly outpatient, art therapy treatment and weekly psychotherapy with his social worker. There were 106 individual art therapy sessions and 12 family art therapy sessions. The underlying family dynamics (language system, the mourning process, and the role of an interpreter) are continually examined.

Case 1: John

At intake, John was a precocious, profoundly Deaf, eleven-year-old child. He had a hearing sibling, Sandy, age 14, a half-brother, Sean, age 3, from his mother's second marriage, and a one-year-old half-brother, Tom, from his father's second marriage. Both his biological mother and father were involved in separate family art therapy sessions.

Mother reported normal developmental milestones for John until age 14 months when he was described as "being into everything" and "hyperactive." At three and a half years, John was placed in a residential school for the Deaf and had difficulty separating from his family. At age 5, John had become used to the separation and was able to adjust to weekend home visits and returns to the institution. Around this time, John was witness to continual verbal and physical interactions between his parents. Frequently, he would display temper tantrums, yet his mother tended to ignore this behavior. At age 6, when the parents divorced, this behavior increased.

Both parents remarried and had one child through the new unions. The births of younger siblings were difficult issues for John so that issues of being displaced surfaced both in his individual and family work.

Presenting symptoms included stealing from his maternal grandmother, assaultive behavior toward family members, inappropriate sexual play with siblings, threatening to cut his mother with broken glass, and overturning furniture when upset. It is also important to note that John blamed mother when father did not show for visitation and continually asked if he could live with him. Moreover, his feelings of guilt were embedded in fantasies that his hearing loss caused their divorce.

John's Timeline

Birth–13 months – normal developmental milestones
14 months – described as hyperactive
3.5 years – diagnosed deaf, placed in residential treatment for deaf children (Rochester School for the Deaf–RSD), experienced great difficulty with parental separation
5 years – parents separate, adjusts to separation from parents at RSD and weekend home visits, witness to parental altercations
6 years – parents divorce, behavioral problems increase both in and out of the home
7–8 years – both parents remarry and have new births occur with these respective new unions
10 years – placed in residential inpatient treatment while attending school at RSD
10.3 years – referred to art therapy
12 years – discharged to RSD and continues with outpatient art therapy
13 years – terminates outpatient art therapy and continues psychotherapy

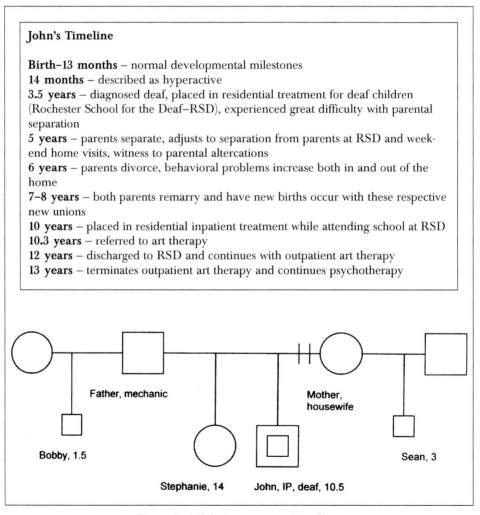

Father, mechanic   Mother, housewife

Bobby, 1.5   Stephanie, 14   John, IP, deaf, 10.5   Sean, 3

Figure 3–1. John's genogram/timeline.

Abbreviated Results of the Diagnostic Art Therapy Tests

Although psychological testing was attempted at his residential school, John was resistant. Testing was unsuccessful in residential treatment until age 10 years, when he was administered the Diagnostic Art Therapy Assessment. The tests administered included the Cognitive Art Therapy Assessment, the House Tree Person (chromatic and achromatic. Horovitz-Darby, 1987, 1988), the Silver Drawing Test (Silver, 1983, revised 2002), and the Kinetic Family Drawing test (Burns & Kaufman, 1972).

John's clay response to the Cognitive Art Therapy Assessment allowed the release of much energy and frustration. The end product, a locked box, reflected John's desire to be valuable, safeguarded, protected, and impenetrable, a theme that was pervasive through all his treatment sessions.

Figure 3–2. CATA Clay Response.

Both John's achromatic and chromatic responses on the House Tree Person Test reflected disorganization, inner chaos, and feelings of vulnerability. Issues raised by drawing the house resulted in the disintegration of its wall structure. The Kinetic Family Drawing (KFD) yielded two responses. In his first attempt, John drew his family with father, mother, sister, Sandy, and half-brother Sean.

Sean's obvious foreground placement represented John's own feelings of displacement. Later, I discovered that failing to provide mother with a mouthpiece was noteworthy since John often told his mother to "shut-up" during family sessions. In the second KFD drawing, John articulated his father and stepmother (not shown). Stepmother was illustrated as pregnant. Displaced, John did not even see himself as part of this family system.

Figure 3–3. KFD #1.

Figure 3–4. KFD #2.

On the Silver Drawing Test, John scored in the fourteenth percentile (14%) for grade 5. The score reflected minimal developmental delay. Cognitively, John seemed to be functioning at the schematic stage of development, aged 7–9 years (Lowenfeld & Brittain, 1975).

Based on his response to the art materials, weekly art therapy intervention was recommended to facilitate ego maturation, appropriate mastery and control of impulses, and cognitive gains.

The Work

There had been 106 individual sessions, 10 family sessions with mother and family and two family sessions with father and stepmother. In the individual sessions, no interpreter was used due to the author's proficiency in sign language. However, in all family sessions, an interpreter was used since ASL is nearly impossible to transliterate coupled with focusing on the dynamics of the family system (Harvey, 1984).

Initially, John used the art materials for sublimation and regressive activity. Themes that continued to surface included his overwhelming need for protection, security, and value, his deep-seated anger as well as depression regarding fears of inadequacy and incompetence, and his feelings of displacement within the family constellation. An example of this displacement surfaced in Figure 3–5, a large, clay fire alarm. John scrawled a vagina on the alarm, covered it with a penis and erased over the penis. He then smeared

Figure 3–5. Fire Alarm.

clay on his genital area and attempted to pull a real fire alarm during cleanup. When asked if he was feeling angry with his stepmother's new baby, John screamed, "The whole family shits." His inability to harness this inner chaos later resulted in regression and resistance to therapeutic intervention.

Several months passed and John's need to master these feelings resulted in a barrage of clay locks and safes. Not only did they symbolize his need to contain his aggressive feelings but more importantly his desire to feel valuable, worthy of safeguarding. Figure 3–6 is an example of his work at this time.

Figure 3–6. Clay lock.

Since the family lived approximately two and one-half hours from the residential program, 30 sessions elapsed before the first family session with John's mother, grandmother and sister. John, extremely resistant to the family interview, became irate when the interpreter asked questions. He insisted that the family issues were "none of (her) business" and that there were "too many people in the room." The presence of the interpreter had already introduced the transference process (Harvey, 1984). Clearly, John was responding to the introduction of this "stranger" and displacing his anger onto the interpreter.

His resistance was also reflected in the art. He refused to make from clay a person in the family doing something. Instead he made a safe, again depicting his need to protect himself and his feelings.

John also ventilated his anger towards his stepfather. He complained of his stepfather's excessive drinking and admitted jealousy of his younger brother, Sean. His mother agreed with John's perception of her husband and added that she "didn't like (him) very much" either. This pattern as described by the family fit the research of Shapiro and Harris (1976), Stein and Jabaley (1981), and Harvey (1984), who described the hearing fathers as often retreating into alcoholic consumption and excessive work.

In an individual session following the family meeting, John's need to be valued and be important to others evolved in a clay crown, which was later painted gold and bedecked with jewels. Alongside, John placed gold coins and gold bullion, which he formed outside of the session.

One month later, his sister and mother came for a second family session. Prior to John's arrival, both complained about the stepfather's excessive alcoholism. Sandy admitted feeling unloved by the stepfather and confessed "pressure" at "always having to sign for John." Thus, Sandy described her role in the family hierarchy as described by Shapiro and Harris (1976), Stein and Jabaley (1981), and Harvey (1984). The mother confided that she was unable to solve these problems, thrusting the responsibility back onto the hearing sibling as reiterated by the aforementioned researchers.

Sandy also discussed her grief over her paternal grandfather's recent death but insisted she didn't want to discuss it in the family session. However, John brought this up when he entered. He asked Sandy if she were "planning to cry at the funeral" and if she had "cried last night." This writer interpreted John's need to ask permission to express his feelings.

Later, John expressed his desire to paint his mother's previous sculpture gold. Again the interpretation was made regarding his need to have value and importance, to which he agreed. He then added that he didn't want the stepfather to attend and looked forward to having separate sessions with his "real mother and father." This author clarified that his need to have sessions with his "real parents" reflected his desire for a parental reconciliation. This initiated discussion of John's guilt regarding the divorce. He admitted feeling responsible because of his Deafness.

The following week, John's father and stepmother attended their first family session. An explanation of art therapy ensued. Members were instructed to make whatever they felt. John's stepmother created a clay heart embossed with "I love you," a light bulb, and a paperweight. Graphically, these items seemed to reflect her desire to communicate her love for John, her attempt to acknowledge his fascination with electricity, and her unconscious feelings about the weight and burden John placed on her family.

John's father's work, Figure 3–7, reflects a man in a fishing boat. Yet, there is only one person in the boat. Symbolically, the father may have been telling John that he needed to man his own boat. John made a lock and wrench, which he later gave to this writer. Although he created items that would interest his father, his decision to offer them to the author eloquently stated his position that the art therapist "fix" the family system.

Figure 3–7. Father's boat.

Discussion revolved around how John was doing with the father and stepmother's new baby. His stepmother replied that John was "very good with the baby–changing him, feeding him," and the like. But John sadly pointed out that he couldn't hear the baby cry, thus referring to what Meadow (1980) described in her review of language acquisition being painfully different for the Deaf child whose linguistic and socialization inputs vastly differ from his/her (hearing) parents. Neither his father nor stepmother responded to John's sadness and isolation. Attempts to initiate dialogue amongst the three were minimal; John avoided eye contact. The father and stepmother's stance modeled the patterns of defensive posture that Stein and Jabaley (1981) alluded to in their research.

The following month John's mother and sister attended a session. John entered angrily and refused to work at the table with his family. When urged to return to the table to be part of the family, John signed that he "wasn't part of that family." John blamed his mother for causing the father to leave. He called her "stupid and dumb" and stated that the father became an alcoholic because of her. His sister defended her mother and pointed out that the father still drank. The mother attempted to explain the reason behind the divorce but John refused to accept her explanations and left angrily. Later, his mother informed me that once outside the door, John told his mother he loved her and hated me. Clearly, he was able to transfer his negative feelings onto me. Yet, mother resisted treatment and conveniently forgot the next session. The balance of power had definitely been challenged (Harvey, 1984) and the family's reaction in this session mirrored their fears, losing their present mode of dysfunction.

John coped well with this rejection and was able to express his feelings and bond more closely with this writer in subsequent sessions. His maturation revealed considerable cognitive development, which had been untapped. Figure 3–8, John's Tutankhamen, mirrored his growth during this period. He had worked diligently for six weeks on this project.

Figure 3–8. Tutankhamen.

In the later family session with his mother and maternal grandmother, he continued his work on King Tut. The grandmother created a squirrel eating a nut and the mother, a bird eating a fish. Both creatures are nurtured and symbolize the women's desire to be more nurturing towards John. They both expressed awe and respect for him and talked fondly about how much potential he had for artistic and communicative expression. The session was pleasant for all.

Later family sessions allowed all members to express joy and fear regarding impending discharge plans from his residential program back to Rochester School for the Deaf. Yet, once John had been discharged and was receiving care via mandated preventative family services, the family's defensive posturing continued and they steadfastly avoided treatment. After three months of aftercare, funding ended. Fortunately, the school psychologist followed up individually with John.

Conclusion and Follow-Up

John's attitude since the inception of family art therapy had changed considerably. He viewed his family's participation in treatment as supportive and caring. The sessions offered John an avenue to release his anger, accept limitation, and acknowledge his feelings of guilt and responsibility toward the family members. Family therapy also permitted the family to perceive John in a different light, forcing all family members to look at their communication system and dysfunction.

The role of the interpreter was tantamount in aiding the mother's assessment of her own inadequacies. As the sessions progressed, the interpreter became an important part of the treatment team, even preparing specific sign language tapes for mother and John to review on the weekends. The interpreter illustrated the dialogue that both child and parent could act lovingly toward each other. As a result, both John and his mother engaged more responsibly in communication with each other. Had the interpreter not been present, communication amongst family members might still have rested on the sister's shoulders.

In John's attachments to all things dear, he had discovered worth in himself and his artworks. In the process, cognitive development and ego maturation had been firmly established. This led to acceptance by his family members, incorporation of that approval and eventual discharge from residential treatment back to RSD. While outpatient art therapy services coexisted with psychotherapy for another six months, it became clear that John's mastery of the art had unleashed an inner power. It was from that helm that he continued to operate.

John's attitude changed considerably during treatment. At termination, he viewed his family's participation in treatment as supportive and caring. The sessions offered John an avenue to release his anger, accept limitations, and acknowledge his feelings of guilt and responsibility toward his family members.

About seven years later, his social worker sent this writer a follow-up note about John: he had graduated from technical school and become a locksmith. Given his propensity, for being safeguarded, protected and valued by his family system, this was no surprise. Coupling this with John's identification with father's mechanical aptitude, his career choice made abundant sense. In coming into contact with the numinous and sacred qualities of art, John had honed his artistic degree into a skilled trade and basked in the power of its consecrated measure. At last, he held the key to being valued and provided the same for others. And through family art therapy, he resolved and unlocked his feelings, experiencing acceptance and was able to "measure up" as a Deaf child operating in an auricular familial system.

REFERENCES

Bowen, M. (1963). *Family therapy in clinical practice.* New York, NY: Jason Aronson.

Brannigan, G. C., & Decker, S. L. (2003). Bender Gestalt II , 2nd Edition. Itasca, IL: Riverside Publishing Co.

Buck, J. N. (1950). *Administration and interpretation of the H-T-P test.* Proceedings of the Workshop held at Veterans Administration Hospital, Richmond, Virginia, March 31, April 1–2, 1950.

Burns, R. C., & Kaufman, S. H., (1972). *Actions, styles, and symbols in kinetic family drawings (K-F-D).* New York, NY: Brunner Mazel.

Dirst, R., & Caccamise, F. (1980). Introduction in Frank Caccamise et al. (Eds.), *Introduction to interpreting.* Silver Spring, Maryland: Registry of Interpreters for the Deaf (RID), Inc.

Haley, J. (1963). *Strategies of psychotherapy.* New York, NY: Grune & Stratton.

Harvey, M. A. (1982). The Influence and utilization of an interpreter for the Deaf in family therapy. *American Annals of the Deaf,* 819–827.

Harvey, M. A. (1984). Family therapy with Deaf persons: The utilization of an interpreter. *Family Process, 23,* June, 205–213.

Horovitz-Darby, E. G. (1987). Diagnosis and Assessment: Impact on Art Therapy. *Art Therapy,* October, *4* (3), 127–137.

Horovitz-Darby, E. G. (1988). Art therapy assessment of a minimally language skilled deaf child. Proceedings from the 1988 University of California's Center on Deafness Conference: *Mental Health Assessment of Deaf Clients: Special Conditions.* Little Rock, Arkansas: ADARA.

Koppitz, E. M. (1968). *The psychological evaluation of children's human figure drawings.* New York, NY: Grune and Stratton.

Levine, E. S. (1960). *The psychology of deafness.* New York, NY: Columbia Press.

Lowenfeld, V., & Brittain, W. L. (1975). *Creative and mental growth,* 6th Ed, New York, NY: Macmillan Co.

Maher, P. & Waters, J. E. (1984). The use of interpreters with deaf clients in therapy. *Journal of American Deafness and Rehabilitation Association, 17* (4), April, 11–15.

Meadow, K. P. (1980). *Deafness and child development.* Berkeley, CA: University of California Press.

Mindel, E., & Vernon, M. C. (1981). *They grow in silence.* Silver Springs, Maryland: National Association of the Deaf.

Minuchin, S. (1974). *Families and family therapy.* Cambridge, MA: Harvard University Press.

Moores, E. (1982). *Educating the deaf: Psychology, principles, and practices.* Boston, MA: Houghton-Mifflin Press.

Padden, C. (1980). The Deaf Community and the Culture of Deaf People in C. Baker and R. Battison (Eds.), *Sign language and the deaf community.* Silver Spring, MD: National Association of the Deaf.

Rainer, J., Altshuler, K., & Kallman, F. (1969). *Family and mental health problems in a deaf population,* 2nd edition. Springfield, IL: Charles C Thomas.

Rawlings, B. (1973). *Characteristics of hearing-impaired students by hearing status.* United States: 1970–1971, Series D., No. 10, Office of Demographic Studies. Washington, D.C.: Gallaudet College.

Schein, J. D., & Delk, M. T. (1974). *The deaf population of the United States.* Silver Spring, MD. National Association of the Deaf.

Scott, S. (1984). Deafness in the family: Will the therapist listen? *Family Process, 23,* June, 214–216.

Shapiro, R. J., & Harris, R. (1976). Family therapy in treatment of the deaf: A case report. *Family Process, 15* (c), 83–96.

Silver, R. A. (1983). *Silver drawing test of cognitive and creative skills.* Seattle, WA: Special Child Publications.

Silver, R. (2002). *Three art assessments.* New York, NY: Brunner-Routledge

Stein, L. K., & Jabaley, T. (1981). Early identification and parental counseling in L. K. Stein, E. D. Mindel, & T. Jabaley (Eds.) *Deafness and Mental Health.* New York, NY: Grune and Stratton.

Trybus, R. (1980). Sign language, power, and mental health. In C. Baker and R. Battison (Eds.) *Sign language and the deaf community.* Silver Spring, MD: National Association of the Deaf.

Chapter 4

ART THERAPY WITH EMOTIONALLY DISTURBED DEAF/HEARING IMPAIRED ADULTS

Sally Brucker

INTRODUCTION

This chapter describes the use of art therapy as a treatment modality with Deaf/hearing impaired adults who suffer from varied forms of mental illness. The majority of the persons described here were patients in a special mental health program for the Deaf at a psychiatric inpatient facility.

The focus of this chapter is on the process and content of one art therapy group and the themes of the artwork of another over the course of a four-year period. Each group is described in terms of the patient population, group characteristics, goals, and treatment effectiveness. The process of the first group (referred to as Group A) is described in detail in an effort to convey the actual experience of conducting such a group. The second group (referred to as Group B) is presented through the spontaneous themes of the artwork that occurred over time. In this way, the inner world of these patients can be more clearly seen and understood. One might also appreciate the struggles, concerns, and even lighter moment in the lives of Deaf mentally ill persons. It is hoped that in some way this might serve to bridge our gaps of ignorance, prejudice, and fear when encountering those who are different from us. The artwork, at times disturbing, but more often eloquent, gives a clear voice to those who often literally suffer in silence.

In order to understand why art therapy has particular value in the treatment of mentally ill Deaf adults, additional background information will first be presented. This will include a brief history of treatment services available to the adult Deaf population, a discussion of mental health problems often related to Deafness, and special considerations for conducting art therapy groups with this population.

Mental Illness and the Deaf Population: Incidence and Availability of Treatment

In the United States, the incidence of mental illness in the adult Deaf population occurs at the same rate as the hearing population, roughly ten per cent. Therefore, of an estimated 250,000 Deaf adults, at least 25,000 persons might find themselves in need of mental health services in their lifetime. Unfortunately, the fact remains that the number of specialized treatment facilities for the Deaf has lagged far behind those available for the hearing.

In the not so distant past, Deaf adults who required inpatient psychiatric hospitalization, found themselves in a difficult predicament. Due to a paucity of services geared to meet their specific communications needs, these persons were often simply "put away" in institutions for the hearing. Few, if any, hospital staff were able to communicate with them and then only through the use of gestures or written communication. Lack of a common language between the helping professional and the Deaf patient proved to be a frustrating and lengthy ordeal (Brauer 1980; Rainer, et al., 1969). Worse still, this situation led to misunderstandings and more often than not, misdiagnoses offering the Deaf, emotionally-disturbed, individual little hope for successful treatment (Altshuler, 1974; Robinson, 1978).

The need for inpatient psychiatric programs geared to the specific needs of the Deaf adult has long been the concern of practitioners in the field of mental health and Deafness. Implementing these programs in the United States has been an uphill struggle. This has been explained as a result of lack of information and understanding among the mental health profession concerning the psychological consequence of Deafness and the special mental health needs of this population (Altshuler, 1974; Rainer et al., 1968).

The first mental health program for the Deaf began in 1955 in New York under the auspices of the New York State Mental Health Program for Deaf People (Oosterhous, 1985). In 1963, Dr. Luthern Robinson, a staff psychiatrist, established the Mental Health Program for the Deaf at Saint Elizabeth hospital in Washington, D.C. in order to meet the special needs of hearing impaired patients who were placed on back wards and received no specialized services. The program accepted patients from throughout the United States and became a model treatment and training program in the field of mental health and Deafness. Since 1963, similar programs have been established throughout the country. The present estimate of inpatient facilities as of 1984 is one hundred (Oosterhous, 1985).

Treatment Modalities: The Expressive Arts Therapies

In the mental health program where I worked, the expressive therapies included art therapy, dance/movement therapy, and psychodrama and are into the overall therapeutic program. These modalities, which rely partially on nonverbal forms of self-expression, offer a means through which the Deaf client is able to explore and express his thoughts, feelings, and behavior. On the surface, this is done in much the same way as it might for hearing, psychiatric patients who similarly may exhibit symptoms which include: confusion of thought, behavioral disturbances, lack of contact with reality or who may be so depressed that words become an inadequate means of self expression. The expressive therapies are particularly important for hearing impaired people who, frustrated in their attempts to express deep feelings, and having experienced a sense of never feeling completely "understood" by others, may have given up trying to communicate. Because the expressive arts therapies allow for the symbolic expression of thoughts and feelings, they are often the key to unlocking years of isolation. The renewed possibility of opening up communication through the expressive modality of dance, drama, or art can thus produce a profound change in outlook and self-concept.

Art Therapy

The frustration of communicating needs and feelings to others may contribute to the behavioral disturbances and social maladjustment problems seen as common problems among some Deaf patients. These disturbances, which often appear as secondary symptoms to more commonly diagnosed mental illnesses such as schizophrenia and bipolar disorders have been noted in some of the literature on Deafness and mental health and include: (1) impulsivity; (2) lack of introspection; (3) egocentricity; (4) emotional immaturity; and (5) an inability to delay gratification (Altshuler, et al., 1976). These problems are said to be caused by, among other things, lack of social input and knowledge of appropriate social behavior, inadequate schooling, lack of reciprocal relationship with hearing parents who could not communicate beyond basic gestures as well as profound isolation from others (Altshuler, et al., 1976). An example of the process of art-making as a sublimatory experience, which may help to reduce such behavioral problems, can be seen in the case of Ralph.

Ralph, 25-year-old male patient, diagnosed as paranoid schizophrenic with a secondary diagnosis of antisocial personality, was often volatile and aggressive towards others. However, he presented few such problems in the art therapy group. He was usually able to maintain some measure of self-control by using intrinsically manageable, art media such as magic markers or pencils as opposed to paints and clay. One day, while watching other patients use finger-paints, Ralph asked if he could do so. Concerned that the regressive nature of this media might cause Ralph to lose his fragile controls, I initially hesitated to comply with his request. Sensing that this was somehow important to him yet against my better judgment and training, I eventually did offer Ralph a large (30"x40") paper and three jars of paint. In the process of smoothing and mixing colors, Ralph appeared to physically relax. The resulting art productions were less important than his obvious pleasure, satisfaction, and ability to maintain self-control. The following week the staff reported a marked decrease in Ralph's acting-out behavior. Ralph spent several more sessions doing finger-paints, but gradually grew tired of this and went on to painting and sculpture.

Art therapy may also be of particular value as a treatment modality with Deaf patients in that the visual messages expressed through their graphic and plastic representations often convey heretofore pent-up or inadequately expressed emotions (Silver, 1962). The art expressions often is the first step in learning to recognize, conceptualize, and convey important inner experiences.

The art materials (paints, clay, etc.) offer Deaf patients tactile and visual stimulation, which is in accordance with their most basic mode of perceiving the world and taking in information. Art media and art-making include structural elements of color, texture, line, form and composition. In producing art, visual, kinesthetic, and motoric responses merge naturally. Through the pressure of the line, selection of color, and choice of composition or theme, the Deaf patient can frequently express immediate feelings and constructively release inner tension.

In the course of the art therapy group, the art therapist may work to assist the patient in merging his or her pure emotion with the self-control and awareness needed to complete a recognizable or finished image. The image itself may then be reworked or even discarded allowing the patient to practice his ability to control, make decisions, test reality, and achieve a level of mastery or competency. More often than not, in discussing the artwork in the group, the issues noted above emerge as shared concerns. When this occurs, patients often experience a sense of relief, which seems to help reduce feelings of isolation. They also discuss ways in which they can use this learning in their lives outside the group.

The finished work of art may become a concrete and permanent representation of the feelings and thoughts, which the patients discuss in the group. In the course of treatment, patients may review their artwork with the art therapist, thus using it as a visual statement of their progress in art therapy. As a stimulus for discussion in groups where hearing loss and the ability to communicate through the use of voice and sign language can vary great-ly, the finished artwork can also take on the significance of "symbolic speech" and memory (Naumburg, 1966). It can become the "jumping off" point for exploring similarities and differences among group members. This may begin simply on the level of looking at different styles of expression and eventually lead to more profound discussions such as: intergroup relation-ships, memories, dreams, feelings about the experience of Deafness, and spe-cific, emotional difficulties. Support and trust develop in the group as each member is allowed time to "talk" about his or her art production and expe-rience the satisfaction of being appreciated, "heard" and "understood" on a deeply emotional level. Often patients who initially come to the group feel-ing frustrated or anxious, report feeling calmer and more relaxed by the end of the group.

Practical Considerations for the Hearing Art Therapist

One of the most important tasks of any therapist is to communicate clear-ly and empathically with her patients. Hearing therapists have learned to place heavy emphasis on eye contact and the additional importance of non-verbal body language (Lowen, 1967). The fact remains, however, that the ability to understand the conceptual and emotional content tonality of the client's communication is crucial to the success of the therapy. The beginning hearing therapist, in trying to understand his or her Deaf patients, may there-fore find him or herself in a position of role reversal. Through lack of expe-rience in sign language in trying to understand what the Deaf client is saying, the art therapist may experience the frustration, isolation, and confusion that Deaf people face daily in the "hearing world." As difficult as this may be, it is an important experience, which may add to empathy and honesty in dis-cussing feelings, especially as they relate to the experience of Deafness.

In order to facilitate communication, the use of an interpreter may be necessary. However, this can be perceived as interfering with the establish-ment of a therapeutic alliance particularly in regard to building trust and maintaining confidentiality (Brauer & Sussman, 1980; Oosterhous, 1985). Be-cause of this, the art therapist is advised to learn the form of sign language most commonly used by his or her patients as soon as possible. An under-standing of the culture of Deafness and the psychological and social devel-opment of the Deaf child is also imperative. In the meantime, the art thera-pist's attitude and openness about the "communication problem" can go a long way in establishing group trust and willingness to discuss and express feelings, which arise as a result of this.

Further considerations in conducting art therapy groups for Deaf/hear-ing impaired adults include:

1. Proper lighting so that visibility of signing and artwork is assured.
2. Seating clients in such a way that they can clearly see one another at all times.
3. Establishing visual cues such as flicking the lights on and off several times to indicate transitional times.
4. Allowing enough time for group discussion due to the fact that some time will be spent clarifying communication and making certain that all group members have understood what has been communicated.
5. Selecting patients for the art therapy group who have similar modes of communication and level of proficiency.

Patient Selection for Groups

At the special mental health program for the hearing impaired where I work, patients are referred for an art therapy assessment upon admission. They are then assigned to one of the two groups based upon information obtained from the assessment. Placement into Group A or B is determined by the following factors: (1) level of skill in communication through total communication (e.g., includes speech-reading, manual sign language, finger-spelling, writing, gestures, mime, etc); (2) severity of presenting symptoms; and (3) level of overall social functioning.

Format of the Art Therapy Groups

Two separate, ninety-minute art therapy groups are conducted weekly in a large, well-lit activity, room. An average of seven patients attend each group. Groups are conducted entirely in sign language and consist of the following structure:

1. Brief group discussion
2. Independent or group art making
3. Break time/cleanup
4. Presentation and discussion of art productions

Group A

Group A consists of six patients ranging in age from 28–43. Chart 1 contains comparative data as to sex, age, diagnosis, length of hospitalization, etiology of Deafness, and mode of communication used in their family of origin. Patients accepted into Group A share one or more of the following characteristics:

CHART 1

GROUP A

	Age	Diagnosis	Etiology & Degree of Hearing Loss	Mode of Communication	Length of Hospitalization
1. Joe	36	Chronic/ undifferentiated schizophrenia	Birth moderate to severe	Voice & sign language-fair	2 years
2. Bob	33	Uncertain alcohol syndrome	Birth untestable- thought to have residual hearing	None	5 years
3. Dora	25	Organic brain syndrome seizure disorder	Birth profound	Speech reading poor sign language skills	
4. Ann	27	Chronic undifferentiated psychosis	Birth profound	Good-sign language	3 years
5. Alice	42	Organic psychosis	Birth severe	Sign language good	1 year
6. Rosa	45	Chronic undifferentiated schizophrenic Mild Mental Retardation	Birth moderate	Voice poor sign	8 months

* Names and other identifying data have been changed to protect privacy.

1. Dual diagnosis with a secondary diagnosis of organic brain syndrome or mental retardation.
2. An inability or extreme difficulty in communicating through American Sign Language (ASL), fingerspelling, speech-reading, cued speech, or gesture.
3. Severe symptomatology such as visual or auditory hallucinations.
4. Behavioral disturbances such as intermittent acting-out and aggression towards others, autistic withdrawal, or extreme social isolation.

Goals for the group include:

1. To utilize the art materials as a primary mode of communicating thoughts and feelings that might otherwise be difficult or impossible to express.
2. To increase the level of functioning in the areas of interpersonal and socialization skills.
3. To improve individual skills in the areas of decision-making, attention span, reality testing, and independent functioning.

4. To improve body image
5. To increase self-esteem

Mode of Communication Employed. Communication with this group is done primarily through a combination of gesture, facial expressions, ASL, written communication, and the visual imagery contained in the artwork. As one might imagine, a great deal of time is spent clarifying communication and making sure that each patient has understood one another. The complexity of this process will become evident in the following section.

Group Process (Refer to Chart #1)

Preliminaries/Initial Group Discussion. At 1 p.m. on Tuesday afternoon, six patients make their way to the art therapy room. Joe, a man in his mid-thirties timidly approaches the door, peers in and hesitates, waiting to be asked to enter. For the most of his two-year hospitalization, Joe has approached others in this manner. Described as extremely passive, dependent, and isolated from others, Joe rarely speaks (which he is able to do to a limited degree). His diagnosis is schizophrenia, chronic undifferentiated.

Bob, smaller in stature and equally unsure of himself, follows Joe. Bob has been an inpatient for five years, initially seen as acutely psychotic and assaultive, he is now described as suffering from brain damage caused by long-term alcohol abuse. Bob is usually found sitting on the ward and doing little else. He was referred to art therapy eight months ago in order to provide him with an opportunity for self-expression since he is virtually uncommunicative beyond a simple head nod. Bob appears to understand sign language to the extent that he can follow the format of the group. Occasionally, he appears to enjoy the artwork of others. He clearly enjoys doing artwork but beyond these observations, we know little of Bob.

In a short while, Rosa, Dora, Ann, and Alice arrive. Rosa, in her mid-forties is perhaps the most communicative of the group. Her diagnosis is chronic undifferentiated schizophrenia with a secondary diagnosis of mild mental retardation. Until recently she had been placed in programs for the hearing and knew little, if any, sign language. While she is learning rapidly, her lack of a common language with the group makes it difficult and frustrating for her to express herself. She has, in fact, had difficulty communicating with others all of her life, which she sees as contributing to her emotional problems. Alice has difficulties seeing others in this group due to a recently diagnosed problem of Usher Syndrome, a degenerative visual impairment also referred to as tunnel vision. She is convalescing from an acute psychotic episode, which brought her to the hospital as well. Her diagnosis is organic psychosis.

Ann, 27 years old, has been an inpatient for the past three years. She exhibits sever symptomatology and unless specifically focused on the group discussion or her artwork, tends to become easily distracted and hallucinatory.

Dora, a young woman diagnosed as having organic brain syndrome, suffers from a seizure disorder. She has a great deal of difficulty controlling her hands when signing and easily becomes frustrated. Interestingly enough, she is able to delineate details in her drawings with little or no difficulty. Perhaps the physiological process of art-making enables her to relax and to coordinate her thought processes with her movements.

After the group is seated, the initial discussion period begins where each person is asked how he or she is feeling and what has happened to them the previous week. In turn, each person asks the same question of the person sitting next to him or her. This is seen as an important part of the group structure and serves the following purposes:

1. Orienting group members to person, time, and place.
2. Allowing the development of social skills
3. Providing an opportunity for developing group awareness and trust.

Today, Ann tells the group that she feels "tired." Dora says she is fine although we learn that she has had several seizures this past week. Alice smiles and states that her psychiatrist told her she may be going home soon for a brief visit. Rosa is upset today. Another patient in the group (Bob) is annoying her because he never responds when she speaks to him. Bob does not respond to Rosa or anyone else in the group. He sits quietly, pencil in hand, waiting to begin to draw. Joe states that he feels "fine" but appears somewhat anxious particularly when questioned about his impending "discharge" from the hospital.

Art-making. Once the initial discussion is completed, the group begins work on ongoing projects, new projects, or group projects. For the most part, group members have surprisingly little difficulty initialing tasks. On occasion, when appropriate, group themes or individual projects are suggested. When given the choice, individuals in the group prefer to work on their own, thus regulating their pace and maintaining control, which is important for them. During the art-making portion of the group, members remain absorbed in their work; although, at times some signed (verbal) exchange does occur.

Break Time. After approximately 40 minutes of work the group prepares for the break. This consists of cleaning up the work area, washing paintbrushes, and putting away supplies. Patients may then help themselves to something to drink and are encouraged to sit in the discussion area, relax, and socialize with one another. Others may leave the room to smoke a cigarette or use the restroom.

Discussion of the Artwork. The discussion usually begins slowly, each member somewhat hesitant to show his or her work. Rosa, as usual, is the first one to volunteer. She describes her picture (not shown) in the following way: "This is the group. I drew four people and two black blobs." In the excitement of describing her picture, Rosa forgets to sign, using her voice instead. She is reminded that no one can understand her. She signs "sorry." Ann is staring off into space and appears to be responding to voices. Bob is in his own world as well. Both are gently tapped on the shoulder and through sign language, asked to try and concentrate on Rosa's picture. (Alice asked Rosa to pass her picture to her since, due to her visual handicap, she was unable to see.)

Alice smiles in acknowledging Rosa's depiction of her. Rosa, still seemingly annoyed, passes her picture to Bob, and then Ann, asking each in turn; "Can you find yourself in my drawing?" Bob does not respond. Ann points to various figures, asking Rosa, "Is that me?" Rosa responds angrily, "No! You and Bob are the two black blobs I drew!" Bob looks up for the first time. Rosa continues: "It makes me mad when you never pay attention to me. I don't know you. You're not real people to me. You make me feel bad!" While Bob looks on, Ann is able to acknowledge how hard it is for her to concentrate and how she cannot often control her "voices." Rosa responds with relief and states that she will try to be more patient with her in the future. She states that she is often frustrated communicating with people in the group and then is able to connect this with communication problems she has with her hearing mother. She also becomes aware of the fact that Bob's lack of response and withdraw in the group makes her fearful that she will regress as well. But in looking at her picture again, she is able to say, "I guess I'm different from Bob because I've drawn myself as a whole figure." She smiles at Bob who seems to smile back.

Ann, Joe, Bob, Dora, and Alice take turns showing their artwork and the discussion focuses on themes, which they contain. Joe has drawn a boat (Figure 4–1), symbolizing his journey away from the hospital. Through the image and the group's questions, he is able to acknowledge his anxiety and fear over the loss of the protective environment of the hospital and how those feelings had interfered with his initial interactions with the group today.

Dora's picture of flowers, trees, and grass is described in concrete terms (Figure 4–2). The group notices that she has also drawn an airplane about to fly into a cloud of lightning. I relate this to her experience of anticipating her seizure attacks by asking, "Does the pilot feel scared he will lose control?" Dora nods her head in agreement.

Alice's picture shows her home in Georgia, which she misses a great deal. In the course of the discussion of this image, ambivalent feelings emerge about her home life, which she is able to express for the first time in the group.

Figure 4–1.

Figure 4–2.

Ann has written words on her page; a confusion of names, some of which she states are hers, and others who are "friends" (Figure 4–3). She appears to be confused, as does the group in trying to make sense of her work. Her fear of nurses and sadness about missing her family are discussed. It is suggested that in the following session, Ann try to draw images of these people as a means of sorting out "what is real from what is unreal." She agrees to do this.

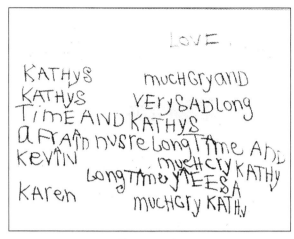

Figure 4–3.

Bob is usually the last person to present his work to the group. He slowly holds up his paper (Figure 4–4). Short lines and small circles appear amidst a proliferation of scribbles, which fill the entire page. Spots of paint are dabbed across the page. This is seen as an improvement for Bob, who previously drew only scribbled pencil lines in a perseverative manner. The emergence of color and form in his artwork may represent a new awareness of his capacity to control the media and to organize his thoughts. The artwork, while lacking in form and order, remains Bob's main means of communication. "Pretty," comments Alice. "What does it mean?" asks Rosa. Bob shrugs his shoulders as if to say, "I don't know." I comment on the change in Bob's work and how, although still difficult for him, he is beginning to make an effort to communicate through his artwork.

This began when, over the past year, Bob was able to tolerate drawing on the same piece of paper with me. In working this way, I lent my "ego support" which helped him to organize his thoughts and to respond in a more direct manner. For Bob, this marked the beginning of a bridge to communication and a therapeutic alliance. It also served to increase his ability to tolerate closeness, which gradually helped him become accepted as a group member.

Concluding the Group. After the artwork has been discussed individually, group members are asked: "What happened today?" This is seen as an important part of the group structure because it serves to increase a sense of

Figure 4–4.

group membership and also to enhance their ability to abstract and utilize information gleaned from the discussion. Comments are made such as: "Rosa let us know how she feels about the group," "Alice learned something about her family," "Bob is improving," "Ann was confused today," etc.

Afterthoughts

In the course of the art therapy group, patients who previously had been unable to communicate with one another due to varying skills in sign language and the severity of symptoms associated with their mental illnesses were able to do so. Their art expressions became the means through which they were able to express feelings about themselves and each other. Sharing the artwork helped to increase self-knowledge and group trust. Socialization skills also improved, as did problem-solving skills. The process of art therapy for Deaf, psychiatric patients (with severe symptomatology and low socialization skills) are slow and often painstaking. It should be noted that the patients described in the previous group session had been in art therapy for an average of nine months. It is clear that in order to achieve the previously stated goals for the group, long-term art therapy is indicated. In such a group, art therapy can be of therapeutic benefit for even the least communicative and withdrawn patients who, like Bob, can utilize art expression as a language in itself.

Group B

Group B consists of four females and three males ranging in age from 25–48 years. For a complete description of diagnostic and demographic data the reader is referred to Chart 2. Patients accepted into Group B share one or more of the following characteristics:

1. An ability to communicate adequately to very well through a combination of speech-reading, signed English, or ASL.
2. Average to good social interaction skills.
3. An ability to utilize abstraction skills in such a way that they are able to benefit from insight-oriented art therapy.
4. No secondary diagnosis of brain damage or mental retardation.

Overall goals for the group include:

1. To express and work through personal problems and conflicts relating to past, and present situations.
2. To establish group trust and to explore group dynamics through self-directed discussions relating to the theme and content of the artwork produced in the art therapy sessions.

CHART 2
GROUP B

	Age	Diagnosis	Etiology & Degree of Hearing Loss	Mode of Communication	At Time of Group Length of Hospitalization
1. Lynn	29	Schizophrenic Acute episode	Birth Profound	ASL (good)	6 months
2. Ann	30	Severe Depression	Birth Profound	ASL (good)	3 months
3. Joe	33	Chronic undifferentiated Schizophrenic	Birth Profound	ASL (poor)	2 years
4. Sandy	27	Borderline Psychotic	Birth Profound	ASL (good)	2 years
5. Ralph	31	Paranoid Schizophrenic	Birth Profound	ASL (good)	6 months
6. Dan	29	Schizophrenic Acute Episode	Birth Profound	ASL (good)	3 months
7. Liza	27	Schioz-Affective Disorder	Birth Moderate	Voice, Some sign language	1 year

Mode of Communication Employed and Role of the Art Therapist. In this group, the basic mode of communication employed is ASL. However, several patients continue to rely on speech-reading and voice due to the fact that their sign language skills were more recently acquired. Although, at times the group is forced to stop and clarify what has been communicated via ASL, this is not as great a problem as it is for Group A.

My role has, over time, been less active than with Group A. Group members initially viewed this as abandonment, producing some anger, withdrawal, and resistance. When this was explored, however, the group was able to assume responsibility for leading discussions, and as a result became more independent and willing to take risks with one another. My stance, at this point, is to facilitate, clarify, and support the group process.

Rather than describe the group process as was done for Group A, the author wishes to present the major themes of the artwork. Discussion will focus on the impact of specific themes on the group and ways in which they served to facilitate therapeutic change and growth.

Themes of the Artwork

I. The Symbolic Significance of the Mouth

In the course of a four-year period, the graphic and plastic representation of the mouth in exaggerated and distorted forms, emerged as an important symbol in the artwork of Group B. Group discussions of this artwork began to focus on early frustrating attempts to have needs met and to communicate clearly with hearing parents. Figure 4–5 created by Lynn, a 29-year-old profoundly Deaf woman diagnosed as schizophrenic, shows a baby seal. The seal, as described by Lynn is "screaming for food, waiting for Mother to feed it, . . . crying." Some group members saw the enormous mouth of the baby seal as empty and indeed needy. Through this image, the group began to understand how their unfulfilled nurturance and dependency needs had left them feeling empty and angry at times. Other patients produced at least nine other images, which emphasized the mouth, spontaneously. This also produced countertransference responses in me since up to this point, I felt occasionally overwhelmed by the groups' insatiable need for attention and nurturance. In understanding the source of this need, and discussing it with the group, members became aware of this and were gradually able to rely less on me and more on each other.

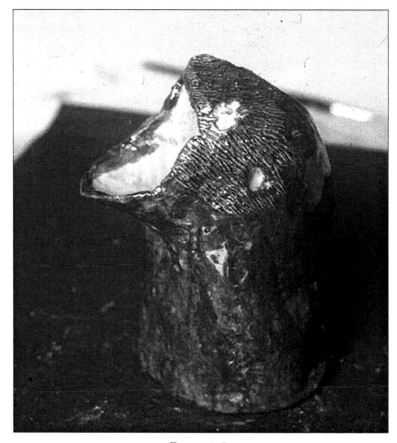

Figure 4–5.

II. Communication

The search for new forms of communication was an ongoing theme of the group. Often group members would produce artwork, which resembled foreign languages or represented an attempt to create a new written language through symbols. Figures 4–6 and 4–7 show two examples of this. In Figure 4–6, we see an oriental design done in several colors. Alice, a 30-year-old profoundly Deaf woman diagnosed as suffering from a severe depression, described this as "Chinese." Group discussion focused on the fact that it was impossible to understand what Alice wanted to communicate since no one spoke or understood Chinese. Alice admitted that she did not either and that it was difficult to communicate what she wanted to say at times. She related her wish that communication be easier and admitted that her drawing grew out of her frustration communicating with her hearing family.

Figure 4–7 shows an attempt by John, a 23-year-old profoundly Deaf

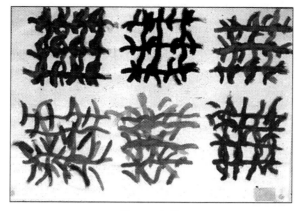

Figure 4–6.

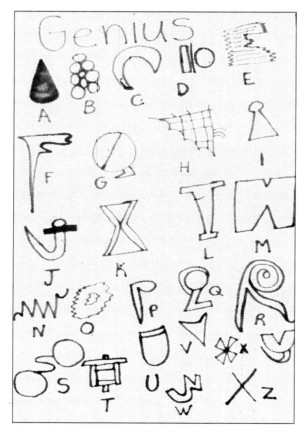

Figure 4–7.

man diagnosed as schizophrenic, chronic undifferentiated, to create an entirely new language for him and the group. When his symptoms were acute, John exhibited bizarre behavior and often lapsed into his own incomprehensible language. The creation of his own language, which not even Deaf people could understand served to give him a sense of power and control lacking in his life.

III. Sense of the Self as Strange

The art of psychiatric patients often depicts the self as strange or different (Prinzhorn, 1972). Self-portraits done by patients in Group B related not only to such distortions, but also to feelings regarding their Deafness. For example, Sandy, a 27-year-old profoundly Deaf woman diagnosed as borderline psychotic, drew several self-portraits, which depicted her as a creature from outer space. One in particular (Figure 4–8) was described as "shooting the bad, baby Martin." This striking image shows a frightened one-eyed creature ("alien") being shot by a spaceman because it is "different, ugly." Full life body tracings done by other patients show similar depictions of body distortions and self-revulsion.

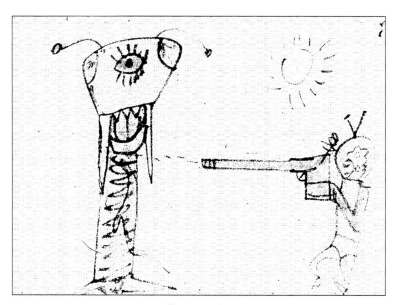

Figure 4–8.

IV. Aggressive Impulses-Anger

Many drawings and paintings produced by the group, illuminated images of overt and covert expressions of rage. Ralph, (described earlier), a 31-year-old profoundly Deaf man diagnosed as paranoid schizophrenic, had been incarcerated for one year prior to being admitted to the program. He was described as assaultive and aggressive. Despite these tendencies, he was able to utilize the art media expressively and with a great deal of control. His self-portrait illustrated a primitive, wild, appearing figure with long, unkempt hair and inappropriately colored green. The teeth are emphasized here and small, colored forms are drawn on them, indicating, according to Ralph, "medications." Although this portrait in no way resembled Ralph, it represented his feelings of being seen as strange, his anger at his hospitalization and need to take medication, his former incarceration, and his potentially explosive, inner rage (see Figure 4–9).

Figure 4–9.

Other patients drew volcanoes or fires and described them in terms of the inner turmoil and range, which they had felt for years.

V. Auditory Hallucinations

The existence of auditory hallucinations in profoundly Deaf psychiatric schizophrenic patients has been reported in the literature (Cooper, 1976; Critchley, 1981, et al.). Approximately five such drawings have appeared spontaneously in this group. In Figure 4–10, Dan, a profoundly Deaf man diagnosed as schizophrenic (acute episode), drew himself as hearing "voices from the devil." When questioned about hearing these statements, he insisted that he did.

Figure 4–10.

Similarly, Liza, a 27-year-old woman diagnosed as having a schizo-affective disorder, made images such as Figure 4–11. The images were said to be self-portraits showing her wish to "stop the voices." The process of externalizing these "inner voices" served to offer temporary relief from them and comfort at being understood by group members.

VI. Hearing Loss and its Effect on Everyday Life

Several patients drew images relating to their wish to hear. Through these images, they were able to share feelings of loss and sadness about their abil-

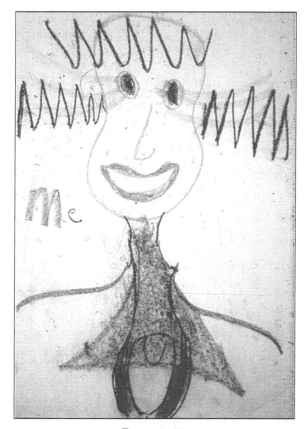

Figure 4–11.

ity to communicate with hearing people their own age. The inability to hear music among this group was seen as the greatest loss.

VII. Looking at the Group

Looking at and expressing feelings relating to the group through the art media marked an important turning point in the life of the group. Until that time, group members had shown little interest in each other, preferring instead to form an alliance with me. This passive dependency on a hearing person as a pattern of learned interaction was thus repeating itself in the group. At each session's end, I often found myself exhausted, having related more to each individual than the group as a whole. While this may be true in the initial stages of many art therapy groups with hospitalized psychiatric patients, it seemed that this occurred with greater intensity and over a longer period of time. This was of course, also due to the fact that I was dealing not only with the symbolic and distorted thought content of mentally ill persons but also with an entirely different language system. For many hearing psychiatric patients, language as a means of communication is often confused and inadequate. This was also true with these patients at times in that their sign language was often incomprehensible even to a trained interpreter or other Deaf staff members.

As a means of looking more closely at group process and group members' perception of one another, the theme of "the group" was suggested during one session. Each member was asked to draw an abstract or realistic representation of either: (a) present feelings about the group; or (b) what they wished or fantasized the group to be. The group responded eagerly to this task. Drawings showed the group as an intertwining of different threads, "tangled" but interdependent at the same time. Other group members created images, which seemed to express that group members could be "closer." Deliberately vague or ambiguous compositions were done to express confused feelings about the group. As a result of this expression and much discussion, the patients began to develop a sense of group identity and were gradually able to assume increased responsibility regarding their own attendance and participation in group discussions. Some members were able to extend this beyond the group in the form of taking responsibility for doing things such as reminding others when it was time for the group to begin. They began to keep track of absences and to encourage others to speak up in the group. From time to time, spontaneous images of the group emerged and group members were able to recognize the intrinsic message of focusing on the group process. The increased interdependence among group members and growing trust in their ability to affect the environment of the group has resulted in a gradual "weaning away" from their dependence on the art therapist.

Afterthoughts

Group B has, over time, been able to utilize art as a means of expressing a wide range of thoughts and feelings relating to their personal and collective concerns. These shared concerns include their attitudes and feelings about their illnesses and their hospitalization, their Deafness, their family and interpersonal relationships, and their experience of being in the group. This has fostered group trust and individual growth in much the same way as it might for any other group. This last point is emphasized because, as with any condition, there may be a tendency to look for either the unusual or the exotic. For example, as an art therapist working with the Deaf, I am often asked if their self-portraits lack the depiction of ears. In six years of conducting individual and group sessions with more than 50 patients, I have found perhaps two or three pictures which show this. Perhaps further research will support or refute this and other subject matter, which have been presented here. Group B, once able to work through past, unproductive ways of interacting, had no more or fewer communication problems than a group of hearing patients with similar diagnoses. The ability to communicate with a common language was a crucial factor here. Members of Group B were for the most part fluent in ASL and therefore had less problems with the semantics of the language than did Group A. That the thematic content of their artwork might be characteristic of Deaf, adult psychiatric in-patients is yet unproven. What is clear is that a strong need to communicate experiences, thoughts and feelings, was felt within the group. The fact that these patients were able to utilize the art media in their struggle to understand themselves and one another speaks to the ability of art as a therapeutic tool and as a visual language.

REFERENCES

Altshuler, K. Z. (1974). The social and psychological development of the Deaf. *American Annals of the Deaf, 119,* 365–376.

Altshuler, K. Z., Deming, W. E., Vollenweide, J., Rainer, J. D., & Tendler, R. (1976). Impulsivity and profound early Deafness. *American Annals of the Deaf, 121,* 331–345.

Altshuler, K. Z., & Rainer, J. (1968). Mental health and the Deaf: Approaches and Prospects. *U.S. Dept. of Health, Education, and Welfare, Social and Rehabilitation Service.*

Brauer, B., & Sussman, A. E. (1980). Experiences of Deaf Therapists with Deaf Client. *Mental Health in Deafness,* No. 4, Fall, NIMH, DHHS Pub. No. (ADM) 81–1047.

Cooper, A. F. (1976). Deafness and psychiatric illness. *British Journal of Psychiatry, 129,* 216–226.

Critchley, E. M. R. et al., (1981). Hallucinatory experiences of prelingually profoundly Deaf schizophrenics. *British Journal of Psychiatry, 138,* 30–32.

Harris, R. I. (1982). Communication and mental health. *The Deaf American,* 34, (4).

Levine, E. S. (1960). *Psychology of deafness.* NY: Columbia University Press, pp. 303–308.

Lowen, A. (1967). *The betrayal of the body.* New York: MacMillan.

Lowenfeld, V., & Brittain, L. W. (1964). *Creative and mental growth,* 4th edition. New York: MacMillan.

Naumburg, M. (1966). *Dynamically oriented art therapy: It's principles and practice.* New York: Grune and Stratton, Inc.

Oosterhous, S. (1985). *Dance Movement Therapy with the Deaf: The Relationship Between Dance/Movement Therapy and American Sign Language.* Unpublished Masters Thesis, Goucher College, Towson, Md.

Prinzhorn, H. (1972). *Artistry of the mentally ill.* New York: Springer-Verlag.

Rainer, J., Altshuler, K., & Kallman, F. (1969). *Family and mental health problems in a deaf population* (2nd ed.). Springfield, IL: Charles C Thomas.

Robinson, L. D. (1978). Sound Minds in a Soundless World. *Dept of Health, Education, and Welfare, Public Health Service, Alcohol, Drug Abuse, and Mental Health Administration,* NIMH, DHEW, Pub. No. (ADM) 77–560.

Rubin, J. A. (1984). *Child art therapy: Understanding and helping children grow through art,* 2nd edition. New York: Van Nostrand.

Schein, J., & Delk, M. (1964). An eye for an ear? Social perception, non-verbal communication, and deafness. *Rehabilitation Psychology, 21,* 56–57.

Silver, R. (1962). Potentials in art for the Deaf. *Eastern Arts Quarterly, 1,* (2), Nov.–Dec.

Vernon, M. C. (1969). Techniques of screening for mental illness among deaf clients. *Journal of Rehabilitation of the Deaf,* 2 April, p. 30.

Vernon, M. C. (1978), Deafness and mental health: Some theoretical views. *Gallaudet Today,* Fall, 78, 9–13.

Chapter 5

ART THERAPY: A CASE OF A MEDICALLY ILL HEARING CHILD OF DEAF PARENTS

Jacob Atkinson and Ellen G. Horovitz

CULTURAL CONSIDERATIONS–CODA'S & KODA'S

CODAs ({Hearing} Children Of Deaf Adults) or KODAs ({Hearing} Kids Of Deaf Adults, referring to very young children) exist in a rather convoluted culture and world. Many of these hearing children grow up in a Deaf culture environment. Numerous children such as Client S (herein referred to as CS) and her brother (herein referred to as E) converse, understand, and communicate in sign even before they can verbalize spoken language (Bull, 1998). Indeed, because of their placement within a Deaf-hearing family, they become interpreters by default, even when extremely young, thus complicating their childhood and forcing them into the "hearing" advocate role for the family system. By proxy, they become "parentified" (Harvey, 1982).

Thus was the scenario for CS and her hearing brother (E). When parents are part of a Deaf culture environment, hearing children automatically participate in Deaf events (Harvey, 1982). Contemporaneously, these children must function in the hearing world: they function by way of auditory modality and attend hearing schools. In time, they form hearing friendships and simultaneously partake in auditory faculty events. Hence, CODAs and KODA's are quite literally trapped between two distinct cultures: they are auricular, yet grow up "Deaf" and become duty-bound to accommodate those with their "Deaf" identities (Harrington, 2001). Subsequently, many adult hearing children of Deaf parents become members of a support group called CODA, which helps them to come to grips with the conflicts involved (Bull, 1998). Still younger children become involved in the KODA support group. But in the meantime, oh, what a weft they weave.

In this case, CS not only struggled with the above cultural issues, but also endured extreme medical illness that compounded the aforementioned. Moreover, both parents were exceptionally bright and accomplished individuals: the father elevated to full partner in a very prestigious law firm and the mother graduated with a master's degree. While Mother S chose to be a "stay-at-home Mom" truly, even had she desired to re-enter the workplace, she had no choice. Someone had to be the caretaker for this very ill child.

Mother S sublimated her feelings by "blogging" openly on the Internet about her daughter and even posted a website that was continually updated with CS's drawings and feelings. Indeed, Mother S also posted her own feelings. So in this rare case, HIPPA fell to the wayside as Mother posted CS's condition, artwork and feelings (sometimes daily) for public scrutiny and review. (We learned this before the first time we met CS at our Art Therapy Clinic at Nazareth College in Rochester, NY.) This was the first time that we worked with someone who so publicly presented "confidential" dynamics to the public. On one level, it created an ethical conundrum for us; on the other hand, Mother S was anxious for some relief since, at referral, CS had become increasingly verbally and physically aggressive towards the mother. However, upon referral during a relay conversation with the mother, Horovitz (author 2) went on to the website (per Mother S's request) to learn more about this unusual medical case.

The dynamics were challenging: CS suffered from Eosinophilic Gastroenteritis (EG), a rare medical condition that preempted her ability to eat almost anything. (See Genogram and Timeline.) Her diet consisted of just a few fruits and vegetables.

> In the U.S. EG is rare, and the incidence is difficult to estimate. However, since the description of EG by Kaijser in 1937, more than 280 cases have been reported in the medical literature. The disease most often involves the stomach and the small bowel. A history of atopy and allergies is present in many of the cases. In children, a history of allergy is even more common. Children and adolescents can present with growth retardation, failure to thrive, delayed puberty, or amenorrhea.

(source: http://www.emedicine.com/MED/topic688.htm)

Yet, for all that she had endured, including retarded growth (due to lack of adequate nutrition even with supplements), CS was amazingly perceptive, artistic, endearing, attractive and intelligent. Thus even with a long waitlist, we made room to work with this very engaging young child. The work has been astounding and the case continues to unfold.

As always, more facts always seem to "spring eternal" post the initial intake and this case was no exception: while Atkinson (author 1) worked with the child, Horovitz (author 2) administered the case, interpreted for the mother (when she dropped off CS and came with both children) and with the other clinical supervisor, Lori Higgins, MS, MS, ATR, Dr. Horovitz obtained a more thorough timeline and genogram from Mother S and was able to (gently) suggest to Mother S that she return to her previous therapist for continued individual therapy. The reasons were myriad but primarily the suggestion came from Mother S's need to work on her issues of loss (regarding her biological family system–e.g., maternal grandmother's (MGM) death and maternal grandfather's (MGF) subsequent depression and alcoholism– her age of 16) as well as her current family systemic issues involving her obvious depression and concomitant rage over having to contend with a "sick" child.

Indeed it became clear, that family art therapy would need to be instituted to aid the family system with CS's parentification issues and cultural divide. But presently, the case has focused on reparation via offering young CS the outlet she so sorely needs to sublimate her feelings concerning her medical illness, social alienation amongst her peer group, and exclusion from normal mealtime situations with both her family and peer group, in addition, to overall anger and depression perceived due to her illness. Couple these antecedent factors with being a KODA and you have one very complicated case (see genogram and timeline in Appendix A of this chapter).

Thus, looking at the presenting symptoms, the case will be presented by reviewing CS's art therapy diagnostic work-up and then some significant sessions. Perusing this case, the reader will glean insight into (a) the Deaf cultural issues that CS faced; (b) CS's ability to cognitively change her behavior; (c) resolve of "parentification;" (d) sublimation regarding her medical condition, Eosinophilic Gastroenteritis (EG); and (e) verbal expression related to excommunication from peers and family.

Art Therapy Diagnostic Assessment

CA: 6.8
Referred By: Mother S
Testing Dates: 02/26/2006, 3/6/2006, 3/27/2006
Test Administered: Complete Art Therapy Assessment (CATA),
          Kinetic Family Drawing (KFD)
          Silver Drawing Test (SDT)
          Person Picking an Apple from a Tree (PPAT)
          Formal Elements Art Therapy Scale (FEATS)
Reason For Referral: Anger towards mother, trauma caused by dietary restrictions
Psychosocial History: See Appendix A, Genogram

Observations and Behavioral Impressions

CS presented as an intelligent, well-groomed 6.8-year-old child, whose physical size appeared closer to that of a four-year-old. (CS's size is the result of her medically restricted diet of fruits and vegetables due to Eosinophilic Gastroenteritis.) Since CS's comes from a family where the mother is Deaf and father is hard-of-hearing, CS communicated by using both speech and sign language. She appeared friendly upon entering the clinic and even more so after her mother left, thus suggesting relaxation of her overall generalized anxiety.

Cognitive Art Therapy Assessment

Paint Response: Schematic Stage, 7–9 years, Lowenfeld & Britain
Clay response: Preschematic Stage, 4–7 years, Lowenfeld & Britain
Pencil Response: Schematic Stage, 7–9 years, Lowenfeld & Britain
Overall Response: Schematic Stage, 7–9 years, Lowenfeld & Britain

Painting Response Subtest

CS chose to paint first. When asked if she knew how to mix colors, she stated that she did not need a demonstration. She began by painting the ground line, followed by outlining and filling in a giraffe. She finished by painting the flower (see Figure 5–1).

CS was quick to solve problems encountered during the painting portion of the CATA, such as requesting black paint for the giraffe's tail, which was not given at the beginning of the assessment. She explained what she was doing while she worked. According to Hammer (1980), a long neck may imply difficulty controlling and directing instinctual drives, perhaps indicating eating in CS's case. Hammer (1980) also suggested that those who have difficulty swallowing or psychogenic digestive disturbances illustrate elongated necks, thus underscoring her current digestive problems. (The painting subtest falls within Lowenfeld & Britain's Schematic stage, approximately age 7–9 years.)

Clay Subtest

CS quickly moved on to work with the clay. She began by verbally expressing things to create, but had difficulty manipulating the stiff clay material. With assistance from the administrant, the client was able to roll the clay flat, which concluded in a circular mass. CS decided that she would

Figure 5–1.

make a pizza and began to add slices of pepperoni to the pizza. She cut herself a "slice," but remarked that it was gross because it was made from clay. Even during play she seemed unable to escape her digestive reality. She then cut a second larger slice, which she drew a smiley face on, perhaps indicating the happiness that nonrestricted foods could bring. Yet, CS next regressed to stabbing the happy slice along with some of the pepperoni and the pizza itself; clearly displaying oral aggression. (These actions were concurrent with her entering the session with wax Dracula teeth.) (CS's clay response was within Lowenfeld & Britain's Preschematic Stage age 4–7 years.) She quickly completed the clay portion and moved onto the pencil drawing, which she said "was best." The fact that she referred to the pencil subtest as the "best" suggested her need to not only veer away from messy or "regressive" materials such as clay and paint, but also her concomitant desire to exert control over her environment by using more restrictive materials (Hammer, 1980).

Figure 5–2.

Pencil Subtest

CS began her pencil drawing with a zebra. She had trouble deciding on the thickness of the zebra's neck but had no problem drawing the rest of the head and stripes. When beginning the drawing, CS commented that she was only going to draw half of the zebra. Her decision to only draft the zebra neck (sans body) clearly points to separation from her own bodily issues. (Again, this might point to her struggle with Eosinophilic Gastroenteritis.) CS expressed confidence about her ability to draw the zebra: "I have practiced a lot to become so good at drawing zebras." Indeed, while drawing, CS stated that she was "almost the smartest kid in her class" and that she "had been reading since she was four." Her desire to impress the administrant indicated deep-seated longing for recognition but also compensation for her illness and consequent physical delay. Once finished with the outline, CS requested colored pencils to fill in the zebra's stripes; she even included the red hair along the top of the zebra's mane. This may have been an attempt to display her knowledge, and again impress the administrant. Next, she detailed a horse, which in comparison to the zebra, looked less practiced. Hammer (1980) suggested that a horse is often indicative of a helper or servant. Neither animal sported a body, indicating resort into fantasy and inferiority of the body (Hammer, 1980). (CS's drawing response was within Lowenfeld & Britain's Schematic Stage age 7–9 years.)

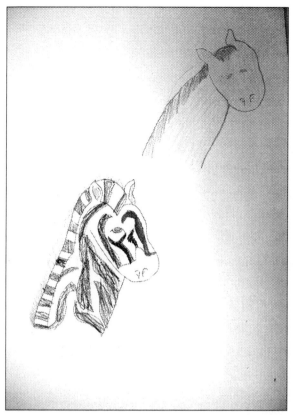

Figure 5–3.

K-F-D Response

CS's KFD consisted (from left to right) of her brother (E) herself (CS), her mother (S), and her father (B). The family is sitting (in that order) on a couch watching the movie "Shark Tale" at home on their big screen television. Again CS seemed to be displaying a need to retreat into fantasy (only drawing the backs of the heads of the family), as well as concern regarding bodily issues, since like the CATA pencil subtest, no body was articulated (Hammer, 1980). The entire family was encapsulated between the couch and the television, creating a barrier for protection (Burns & Kaufman, 1972). While in reality, CS is 6.8, her brother (at three years old) is nearly the same size as she; yet in this picture, both are drawn as the same size as the parents, suggesting parentification. All four family members were drafted at the same height and scale, again suggesting lack of control and parentification (Burns and Kaufman, 1972). CS expressed that she often felt parentified by her mother. She told of getting her brother's attention and communicating with

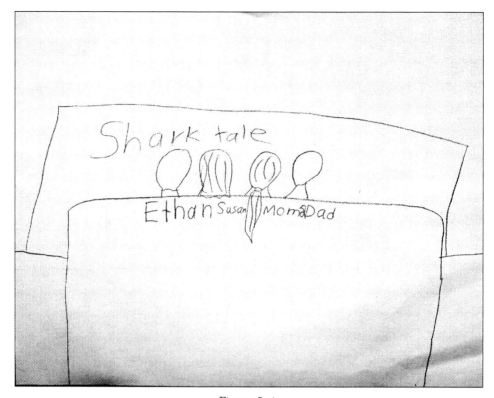

Figure 5–4.

him, as it is sometimes difficult for her mother to do so by speaking in sign language. The fact that no one was facing the viewer might also indicate feelings of rejection, perhaps by the family or rejection towards them (Burns & Kaufman, 1972). Oftentimes, the television has been relegated as indicative of a need for warmth and love. If this is the case for CS, a lot of warmth and love is needed as expressed by the oversized television set (Burns & Kaufman, 1970; Appendix B).

Silver Drawing Test (SDT)

Predictive Drawing:	9
Drawing from Observation	8
Drawing from Imagination	12
Total Score	29

(See Appendix C for complete SDT)

CS Received a total score of 29 out of 45 possible points. This overall score placed her in the 99+ percentile, with a T–score of 76.39 for six to

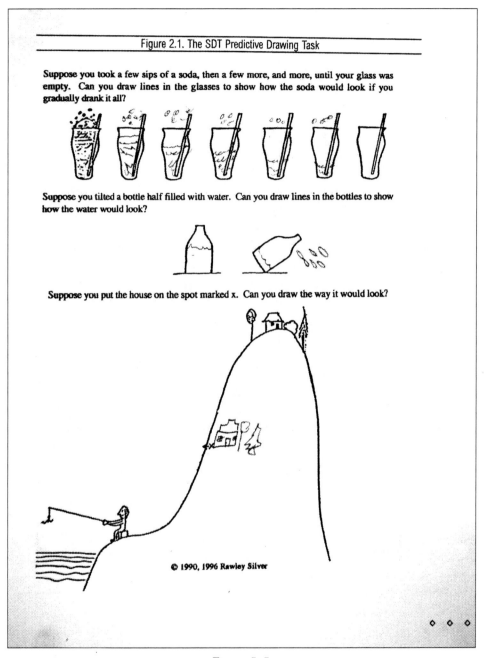

Figure 5–5.

seven-year-old first graders (Silver, 2002). CS was able to accurately depict sequencing in task one of the Predictive Drawing subtest. Her response to

Examples of Scored Responses

Figure 2.9. The SDT Drawing from Observation Task

Have you ever tried to draw something just the way it looks? Here are some things to draw. Look at them carefully, then draw what you see in the space below.

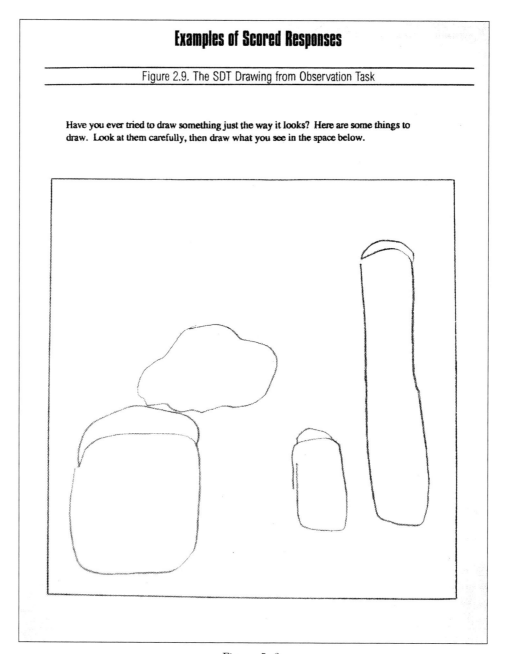

Figure 5–6.

task two of this subtest demonstrates that she has not yet acquired the ability to predict horizontality. CS does have water spilling out of the jug, which in reality would occur if the second jug were as full as her first jug when tipped. Her response to the third task in the Predictive Drawing subtest shows that CS is beginning to grasp the concept of verticality, but does not fully comprehend it. She scored in the 97 percentile for her age in this subtest (Silver, 2002). CS's second subtest, Drawing from Observation, displays that her ability to form spatial relationships is still developing. She scored in the 75 percentile for her age group in this subtest (Silver, 2002).

Her response to the first task in the Predictive Drawing subtest shows that CS is beginning to grasp the concept of verticality, but does not fully comprehend it. She scored in the 97 percentile for her age group in this subtest (Silver, 2002). CS's second subtest, Drawing from Observation, displays that her ability to form spatial relationships is still developing. She scored in the 75 percentile for her age group in this subtest (Silver, 2002).

CS's Drawing from Imagination Subtest was a cat on its back playing with a ball of string; nearby, a dog observes the cat. In this subtest, she demonstrated the ability to select, combine, and represent in the 97 percentile for her age group (Silver, 2002). The story that she created to accompany this image is very telling. Her story involved the cat and dog switching attributes, then going to the veterinarian. The veterinarian told them it was just "a case called opposite case" and that "it wasn't serious." The story appeared to be reminiscent of her many experiences of going to doctors, and a cry for normalcy. Also implied, is the role reversal that she may be feeling towards her mother as CS has often expressed feelings of parentification. The image seemed to reflect this as the cat (CS) trying to balance the ball (health, school, family, etc.) and the dog (Mom) just watching–e.g., role reversal, the mother should be doing the balancing and the child should be observing ("a case of opposite case").

Person Picking an Apple from a Tree (PPAT) and Formal Elements Art Therapy Scale (FEATS)

CS was handed a white 12x18 sheet of paper, along with the appropriate markers assigned to the PPAT. CS was then instructed to "Draw a person picking an apple from a tree." The administrant utilized the FEATS rating and content tally sheets (see Appendices D and E). CS's overall rating score was a 52.5 out of a possible 70, and she fell into the FEATS nonpatient grouping (Gantt & Tabone, 1998). In her drawing, CS made the apple overly large and orange. The overemphasis of the fruit size might again mirror a desire for increased nurturance both physically and emotionally. Though the girl in the drawing leaned quite far forward for the apple, her ladder appeared stable and supportive of her imbalanced position. Only half of the tree was illustrated, which might imply poor planning. This might also reflect partial nurturance (perhaps from only one parent) as there is only half a tree

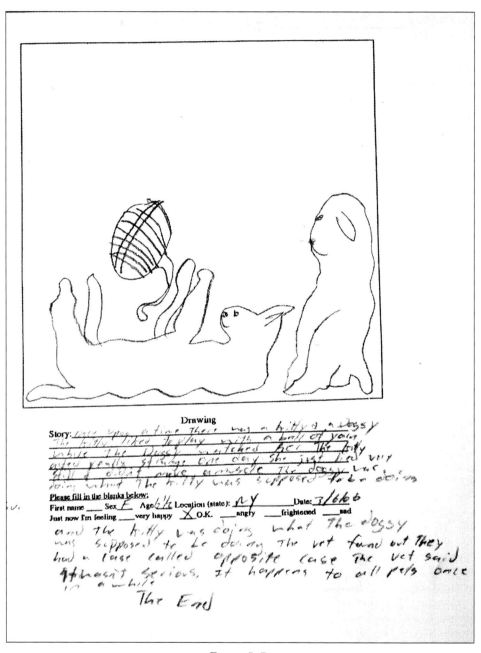

Figure 5–7.

and one apple from which to choose. Also there are no roots connecting the tree to the ground line which might highlight repressed emotions (Oster & Crone, 2004)

Figure 5–8.

Significant Sessions

Session 1 "I Feel Bad" 2/27/06

CS concluded the first diagnostic session by creating a drawing, and discussing her work with Atkinson (author 1), supervisor, Lori Higgins, and Dr. Horovitz (author 2). CS attempted to share and explain her feelings about her "I Feel Bad" drawing with her mother after she arrived to collect CS. As Shoemaker (1977) explained: a patient's problems, strengths, and potential for change and growth can often be seen in the first image. CS was able to explain her problem both artistically and verbally. She clarified that she was the puppy being left out (by the line drawn between other family members) and that the other three puppies were her brother, her mother, and her father; and that all of them were being fed by her "Nana" (PGM). Initially, the drawing only included the puppies and the mother dog; however, while discussing her feelings with Dr. Horovitz she added the blue line that separated the puppy on the left (CS) and the words (in sign language), "I Feel

Figure 5–9.

Bad." After the session, CS told her mother that she often felt badly and "left out," again indicating a need for warmth and love. As CS, her mother and brother were leaving the clinic, CS asked Mother S to carry her. It was suggested by Dr. Horovitz (author 2) that her mother carry CS to the car instead of her brother (E); however, Mother S did not acknowledge the suggestion. CS sadly left without her need being met.

Session 2 "The Feelings Book" 3/6/06

This session began with the administering of the SDT. During this session CS began expressing her feelings of parentification as she told the administrant that she was often expected to care for her brother. She also stated that her mother often forced CS into the role of interpreter, which caused CS to feel shy and embarrassed. CS was given a blank book in which she could express her feelings. She titled the book "The Feeling Book" and drew four faces on the cover: shy, sad, scared, and happy. CS attempted to draw bodies for the faces but ended up scribbling the bodies out. Once again, this seemed to suggest fear of bodily harm, anxiety regarding bodily issues and body image, and frustration over the lack of control surrounding her medical condition (Oster & Crone, 2004). The session ended before there was ample opportunity to discuss all of the feelings she had drawn, but the issue of parentification had been raised. More importantly, since she requested to take this book home, it allowed for continuity and the continuance of this discussion with Mother S. Indeed, this is where it rightfully belonged. Again, a transitional object had served CS in making these cognitive and behavioral connections (Winnicott, 1953).

Session 5 "Can I Take Them With Me?" 4/10/06

According to Ainsworth (1969), there are three approaches to the origin and development of the infant-mother relationship: "psychoanalytic theories of object relations, social learning theories of dependency (and attachment), and an ethologically-oriented theory of attachment" (p. 969). The structure of attachment (and/or lack thereof) contribute to the complexity of bonding and attachment:

> Object relations, dependency, and attachment, although overlapping, are seen to differ substantially . . . reinforcement as compared with activation and termination of behavioral systems and with feedback, strength of attachment behavior versus strength of attachment, inner representation of the object, intraorganismic and environmental conditions of behavioral activation, [as well as] . . . the role of intraorganismic organization and structure. (p. 969)

For CS, these issues were complicated by a mother who (on intake) described her family as completely "different" from her husband's. Indeed, before she relayed the story of her mother's (MGM) untimely death, she reiterated how difficult it was for her to grow up Deaf in a hearing environment. (Unlike CS's Father B, Mother was a Deaf child born to hearing parents. She was the opposite of a CODA and her experience replicated the research of Schein and Delk [1974]: 90% of the Deaf population in the United States have hearing parents of which 88% do *not* know sign language.)

Attachment for CS like that of Mother S was a very complicated issue from myriad standpoints: (a) growing up as a CODA; (b) contracting premorbid medical conditions of Eosinophilic Gastroenteritis (EG) at early onset; (c) dealing with significant abandonment issues regarding attachment to mother because of her numerous hospitalizations; and (d) finally, attachment to Mother (S) who had not resolved her own attachment issues due to the Deaf-hearing culture barrier experienced with MGM and MGF and early bereavement of her MGM.

Because of CS's struggle with the above issues, Atkinson (author 1) suggested creating family members when CS began forming puppets for a puppet show. CS promptly retorted that the show was only for the oldest animal. This reaction was changed when her brother (E) entered after the session and she offered to perform a puppet show for and with him at home. CS also

Figure 5–10.

asked to take the puppets with her, perhaps as a transitional object, to help her write "lines" for the puppet show while away at her cousins and revisiting the hospital. Her desire to take these transitional objects from the therapy room suggested her need for continuity between sessions, especially in light of her upcoming hospital stay.

While CS met with Atkinson (author 1), Mother S reported to Dr. Horovitz (author 2) that both physical and verbal altercation had ceased at home and that in-between sessions, CS had been able to express her feelings (through sign language) and articulation of her drawings. This was a momentous moment for the case as it seemed that CS was beginning to connect her past cognitive behavior with her own sense of loss regarding medical condition, alienation from peers, etc. This was further evidenced when Mother S relayed a story about CS's friends coming to her house and during snack time, Mother S informed Dr. Horovitz (author 2) that all of the friends first ate food with CS (her restricted diet of strawberries) before going on to their other snacks. This pleased CS greatly, that is to "break bread" (so to speak) with her friends and feel more normalized despite the dietary restrictions.

Session 7 "Her Family were Her Friends"

This session was filmed by author 2 (Dr. Horovitz) so a DVD could be made for CS of the puppet show. CS began by continuing to work on lines for her play, which she had started to write during the previous session. The play is about a kitty that has no family or friends because she has gotten lost. The kitty meets a bluebird that introduces the kitty to her friends; a dog, a bunny, and a tiger. After the introductions are made, they all become friends.

During this session, CS revealed that she did not have any friends at school and, again, expressed feelings of being "left out" at home, referring to her dietary restrictions and the associations to that issue. Part of her story is about a note that the kitty receives, telling her that she was missed.

A few weeks prior, author one (Atkinson) sent CS an e-mail of encouragement, as she was undergoing more testing in the hospital for EG. This verbal associate to her artwork amply illustrates how CS communicates her personal experiences through her creations.

Originally, the final line CS wrote for the play was the kitty stating, "Her family were her friends." This statement appeared to hold true for CS's personal life and seemed to strike a personal chord with her. Almost immediately after writing this, she changed the line to "Her friends were her family." The story of the kitty is a clear parallel for CS and her desire for friendships and to be accepted by others. CS ended the session by performing the puppet show with author one (Atkinson), while author two (Dr. Horovitz) continued to film. (See Figure 5–11, image from last part of CS's story.)

Figure 5–11.

Conclusion and Recommendations

CS is a bright child whose overall artistic response is within Lowenfeld & Britain's Schematic Stage age 7–9 years. She displays attributes in her art that suggest a need for nurturance, warmth, and love, as displayed by all of her batteries throughout the diagnostic testing. Hammer (1980) also suggested that individuals who suffered digestive disturbances drew figures with elongated necks, which is congruent with CS's art and physical diagnosis. Continuing individual art therapy has been recommended, as CS has demonstrated a strong ability to communicate her feelings through art and extend that into her interactions in the home. Continued sessions will allow CS the opportunity to learn appropriate strategies for coping with and expressing her feelings. Also family art therapy has been recommended to help bring CS's need for increased emotional nurturance to the attention of her family and allow for exchange regarding the Deaf-cultural divide (from CODA perspective) as well as support CS's need to attach to the parental units and avoid the role of interpreter and parent.

APPENDIX A: Genogram and Timeline

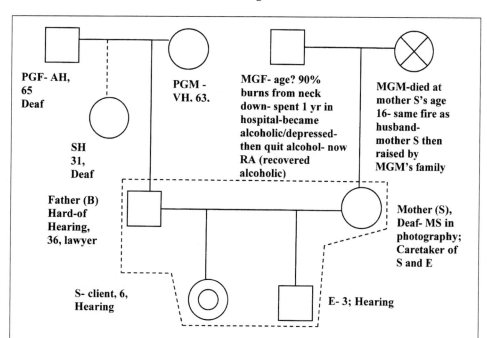

Timeline for Client(CS):

- Mother is deaf; Father is hard-of-hearing
- Both paternal grandparents (PGF and PGM) are deaf; maternal grandfather MGF is hearing; maternal grandmother MGM (deceased) was hearing
- 1 yr, CS becomes ill
- 3 yrs, CS is diagnosed with Eosinophilic Gastroenteritis (EG) which currently only allows her to eat selected fruits and vegetables; disorder has caused multiple surgeries and tests
- Brother E is born
- 6 yrs, CS becomes frustrated with food restrictions
- CS spends over a month at the KKI (Kennedy Krieger Institute) hospital in Baltimore for EG in November, 2005
- February, 2006, CS begins Art Therapy–referred for physical acting-out and aggression towards Mother S; symptoms subside within 3 weeks of individual art therapy treatment.
- Spring of 2006, CS reenters KKI (Kennedy Krieger Institute) for additional testing and treatment
- Returning to hospital for weekend checkup in April, 2006

(**N.B.:** Mother S's history: Mother S's mother (maternal grandmother–MGM) dies in fire at mother's aged 16. Mother S's father (maternal grandfather–MGF) was hospitalized for up to one year having sustained and survived the same fire. Ninety percent of MGF's body was burned, neck up–spared by fire. MGF suffered disability from fire and no longer works. After one year in the hospital, MGF was released, became depressed and alcoholic for a period of four years. Mother S lived with relatives during this period of time. Mother S helped get MGF into treatment. Currently MGF is RA [recovering alcoholic].)

N.B.: Editor's Note: Eosinophilic Gastroenteritis (commonly referred to as EG) is a rare disease in which the lining of the stomach, small intestines and large intestines become infiltrated with eosinophilis. Eosinophilis is a type of white blood cell. Eosinophilic Gastroenteritis can spread to other organs. It mostly affects children and young adults. The most common symptoms are: (a) abdominal pain; (b) weight loss; (c)nausea and vomiting; (d) diarrhea; and (e) bloody diarrhea. Exact cause of EG is unknown at this time. Treatment options such as Corticosteroid medications are usually successful in treating Eosinophilic Gastroenteritis.

(*Source:* http://www.mamashealth.com/stomach/eosingas.asp)

APPENDIX B

K-F-D ANALYSIS SHEET

Name __S__   Age __6__   Sex __F__   K-F-D Analysis Sheet

I. STYLE(s) (Circles)
- A. Compartmentalization
- B. Edging
- (C.) Encapsulation
- D. Folded Compartmentalization
- E. Lining on the Bottom
- F. Lining on the Top
- G. Underlining Individual Figures

II. SYMBOL(s)
- A. _T. V._   D. _____
- B. _____   E. _____
- C. _____   F. _____

III. (A) ACTIONS OF INDIVDUAL FIGURES

Figure	Action
1. Self	Watching T.V.
2. Mother	watching T. V.
3. Father	watching T. V
4. Older Brother	
5. Older Sister	
6. Younger Brother	watching T. V.
7. Younger Sister	
8. Other	

(B) ACTIONS BETWEEN INDIVIDUAL FIGURES

Figure	Action	Recipient
1. Self		
2. Mother		
3. Father		
4. O.B.		
5. O.S.		
6. Y.B.		
7. Y.S.		
8. Other		

IV CHARACTERISTICS OF INDVIDUAL K-F-D FIGURE

A. Arm Extensions
1. Self   5. O.S.
2. Mother 6. Y.B.
3. Father 7. Y.S.
4. O.B.   8. Other

F. Omission of Body Parts
(1.) Self   5. O.S.
(2.) Mother (6.) Y.B.
(3.) Father 7. Y.S.
4. O.B.   8. Other

B. Elevated Figures
1. Self   5. O.S.
2. Mother 6. Y.B.
3. Father 7. Y.S.
4. O.B.   8. Other

G. Omission of Figures
1. Self   5. O.S.
2. Mother 6. Y.B.
3. Father 7. Y.S.
4. O.B.   8. Other

C. Erasures
1. Self   5. O.S.
2. Mother 6. Y.B.
3. Father 7. Y.S.
4. O.B.   8. Other

H. Picasso Eye
1. Self   5. O.S.
2. Mother 6. Y.B.
3. Father 7. Y.S.
4. O.B.   8. Other

D. Figures on Back
1. Self   5. O.S.
2. Mother 6. Y.B.
3. Father 7. Y.S.
4. O.B.   8. Other

I. Rotated Figures
1. Self   5. O.S.
2. Mother 6. Y.B.
3. Father 7. Y.S.
4. O.B.   8. Other

E. Hanging
1. Self   5. O.S.
2. Mother 6. Y.B.
3. Father 7. Y.S.
4. O.B.   8. Other

V. K-F-D Grid
A. Height
1. Self __3__   5. O.S. _____
2. Mother __3 + 3__ 6. Y.B. __3__
3. Father __3__ 7.Y.S. _____
4. O.B. _____   8. Other _____

B. Location of Self
Between Y.B and mother

C. Distance of Self From:
Mother __1 CM__
Father __4 CM__
Other (Specify) __.5 cm - YB.__

APPENDIX C

RESPONSES TO SDT

Administering and Scoring the SDT

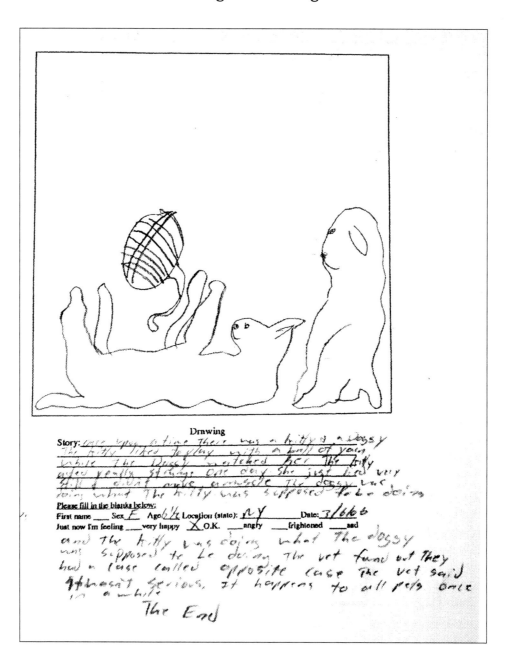

Drawing

Story: _Once upon a time there was a kitty & a doggy. The kitty liked to play with a ball of yarn while the doggy watched her. The kitty after really strange car day she just had very stiff & couldn't quite complete. The doggy was doing what the kitty was supposed to be doing_

Please fill in the blanks below:

First name _____ Sex *F* Age *6½* Location (state): *N Y* Date: *3/6/66*

Just now I'm feeling ____ very happy *X* O.K. ____ angry ____ frightened ____ sad

and the kitty was doing what the doggy was supposed to be doing. The vet found out they had a case called opposite case. The vet said it wasn't serious. It happens to all pets once in a while.

The End

APPENDIX D

FEATS RATING SHEET

Picture #: *1*

Rater: *JAKE*

FORMAL ELEMENTS ART THERAPY SCALE (FEATS)©
RATING SHEET
Linda Gantt, Ph.D., ATR-BC, & Carmello Tabone, M.A., ATR

The FEATS uses scales that measure **more or less** of the particular variable. Look at the degree to which a picture fits the particular scale by comparing the picture you are rating with the examples in the illustrated rating manual. **You may mark between the numbers on the scales.** Approach the picture as if you did not know what it was supposed to be. Can you recognize individual items? If you have a picture that is hard to rate, do your best to compare it to the illustrations and the written descriptions. Do not worry whether your rating is the same as another rater's. Concentrate on giving your first impression to the variable being measured.

#1 - Prominence of Color

Color used for outlining only   0 | 1 | 2 | 3 | ④ | 5   Color used to fill all available space

---

#2 - Color Fit

Colors not related to task   0 | 1 | 2 | 3 | ④ | 5   Colors related to task

---

#3 - Implied energy

No energy   0 | 1 | 2 | ③ | 4 | 5   Excessive energy

#4 - Space

Less than 25% of space used   0 | 1 | 2 | 3 ③ 4 | 5   100% of space used

---

#5 - Integration

Not at all integrated   0 | 1 | 2 | 3 | ④ | 5   Fully integrated

---

#6 - Logic

Entire picture is bizarre or illogical   0 | 1 | 2 | 3 | 4 | ⑤   Picture is logical

---

APPENDIX D

FEATS RATING SHEET *(continued)*

#7 - Realism

Not realistic (cannot tell what was drawn)　　0 | 1 | 2 | ③ | 4 | 5　　Quite realistic

#8 - Problem-solving

No evidence of problem-solving　　0 | 1 | 2 | 3 | 4 | ⑤　　Reasonable solution to picking apple

#9 - Developmental Level

Two-year-old level　　0 | 1 | 2 | ③ | 4 | 5　　Adult level

#10 - Details of Objects and Environment

No details or environment　　0 | 1 | 2 ② 3 | 4 | 5　　Full environment, abundant details

#11 - Line Quality

Broken, "damaged" lines　　0 | 1 | 2 | ③ | 4 | 5　　Fluid, flowing lines

#12 - Person

No person depicted　　0 | 1 | 2 | 3 | 4 ④ 5　　Realistic person

#13 - Rotation

Pronounced rotation　　0 | 1 | 2 | 3 | ④ | 5　　Trees & people, upright, no rotation

#14 - Perseveration

Severe　　0 | 1 | 2 | 3 | ④ | 5　　None

From: L. Gantt & C. Tabone, 1998, *The Formal Elements Art Therapy Scale: The Rating Manual*, Morgantown, WV: Gargoyle Press. Copyright © 1998 Linda Gantt.

This is a revised version of the rating sheet for the Formal Elements Art Therapy Scale, © 1990, Linda Gantt. This rating sheet may be reproduced in quantity by researchers. For other uses, written permission is needed.

APPENDIX E

PPAT CONTENT TALLY SHEET

CONTENT TALLY SHEET
"Draw a Person Picking an Apple from a Tree"

Picture #: _1_
Rater: _JAKE_

Instructions for Coding: Approach the picture as if you did not know what it was supposed to be. Can you recognize the individual items? Place a check for all items you see in the picture. If there is no category for an item try to describe it in the section called "Other Features" (Section 13). If there are two or more persons in the picture designate the person on the left as Person #1, the next person to the right as Person #2, and so on.

1. Orientation of Picture

Horizontal		Vertical	✗

2. Colors Used in the Whole Picture
(Check all colors used)

Blue	✓	Turquoise	
Red	✓	Purple	
Green	✓	Dark green	✓
Brown	✓	Black	
Pink	✓	Magenta	✓
Orange	✓	Yellow	

3. Person (If this is marked skip to Section #9.)

Cannot identify any part of the drawing as a person	
(If this is marked, score Section #3 & 8)	
Only arm or hand seen reaching for or grasping apple	

4. Color Used for Person
Check all colors used for the person(s) (or arm or hand) including the clothes. If you cannot identify the person do not code this section.

	Person #1	#2	#3
Blue	✓		
Turquoise			
Red	✓		
Green			
Dark green			
Brown	✓		
Black			
Purple			
Pink	✓		
Magenta	✓		
Orange			
Yellow			

5. Gender

	Person #1	#2	#3
Cannot tell (ambiguous or stick figure)			
Definitely male			
Might be male			
Definitely female	✓		
Might be female			

6. Actual Energy of Person
(The categories are not mutually exclusive - ex., person could be sitting and reaching toward apple.)

	Person #1	#2	#3
Prone			
Sitting			
Standing on implied or actual ground			
Standing on box, ladder, or other object	✓		
Reaching toward nothing			
Reaching down or up toward apple or object			
Floating (feet higher than base of tree with no groundline or visible support for feet)			
Hanging (appears suspended from tree or branch)			
Jumping up (may have "action lines")			
Jumping or falling out of tree			
Climbing tree without ladder			
Flying			
Other (if you cannot use one of the above categories describe it as best you can):			

7. Orientation of Person's Face
How much can you see of the person's face?

	Person #1	#2	#3
Cannot tell			
Front view - no features			
Front view with at least one feature (ex., eyes)			
Profile	✓		
Three-quarters view			
Back of head			

8. Approximate Age of Person

	Person #1	#2	#3
Cannot tell (ambiguous or stick figure)			
Baby or child			
Adolescent or adult	✓		

APPENDIX E

PPAT CONTENT TALLY SHEET *(continued)*

9. Clothing

Person	#1	#2	#3
Hat			
No clothes (stick figure or hand)			
Nude			
Some suggestion of clothes (may be a line indicating neckline or hem; may be same color as person; may be a sleeve or suggestion of sleeve if only hand is shown)			
Well-drawn clothes done in different colors than person (ex., street clothes or work clothes, dress, jumpsuit)	✓		
Costume (specify):			

10. Apple Tree

If you cannot identify any part as an apple tree, a branch, or a stem, check the first box and skip to Section #11. Count the total number of apples you can see, whether they are in the person's hand, on the ground, in the tree, or in a container.

No identifiable apple tree or branch or stem	
Only one apple in the picture:	■
Only a stem or branch with one apple on it, no tree trunk	
Trunk and top visible (may run off edge of paper) with one apple	✓
2-10 apples	
More than 10 apples	
Apples placed on perimeter of top*	

* Code if the apples are placed around edge of tree top, on stems sticking out from edge of top, or only at the ends of branches rather than in the tree.

11. Color of Apple Tree

Trunk:	■
Brown	✓
Black	
Other (specify):	
Top (may be distinct leaves or lollipop top or rounded form):	■
Green and/or dark green	✓
Other (specify):	
Apples:	■
Red	
Yellow	
Green/dark green	
Other (specify): *orange*	✓

12. Environmental Details

If you cannot identify any details in the categories below check the first box and skip to Section #12.

No identifiable environmental details	
Natural details:	■
Sun, sunrise, sunset	
Moon	
Grass or horizon line	✓
Flowers	
Tree (other than apple tree)	
Clouds, rain, wind	
Mountains or hills	
Lake or pond	
Stream, river, or creek	
Sky (filled in or sky line)	
Rainbow	
Animals:	■
Dog	
Cat	
Bird	
Cow, sheep, farm animal	
Butterflies	
Other (specify):	
Imaginary items, machines, or animals (specify):	
Inanimate items:	■
Fence	
Sign	
House	
Walkway, path or road	
Car, truck, or wagon	
Other (specify):	
Ladders	✓
Baskets, boxes, or containers	
Apple pickers or sticks	
Other (specify):	

13. Other Features

Writing (not a signature or on a sign)	
Numbers (not a date or on a sign)	
Geometric shape(s)	
Seemingly random marks	
Other (specify):	

REFERENCES

Ainsworth, M. D. S. (1969). Object Relations, Dependency, and Attachment: A Theoretical Review of the Infant-Mother Relationship. *Child Development, 40* (4), 969–1025.

Bull, T. H. (1998). *On the edge of deaf culture: Hearing children/deaf parents.* Alexandria, VA: Deaf Family Research Press.

Burns, R., & Kaufman, S. (1972). *Actions, styles and symbols in kinetic family drawings (K-F-D): An interpretive manual.* New York: Brunner/Mazel.

Gantt, L., & Tabone, C. (1998). *The formal elements art therapy scale: The rating manual.* Morgantown, WV: Gargoyle Press.

Hammer, E. F. (1980). *The clinical application of projective drawings.* Springfield, IL: Charles C Thomas.

Harrington, T. (2001). http://library.gallaudet.edu/dr/guid-hcodp.html

Harvey, M. A. (1982). The influence and use of an interpreter for the Deaf in family therapy. *American Annals of the Deaf,* 819–827.

Horovitz-Darby, E. G. (1988). Art therapy assessment of a minimally language skilled deaf child. Proceedings from the 1988 University of California's Center on Deafness Conference: *Mental health assessment of Deaf clients: Special conditions.* Little Rock, Arkansas: ADARA.

Oster, D. G., & Crone, P. (2004). *Using drawings I assessment and therapy* (2nd Ed.). New York & Britain: Brunner-Mazel.

Silver, R. (2002). *Three art assessments.* New York, NY: Brunner-Routledge.

Schein, J. D., & Delk, M. T. (1974). *The Deaf Population of the United States.* National Association of the Deaf, Silver Spring, Md.

Shoemaker, R. (1977). The significance of the first picture. *Proceedings from the 8th Annual American Art Therapy Association.* Illinois: AATA.

Winnicott, D. W. (1953). Transitional objects and transitional phenomena–A study of the first not-me possession. *International Journal of Psychoanalysis, 34,* 89–97.

Chapter 6

ART THERAPY AND THE MULTIPLY HANDICAPPED DEAF CHILD

David Henley

As art therapist at a residential school for the Deaf during the 1980s, I was often called upon to take referrals for Deaf children who, for various reasons, could not benefit from verbal or language-based therapy. One such referral concerned a Deaf/legally blind boy named J, who was then nine years of age. My first observation of J took me to the playground where I found him perched upon the uppermost bar of a jungle gym. He was gazing up into the sunlight rocking his head gently so that the light would play off of the thick lenses of his glasses. Suddenly, he emitted a strange yet gleeful cry and leapt with total abandon into the air then landed nimbly in the sand pile below. This was repeated perhaps twenty-five times within the hour with the child literally throwing his small yet obviously fit body into the air. As he relentlessly hurled himself through space, eventually he came upon another child clinging to a mid-level bar. Without any discernable emotion, J seized this child and threw him off the gym as if he were merely an object of play. The boy sailed through the air much to the horror of his ever-watchful supervisors. Luckily, the sand was deep and cushioned the flailing body. Clearly I reasoned, this was not the play process of an ordinary hearing-impaired child. I soon found that his art process and artwork were no less extraordinary.

In his first art therapy session, he boldly sifted through the stack of drawing papers and settled upon a large sheet of smooth, white rag paper. He then grabbed the nearest oil crayon and began to scribble—not an ordinary, infantile scribble but a rapid, intense drawing stroke that possessed a kinesthetic quality. Multiple squares, rectangles and lines sprang up in profusion. Great arcing lines struck out to the edge of the paper, then swept over the entire

110

piece as if serving as vicarious leaps through space. Eventually, recognizable images emerged from the frantic entanglement of lines: A gabled house, a lamppost, shrubbery. A sun radiated it's yellow and white light through the black scribbled canopy of a solitary tree. Again, I was struck by the second instance of metaphor, with the child conveying his obsession with light and its prismatic changes. Then, something which looked like a bed was sketched inexplicably parked outside of the house. Two oval forms with rudimentary faces were rendered tucked into this bed and then were scribbled completely out of the picture. He then stopped drawing and began to visually pour over his piece, checking each area with his glasses virtually grazing the surface of the paper. Next, he pushed this piece aside and without prior deliberation, began scribbling the next picture with the same sense of urgency as the first. In our first session together, he produced six fully embellished 18" x 24" pictures in less than 20 minutes. At the session's conclusion, he neglected to pause during his work to acknowledge my presence except in one instance to move me out of his way.

This chapter will explore the creative, art therapeutic and educational processes of multiply handicapped, Deaf children. It will draw upon J's case account for two reasons; first, his case embodies many of the problems and issues that arise when working with such an individual and second, he demonstrates the extraordinary potential that select individuals of this population possess in the way of the visual arts. As part of our discussion of multiply handicapped, autistic and Deaf/blind children, I will be describing the art therapeutic and studio-art process that focuses upon the specialized needs of this population. For contrary to many professionals' impressions, the multiply handicapped child is not a Deaf individual who cannot see nor is he a blind child who cannot hear. The nature of the problem is not an additive or compounding one, but is extraordinarily convoluted and complex. The subtle yet profound interactions between congenital and environmental trauma defy their being isolated since both medical and behavioral symptoms are rarely manifested in clear terms. Cognitive deficits, sensory distortion, language incapacity, autistic behavior, somatic defects all freely interact and aggravate the child's functioning. In appreciating the magnitude of these problems, one thing does become clear; that treatment programs and support systems must be modified to accommodate this exceptional population of Deaf children.

This new approach was placed practice by myself and associate, Cynthia Orsini, as part of a Deaf/Blind Program within a larger school for the Deaf. Working with J and other similar multiply handicapped children, we utilized a psychoeducational approach to art programming. Within the art studio, the children were provided with a secure yet sensorially enriched environment with which to explore, experiment and participate. They were encouraged to utilize this environment along with its tantalizing art media on their own terms, in ways that were meaningful and productive for the child. These environmental considerations were complemented by carefully measured, art-based interventions by the therapist/teacher. With therapeutic and instructional support, the program sought to provide these children with a vital means of communication–an alternative medium which effectively articulated their ideas and concerns without relying upon the conventional medium of language and interpersonal skills. Such normative ways of relating were a constant source of frustration and alienated these children in their academic and daily lives.

This chapter will describe the theoretical and practical implementation of a viable therapeutic and educational alternative–one that fosters both the acquisition of art-based skills and resolution of emotional conflicts in the studio sphere (Henley, 1987).

Etiology

Many multiply handicapped, Deaf children unfortunately share an etiology based upon the prenatal attack of the Rubella virus upon the still developing fetus. Although German Measles is a mild illness for the mother, it can devastate the unborn child if contracted during the first trimester of pregnancy. The birth defects that result in such a case, are profoundly debilitating and affect many areas of the child's functioning. Heart defects, cataracts, glaucoma, hearing loss, loss of vision, and brain damage may be sustained in any combination. As if these defects were not insidious enough, the child must fight off this attack if he is to survive at all, when still an unborn infant. One can scarcely imagine the stresses invoked upon the child at this stage of development which we normally associate as being a time of blissfulness and security within the soft confines of the womb. Many clinicians postulate that the virus not only attacks the child from the time of gestation, but contributes to assault the child throughout his life (McInnes & Treffry, 1982).

The most conspicuous disability is the obvious damage to the vision and hearing apparatus. The inability for the child to visually and auditorially process his environment deprives him of developing distortion-free impressions whether it be of his own body or other pertinent objects in the environment. The child is unable to gain a solidly-oriented sense of permanence, scale, movement, or cause and effect. He is unable to anticipate changes which make even the most benign experiences potentially traumatic.

> The lack of visual and auditory input deprives the multi-sensory deprived infant of and ability to anticipate coming events from environmental cues. Mother's entry into the room does not signify comfort, food or cuddling. The inability to anticipate changes makes each experience a new and fright-

ening one. To be picked up–snatched away from solid physical support; to be fed new foods–without mother's reassuring voice and smiling face; to be changed–suddenly pulled, lifted, and rolled about–all become potentially terrifying. (McInnes & Treffry, 1982, pg. 9)

Deaf/blind children are deprived of vital senses, which essentially seal them off in profound isolation. It must be stressed once again that it is not merely the lack of possessing these two senses that is so debilitating; it is also the residual, indecipherable distortions that are so painful to endure. Without an adequate means of communication, the child has difficulty in progressing through the developmental and cognitive stages of development. Unless given the tools needed to perceive his environment accurately and respond meaningfully to those around him, the child's motivation process will inevitably falter.

Aside from the medical complications and disabilities that result from rubella, are the behavioral or emotional maladjustment symptoms that eventually emerge in childhood. Many of these symptoms are associated with autism, which in itself, is an equally intractable and debilitating emotional disorder. Again, any number of symptoms may be manifest singularly or in combination and will defy whether they are congenital or environmental in origin.

The first autistic response that is recognized may be the lack of effect or interest the child shows in the parent. Without the proper environmental cues, the child is deprived of extrinsic motivation which appeals to his sense of anticipation and curiosity (Henley, 2005). Further aggravating the situation is again the issue of sensory distortion. Damage to the sensory apparatus may inhibit the child's ability to modulate incoming sensory stimuli accurately. This may take the form of being hypersensitive to certain sensations such as the tactile senses received when being stroked, kissed, fed, or other interactions that involve handling. The child's perception to such seemingly benign interactions may be decidedly exaggerated, even traumatic. We shall see in throughout this chapter, instances where a hyperreaction to normative stimuli is inaccurately perceived, distorted and strongly reacted to. This may include aversions to certain textured foods, clothing or play things, sounds such as the ticking of a clock or the vibration of footsteps. Certain sights such as the play of shadows or the glare of light may elicit strong responses. Any sensation that can be distorted, removed from its context and inaccurately perceived can cause tremendous stress and anxiety in such children. Frequently, the response is based upon the "flight or fight" dictum (Tinbergen, 1983). The child may react by resisting or avoiding those in the environment, which he perceives as being uncontrollable and threat provoking. Conversely, there may be an aggressive response in which the child attempts to repel the threatening stimuli. There are innumerable combinations of these behaviors, with the most pronounced example being self-inflicted head banging. This response is often associated with both mentally handicapped children and autistic children and represents the dual expression of panic and rage. In such children, uncomprehended and profound fear often gives way to intense pathological aggression that is in turn, turned against the self. The child soon realizes his head-banging as a desperate measure of managing and manipulating those in the environment. Its effectiveness is inarguable since it constitutes a behavior that few clinicians or parents can ignore (see Henley, 1986b).

As an avoidance measure, multiply handicapped-autistic children seem to take refuge in the world of objects (Henley, 1995). Here there is sense of predictability and permanence. The scale is more manageable and benign. There is enough variety for the child to select objects with neutral tactile properties. In some cases, the child will perseverate with one specific object or type of object which may in some ways take on the properties of a transitional object (Winnicott, 1965). It is the obsession with the object that allows the art therapist some measure of leverage and a point of departure with this type of child. Without relying upon interpersonal skills, or the capacity to use language, the art therapist can engage the multiply handicapped child by drawing upon the rich stimulation provided by the art environment.

Environmental Considerations

The multiply handicapped Deaf child's learning and therapeutic environment must comprise of space, furniture, objects and materials which can be assimilated with a minimum of individual distraction and stress. Should the child be unable to tolerate complex or large volume sensory stimuli, the environment must be adjusted to accommodate this need. In some cases there may be hypersensitivity to the room itself. Does it appear caverness to the child, are it's pathways obstructed or bewildering, is the color disturbing, do the windows rattle, is the door too heavy to operate, or is it imbalanced so that is slams unpredictably and so on. Sometimes it is the motivational objects of the studio that are a source of anxiety. Pictures on the wall, hanging plants or mobiles, collections of natural objects or other props may be selectively noxious to sensitive children. In some cases, it is not the tactile or visual qualities of the object but it is quality of impermanence or portability that disturbs a child (Bettelheim, 1952). It may be that, the objects in the child's immediate surroundings be securely fastened in place so as to promote a sense of permanence and security. Light sources as cited earlier, can affect a child's performance and behavior. One child reacted strongly to the incessant hum or the blinking of a florescent light fixture. The art therapist is responsible for carefully monitoring the child's response to the studio environment. As the child's tolerance grows, the type and strength of the stimulus can be slowly increased (Henley, 1992).

Conversely, the multiply handicapped Deaf child may be sensory deprived as well as sensory distorted. Because of severe sensory deprivation he may display decidedly hypo-responses to environmental stimuli. Motivation to explore his surroundings may not be forthcoming in these children unless vigorously prompted to do so. Props, objects, sounds, smells, textures, movement and other stimulation should be introduced in carefully measured interventions. The child's developmental stage, and emotional state of being should be considered in this sensory stimulation process. One should not be forcing the multiply handicapped Deaf child to conform to external demands or the expectations of a generic program. The environment along with staff's interventions are structured so as to *elicit* responses from the child when he demonstrated the readiness to assimilate and utilize such input. Only then will the child begin to comprehend and effect some meaningful control over his surroundings. With a greater sense of control, comes increased confidence and a willingness to initiate participation despite trepidation. Once the child has been aroused, the art therapist must insure a degree of routine, consistency and stability in the program, so as to not upset the child during the crucial phase of exploration and risk taking. Many children have been brought to the point of participation only to have them regress in the face of too much stimulation too soon.

Materials

The set-up of materials, motivational props, and tools should be accessible so that the child is encouraged to consider, choose, and act upon his decisions (Henley, 1992). For instance, paper should be stacked within visual and tactile reach, and brushes, sorted in cans so that their size and texture are discernable. Bulletin boards with pins stuck in one predictable corner should also be close to the work area so that the child can as a matter of routine, mount his freshly completed works. Routine is a vital part of these children's ability to adjust to their environment. Each child should be allowed to wander and explore the premises under supervision, so as to increase their sense of security and familiarity with the studio. Once materials, tools, props, and furniture are clearly and consistently secured in their respective places, the child may then function with a degree of independence, self-control, and responsibility.

The selection of materials is a crucial part of the treatment program (Henley, 1992). Brushes should be thick and stout for better control, with the bristles being stiff enough to offer resistance in the face of the child's lack of fine motor control. They should also be resilient and stand up to heavy scrubbing. Crayons, craypas and other dry coloring sticks should also be stout and flat on one side to inhibit rolling. Paper should be heavy grade with high rag content, and should also stand up to robust brushing and marking. Masking tape should be securely applied around the entire paper, creating a tactile frame that cues the child as to the papers parameter. Sculptural materials, like clay, are an ideal medium for the multiply handicapped Deaf child. Any high grade nontoxic potters' clay or polymer clay with fine grog content will offer a plastic, responsive and resilient material for the child to roll, cut, or carve (Henley, 2002).

Many different kinds of media can be introduced to multiply handicapped Deaf children. Developmental considerations, sensory capacities, and the child's cognitive level of functioning will all govern the materials introduced. Despite the range of multiply handicapped Deaf children's deficits, they do demonstrate strong preferences in regard to media, manner of working and content. The art therapist may strategically introduce materials, to mix, match and adopt so as to allow this discrimination process to proceed. As Kramer (1975) points out, we set the stage for the art experience to move forward. To do this, we draw upon our own intimate understanding of media and technique to effectively anticipate the creative needs of these children.

The Role of the Art Therapist

The art therapist plays a pivotal role in the development of the child's expressive abilities in the art studio. However, art therapy advances furthest with this population when we rely upon our ability to remain unobtrusive and nonconfronting in our interventions. Most multiply handicapped Deaf children are quite sensitive to interpersonal contact. They are in many instances, unsure of their own body and their own sense of self is tenuous. This confusion over body image and object relations is compounded when they are expected to relate normally to those around them. From the child's viewpoint, any unfamiliar person (which in severe instances can include the mother) poses a potential threat. When this unfamiliar individual attempts to coerce or even encourage the child to engage in even the most benign activity, this again can be extremely provocative. Regardless of the person's good intentions, he is perceived as a hostile entity that is capable of causing great anxiety (Henley, 2005, 2001, 1994). This autistic symptomatology that is associated with multiply handicapped Deaf children, may involve a panic reaction in response to those outside the child's interpersonal orbit. Thus, if the art therapist is to advance the therapeutic process, he/she must establish some sort of trust bond with the child. This act of developing rapport is a clear enough objective but in actuality constitutes a formidable obstacle in the therapeutic process.

I have worked with many multiply handicapped Deaf children for some-times years at a time, without having developed a truly stress-free bond. In J's case, four years of consistent contact that made use of cautious, art-based interventions produced only, an uneasy coexistence. It was never clear what J thought or felt for me, except that it was obvious that he associated me with the art studio. J was able to use parts of me—my artistic skills, and technical guidance, and especially my janitorial expertise (much time was devoted to maintaining his studio space as a kind of apprentice). I became something of a fixture—inextricably tied to the process he loved and was thus accepted as a necessary evil. Yet, even this tenuous bond or alien form of rapport was suf-ficient for the art process to move forward and eventually reach fruition.

Thus, the effective art therapist will respect autistic features of the multi-ply handicapped, Deaf child's need for solace by maintaining a comfortable distance that does not provoke or inhibit. It is the medium or a special prop that motivates the child to participate and express himself. Again, I am sat-isfied to function as the washer of brushes and filler of water bowls while the child concentrates on the task of art-making. It is a most suitable point of departure from which to initiate a relationship, regardless of its degree of inti-macy with the child. From this point, the art therapist can begin to interact more boldly with the child, through interpersonal and art-based interven-tions such as cuing him to keep his brush properly loaded, helping him main-tain his palate and his colors clean, et cetera.

Once the child can tolerate these art-based interventions, the therapist may then attempt to lean more toward personal interactions such as having him pause long enough to answer a yes or no question or ask him which color he wants and so forth. In the later stages of treatment with J, I grew even bolder by encouraging him to answer simple questions before he began painting (an activity he endured only because he was confident that eventu-ally he could get on with the real task at hand; his painting).

Eventually J did tolerate both art-based and interrelational interventions without becoming overly frustrated or stressed. In the end, he was able to feel sufficiently at ease in the studio environment so that creative risks could be taken. These creative risks stood as a metaphor for the intrapsychic changes that were taking place within the child himself.

Early Art Process and Work

As early as his kindergarten year, J's classroom teachers recognized his insatiable need to make art. Although they viewed his work as somewhat strange and alienating with it's intensity and obsessional qualities, they still allowed him free moments to work. Indeed, they felt little choice in the matter since J's ability to endure the classroom depended upon his being able to direct his energy through some form of appropriate outlet. Unless allowed drawing time, J's self-stimulatory and other aberrant behaviors would have undoubtedly escalated, making academic work increasingly more difficult to sustain. Thus, since his preschool days, J was afforded a corral where he could retreat from the demands being placed upon him in the classroom, to a safe and predictable place to draw.

Chiefly, his parents recognized the importance of his artistic outlet and preserved the primary school works. They reasoned correctly that his work constituted a very real strength—one that should be nurtured and developed to it's fullest extent. It seems that he drew constantly since age four, with the pieces of this period being a collection of figure drawings and landscapes that were precocious even by the standards of an intact child. (It should be noted that these works were created spontaneously, without the encouragement or direction of any adult.)

It wasn't until J reached the age of ten that he began receiving art education and art therapy. His portfolio at age seven demonstrates that a highly evolved idiosyncratic style had already developed. Working in his patented kinesthetic style, J created innumerable interior architectural drawings mainly in crayon and marker. In viewing these works one is immediately struck by the precocious and unusual use of perspective. His representational qualities are remarkable even for a normal child of this age.

Objects such as chairs, tables, and other furnishings are not rendered as conceptual stereotypes, which are an ordinarily expectation of a seven-year-old. When seen in this light of his severe disability, the ability to work from a perceptual standpoint is all the more remarkable. He had already developed a favored visual vocabulary of interior objects, which he drew directly and simply as he saw them.

Chairs are rendered from the perspective of a child who studies the seat from eye level and the back from well below. The entire environment is rendered from a perspective that indicates the child's small stature. It is unusual that we ever see this in the art of a six-year-old since they are ordinarily incapable of rendering in three-point perspective at this stage of development. In viewing these works, one gains the impression that the towering assemblage of spaces and objects might have filled this child with awe and possibly bewilderment.

There is also a sense of urgency and even desperation about these pictures. These are not the casual drawings of a child at play but are deadly serious in their intent—as if vital impressions and information were being processed through the creative art. Coping with his distorted sensory input, J had to draw upon the only compensatory mechanism available to him so as to aid in translating environment stimuli into meaningful information. His art process constituted this vital avenue of connection with the outside world; one that assisted him in coping, assimilating, and conceptualizing his environment.

In viewing the volume of work from this period, it seems as though J was calling up image after image to exert some measure of control over this vast environment, which perhaps threatened to overwhelm him. Maybe the act of creating these images in rapid succession assisted him in keeping the world at bay or possibly, in it's place. For a Deaf/blind child, the world is fraught with countless unexpected and uncontrollable things and occurrences. By creating them symbolically, J was possibly identifying with the aggressive environment and thus defending himself in the process. Yet, despite all this psychodynamic theorizing, there is a sense in these works that J was fascinated, as any artist would be, with the myriad of forms, structures and spaces of his environment.

Given the fact that most other modes of inquiry were denied him, it is only reasonable that he pour his energy into the mode that was relatively intact. Like a true artist, J relentlessly transcribed his impressions with style and design sensibility that even included a touch of grandeur.

The human figure drawings from this period are equally remarkable for their precocity and the presence of psychopathology. First, it is unusual that he drew human figures in several styles that indicated disparate levels of developmental and cognitive functioning. Figure 6–1 shows a figure that was elicited by the classroom teacher. Perhaps because it was the product of a directive, it is stereotypical with minimal embellishment with little or no emotional investment.

Figure 6–2, which was a spontaneous drawing, is radically different. It is a fully articulated figure placed in context with a familiar environment. It is drawn with conviction and passion, using fairly sophisticated, design devices. Note the intensity of the coloring and the unusual cropping of the figure's form. One is reminded in looking at these two pictures, of the renown autistic individual known as Nadia (Selfe, 1977; Henley, 1989). This child was also able to draw in a precocious perceptual mode at an early age, so long as it was on her terms. Once pieces were elicited from this autistic child, she, too, regressed back to more stereotypical images.

The figures also indicate the presence of the autisms that are part of this child's emotional life. As precocious as the figurative works are, there is a strangeness that pervades them. The cropped frontal view, while being a perceptive and sophisticated design device is also disturbingly close and intrusive. While we can attribute the figures domination of the composition to the importance assigned to it in the child's estimation, it also bespeaks of anxiety and threat. The figure seems at odds with the predictable nature of the object world—instead it's blank, yellow face and powerful, black shoulders

Figure 6–1.

Figure 6–2.

and hair seem volatile and provocative.

Once this child began working with human figures, the nature of his work changed. Throughout his works, from age six to twelve, these faces appear and reappear, filling the composition with their disturbing expressions.

By the age of ten, J began to work with me in individual, therapeutically-based art sessions. Initially, his works involved exterior views of buildings and the surrounding landscape. Although his style was still an intensive controlled scribble, his visual vocabulary had expanded considerably from the portfolio from age six. His images, in fact, had evolved to an almost encyclopedic inventory of visual impressions. He recorded hundreds of views of different scenes and objects all in his patented style of scribbling.

In the opening vignette, I described the process whereby J would virtually attack any drawing surface he could find and draw for as long as he was permitted. This aggressive, obsessive manner of working continues unabated to this day. He works in a most intense manner without any overt preliminary planning. His perceptions are recorded without a thought to decoration or aesthetic pretension. He simply draws what he sees in the energetic style, developed over seven years of constant working.

The exterior works of this period are predominantly facades, rooflines and the immediate landscapes of residential houses. Windows, doors and roofs are given particular attention, while other embellishments are held to a minimum. Hundreds of these houses were rendered from all different perspectives. Many are done from improvable angles such as corners drawn from below grade such as Figure 6–3. It is at this point in J's artistic evolution that I began to intervene as his art therapist.

Figure 6–3.

Art Therapy Process and Interventions

During the first six months of art therapy, I sought to acclimate J to the new studio with it's materials, props, furniture layout, and most importantly, the routines of the sessions. Beginning with the most mundane and simple activity, I hoped to ease J into this new environment as quickly and as painlessly as possible. Thus, traveling back and forth to the art room, finding the work apron, selecting paper, working the light switch of his tensor lamp all became regimens that began each session. I, too, sought to become part of this regimen. I guided him through the room, helped him select media, kept his work space relatively clean and free of clutter and in short, made myself useful. I attempted to remove myself from a teacherly role—one that I am sure he anticipated and would be resistant to, in favor of a more neutral, supportive one. In doing so, I hoped to provide a sense of consistency, security, and stimulation in an environment conducive to work and growth (Henley, 1995a).

My initial interventions were exercised exclusively through the art process. These art-based interventions involved adopting the media, the technique or environment in such a way, that aesthetic, cognitive, and therapeutic issues could be addressed. These issues included fostering flexibility, encouraging decision-making and experimentation, promoting aesthetic awareness and developing appropriate behaviors—all of which were addressed during the art process.

The first objective to further these aims was to develop J's capacity for reflection. This involved affecting J's unadulterated style in such a way so as to begin to shift the emphasis from purely kinesthetic involvement with the process toward increasing his awareness of the art product. By increasing his awareness and appreciation for his completed pictures, I hoped to instill in him the capacity to pace himself, plan, make decisions, solve problems, and eventually reflect upon his finished results.

Achieving the objective of reflection implied sweeping changes in J's manner of working—a system, which had been locked into place for years. I therefore had to move cautiously at loosening very rigid and vital defenses. Instead, I attempted to replace these with a more flexible, yet equally secure system with which the child could successfully function (Henley, 2004).

Inevitably, promoting changes in a system as hard-driven and rigid as J's meant there would be a certain amount of resistance and frustration (for both of us). Any intervention would need to respect J's system (since it has allowed him to proceed successfully thus far) so as to not compromise the child's creative energy. Yet, I hoped to unlock him from the sheer compulsivity of his process—to replace unyielding preservative behavior with more flexible defenses, so that the growth process could move forward.

The investigation began with J scrubbing furiously with his colors, snapping the thickest crayons and crushing the hardest colored pencils without respite. I had previously responded by providing a steady stream of repaired materials without interrupting his work. Eventually, I felt it would be possible to encourage J to sharpen his own pencils, not only to promote responsibility and respect for the media but more importantly, to create a respite during the drawing process; or an opportunity for reflection. Standing wistfully at the sharpener, J would sometimes look over to the table as I would prop up his work in progress and attempt to gain some eye contact. While this intervention met with mixed results, it did allow for breathing space during the session and established itself as a ritual in it's own right. J was now in a position to be more aware of his medium and how the medium properties could affect the pace of the session (Henley, 1995b).

At one point, I decided to discourage his arbitrary selection of media, by increasing his awareness of colors, textures, and other properties of the media. I asked him via sign language, to choose colors, paper size, and media. J resented all this talk and made his feelings known first by ignoring my signing completely. Pushing him further, on one occasion he bit his own finger and ripped the paper. After approximately six sessions, J began to tolerate these demands. He would humor me by choosing a finite set of colors, (I'm sure uncaring as to which) so as to satisfy me and allow him to go on to the real task at hand. Yet, we did begin some modicum of interaction—again, based solely upon the dynamics of the art process. Another issue that I soon addressed was J's propensity to overwork his pieces by saturating the paper with countless layers of crayon wax or pencil lead. J would rarely take the time to change papers after finishing a piece. He would literally start another drawing on top of the finished one, thus attesting to his lack of concern for a finished product. It was difficult to both mediate this process and remain unobtrusive. It was certainly intrusive to try and stop him. (Indeed, one would have to literally wrestle the piece away from him). Eventually, I turned him toward me and signed "Finished?" After the second year, J did eventually compromise and would reluctantly part with his highly burnished (almost repousse) pictures, after reluctantly signing back "Yes, J finished."

With consistent interventions, J eventually accepted the fact that he could no longer work furiously, break crayons, go through unlimited supplies and bite his finger if he didn't get his way. He learned somewhat that his selection of materials, their working condition, and his ability to endure a modicum of interactions had a direct bearing upon his performance. Along with these expectations and limitations, J also found that I was different from the usual classroom teacher. He was able to become frustrated and angry without being admonished. He was left to work for long, uninterrupted periods without being forced to shift gears to another activity. He was also given a relatively free rein of the studio space, free to explore and experiment at the expense of his productivity.

By the eighth month of individual sessions, the art therapy was affecting both his behavior and his artwork. Figure 6–4 attests to the fact that J had achieved many of the goals set for him. His forms now seemed more clari-fied; the composition was relaxed with only slight sacrifice to its vigor. J still worked robustly but with great control and at a slower pace. It may be sig-nificant that with this piece J renewed his interest in interior space. It is tempting to suggest that his well-ordered, strongly drawn interior parallel changes occurring intrapsychically as J moved closer toward a state of reflec-tion.

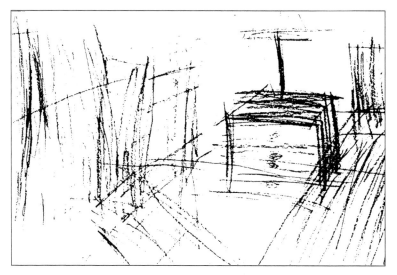

Figure 6–4.

Working within a more mature style, J eventually reintroduced the human figure. Using many of the earlier design devices, he continued to ren-der familiar objects. But, as Figure 6–5 attests, he incorporated the subject not as a realistic human being, but as one more inanimate accessory in the room furnishings.

These two figures are confined to the television and a picture on the wall and are thus powerless. It is again, an astounding example of problem solv-ing, whereby the child has taken a threatening and provocative theme and incorporated it into a semi-neutralized solution. Although it is symptomatic of this child's autistic/affective disorder, it makes for a fascinating example of resolving conflict through the projection of symbolic imagery.

Figure 6–5.

It is possible that this autistic-like, design device served an additional purpose with the advent of relatively provocative interventions on my part, with such demands to a certain degree that regression was to be expected. It can be seen as the price I paid and indeed, the child paid, for engaging in the growth process. It underlines how growing pains are part of the therapeutic and artistic experience. This question of regression was confirmed in the following figurative picture.

Figure 6–6.

In this next piece, Figure 6–6, J returned to the portrait-dominated com-position which has undergone a fascinating and regressive transition. The fig-ure now leans into the picture as if springing out from behind the doorway. Behind him are the long tunnel-like walls and ceilings as seen by the small child. The facial expression is unchanged from the earlier portraits, yet evokes a woeful and even sinister quality. It communicates clearly what the consequences are once the figure is released from its inanimate confines. It is a threatening and provocative person who, incomprehensibly, may be lurking beyond the distorted peripheral view of the child's perceptions.

It was about this time that J began painting with art therapy intern, Cynthia Orsini. As a project, we agreed that J might benefit from retreat from figurative work to a change of scale and medium as long as he dis-played the readiness to adjust to the transition. Beginning with colored pen-cils with a water color wash, J was instructed in the use of the paint brush, paint tray, watercolor paper, the use of water and in blending and diluting. Quickly he mastered these techniques. The adaptations in medium and tech-nique were really quite minimal. A stiff bristled stenciling brush with a thick handle stood up well under J's intense scrubbing. Heavyweight paper was secured with wide masking tape as were the water bowl and paint tray.

After several months of working in watercolor and diluted tempera, J was given cups of acrylic and sheets of canvas, which were also taped to the table's surface. With hand-over-hand instruction, J gained experience in loading his brush, stroking the canvas and blending the colors on a palette, (which in this case was a cafeteria tray). Once familiarized with this process, J was put in front of a 4' x 4' stretched canvas on an easel and with close mon-itoring; J was encouraged to create on a grand scale.

Contrary to our expectations, J was able to handle the switch to painting medium with uncommon self-control. His response was one of being soothed instead of the expected uprush of passion and excitement that is so often seen with viscous colored medium. J almost systematically stroked the two-inch house-painting brush, delineating his becalmed images in the most thoughtful way.

Figure 6–7 depicts both Orsini and the artist interacting during this process. The painting demonstrates how the agitated tangles of line and form give way to large planes of unfettered color. Objects have become simplified and less in number, yet they retain their vigor and intensity. As we can expect in painting, moods are established with less regard to achieving real-istic precision. The only hint of regression was the conspicuous absence of the human figure. J now routinely includes portraitive and figures in his can-vases. By switching to the painting medium at a time in J's therapy when the figure constituted a highly charged issue, it was only natural that he elimi-nated the human form problem.

Figure 6–7.

When I left the school, J was still working with Orsini, and seemed to be thoroughly acclimated to large-scale acrylic painting Figure 6–8. While he still overworked his pieces, they gained clarity, purity of color, and sophistication of design. Under Orsini's guidance, J reintroduced the figure into his canvases, painting with greater "relatedness" and interpersonal awareness (Orsini, 1988). Maturation continued to advance with long-term therapy, yet it remained an erratic process, whereby regression and stagnation took hold as readily as progress.

Figure 6–8.

CONCLUSIONS

I have drawn upon the case of J because of its richness in illustrating the extraordinary problems, the contradictions, and the enormous potential of the multiply handicapped Deaf artist. As in the case of J, many in this population possess a wide range of disparate qualities—some profoundly deficited and others remarkably positive. What is fascinating is the nature of the multiply handicapped Deaf child's creativity; it is often inextricably bound by both pathology and giftedness. It is obvious that J's artistic talent was deeply affected by the distortions, and idiosyncrasies that were inherent in his physical/cognitive and perceptual make-up. Where J's giftedness began and his pathology left off is an issue worth debating. It again brings to mind the case of the autistic savant, *Nadia* (Selfe, 1977) who displayed extraordinary drawing ability at age five despite profound cognitive and behavioral deficits. In this case the balance of giftedness and pathology was a tenuous one—once it was disturbed by intensive speech and cognitive training it diminished dramatically. This points decisively to the delicate relationship between the giftedness and its accompanying pathology; as if one could equate the gift as an elaborate and sensational symptom in itself. Regardless of this theorizing, a salient problem remains; how does one work therapeutically with this population (which infers maintaining empathic regard and acceptance of symptomatology) while still maintaining limits and exceptions for their adaptation and relative normalization?

Throughout my program for multiply handicapped Deaf children, I have aspired to strike a balance between these two contradictory demands. I have attempted to promote maturational growth without making the process unendurable for the child. Focusing upon the whole child, I rarely discriminate between what is a behavioral/cognitive approach or psychodynamic therapy. I feel strongly that each of these areas is the domain of the art therapist.

For example, we can hardly affect a change in a child's behavior without addressing what is making him angry or whether or not he can understand what is expected as being behaviorally appropriate. Each function is interconnected and any intervention that strives to ameliorate only one facet will be ineffective. Therefore, as art therapists we also take on roles as behaviorists, teachers, adult role models, parents and especially, as mature working artists.

We need to utilize our training as artists so as to understand and act upon the creative struggles and endured by children as described in this chapter. Without this artistic empathy one cannot expect to *anticipate* the child's problems or concerns. Unless we can anticipate these issues we cannot hope to devise appropriate strategies to address the child's concerns. As Kramer

(1975) points out, there is inherent power in the art process–power that can prompt change and growth far more effectively in this nonverbal sensory-deprived population than any talking therapy. To wield this power we must be rational, sensitive and sure in our interventions. Additionally, we must be firm in our belief for the child's potential.

In this chapter and in other writings (Henley, 1995, 1986, 1987), I have argued that latent potential resides in even the most handicapped child. In my years of clinical experience, I have encountered profoundly autistic, mentally retarded, and Deaf/blind children who possessed the creative spark–just waiting to be tapped and developed. We must therefore approach this population by insuring that our appreciation of the child's potential remains untainted by prejudice or self-fulfilling prophecy. We must look past the gross physical abnormalities and bizarre behaviors and ferret out any strengths in evidence.

REFERENCES

Bettelheim, B. (1952). *The empty fortress.* New York: The Free Press.

Henley, D. (2005). Attachment disorders in post-institutionalized adopted children: Art Therapy approaches to reactivity and detachment. *Arts in Psychotherapy, 32* (1), 29–46.

Henley, D. (2004). The meaningful critique: Responding to art from preschool to postmodernism. *Art Therapy, 21* (2).

Henley, D. (2002). *Clayworks in art therapy.* London: Jessica Kingsley Publishers.

Henley, D. (2001). Annihilation anxiety and fantasy in the art of children with Asperger Syndrome and others on the Autistic Spectrum. *American Journal of Art Therapy, 39.*

Henley, D. (1995a). A consideration of the studio as therapeutic intervention. *Art Therapy, 12* (3), 188–190.

Henley, D. (1995b). Five scribbles: An inquiry into artistic intention and critical empathy. *British Journal of Art & Design Education, 13* (3).

Henley, D. (1994) Art of Annihilation: Early onset schizophrenia and related disorders in childhood. *American Journal of Art Therapy, 32* (4).

Henley, D. (1992). *Exceptional children, exceptional art.* Worchester, MA: Davis Publications. 1992. (Hardbound text in use in over 23 universities nation-wide.) (See reviews).

Henley, D. (1989). Nadia revisited: Regression in the autistic Savant Syndrome. *Art Therapy, 6* (2), 43–56.

Henley, D. (1989). Incidence of artistic giftedness in the multiply handicapped. *Advances in Art Therapy,* H. Wadeson, (Ed.), New York: John Wiley.

Henley, D. (1987). Art therapy with the special needs hearing impaired child. *American Journal of Art Therapy, 25* (3), 81–89.

Henley, D. (1986). Approaching artistic sublimation in low functioning individuals. *Art Therapy, 3* (2).

Henley, D. (1986b). Art with self-injurious clients: Educational/therapeutic interventions. *The Arts in Psychotherapy, 13* (1).

Kramer, E. (1975). In *Art and emptiness: New problems in art education and art therapy.* Edited by Elinor Ullman and Penny Dachinger. New York: Schocken Books.

McInnes, J. M., & Treffry, J. (1982). *Deaf blind infants and children: A developmental guide.* Toronto: University of Toronto Press.

Orsini, C. (1988). *An art therapy/educational approach with a gifted multiple-handicap rubella child.* New York: New York University Press,

Selfe, L. (1977). *Nadia.* London: Academic Press.

Tinbergen, N. and E. A. (1983). *Autistic children: New hope for a cure.* London: George Aken and Unwinn Ltd.

Winnicott, D. W. (1965). *The maturational processes and the facilitating environment.* New York: International Universities Press.

Chapter 7

INTERNATIONAL PERSPECTIVES ON DEAFNESS: IMPLICATIONS FOR ART THERAPISTS

AMY SZARKOWSKI

INTRODUCTION

For this book to be useful to art therapists around the world, it is necessary to consider the implications for such work in various areas of the globe. This chapter will explore the meaning of "Deaf Culture" in several locales, and reflect upon differences found in the definitions of both *Deafness* and *disability* worldwide. Current paradigms in Disability Studies will be addressed, as will the application of Disability Studies to the field of Deafness.

Art therapists working with Deaf clients need to understand the cultural context in which they live and work. This chapter will provide some "food for thought" regarding various ways to perceive of the influence of Deafness on the lives of those who are Deaf. By considering these issues within a global context, the professionals working with Deaf clients, whether Hearing or Deaf themselves, can better understand the impact on clients of being Deaf in the places in which they live. This chapter will also outline commonalities and differences in the lived experiences of Deaf people around the world. It will consider the positive perspectives adopted by some cultures regarding Deafness and will seek to understand how this level of acceptance might be further adopted by other communities and cultures. Lastly, this chapter will address the implications for Art Therapists specifically in working with the Deaf internationally.

What does "Deaf Culture" mean in the international arena? For professionals working with *Deaf* or *deaf* individuals, whether art therapists or others in the mental health field, the implications of "location" are enormous. Differences exist between countries in terms of their perspectives of the Deaf as a minority group, and their perceptions of Deafness as a disability (Marshall, 1996; Calderon & Greenberg, 2003). Even within cultures or nations, the experiences of Deaf people will vary (Sedano, 1997).

Background

I came to be involved in working with Deaf people through my personal experience of having a friend who learned of his progressive hearing loss at the age of 20. He was subsequently informed that he could anticipate becoming Deaf by 25 years of age and I took a class in American Sign Language to support him. I quickly fell in love with the language itself and found myself drawn to communicating through gestures, facial expressions, and "pictures." After being introduced to Deaf people, I became not only interested in their language, but also in their lives. As I continued to progress in subsequent ASL classes, I learned about Deaf Culture and was determined to pursue this as my occupation.

Following my undergraduate work, I attended a master's program in Clinical Psychology and obtained Certification in Deafness and Mental Health. Later, I moved to Washington, D.C. to pursue my Ph.D. in Clinical Psychology from Gallaudet University. While attending Gallaudet, I learned a great deal more ASL and delved into learning about Deaf Culture. I was fortunate enough to be granted a Fulbright award to go to Rome, Italy, to work at their National Research Center with well-known scholars in the field of Deafness. That experience opened my eyes to the experiences of other Deaf in the world. Living outside of the U.S. for a time allowed me to gain greater understanding about the situation of Deaf people. At my first international conference, I presented a poster at the European Congress on Mental Health and Deafness in Bad Ischel, Austria. There, I had the opportunity to meet and interact with scholars whose work I had read and admired. My eyes were further opened to the global situation of mental health and Deafness. Following that conference and my time in Italy, I returned to the U.S. and completed my clinical internship in New Mexico, in the Southwest. Exposure to the large Hispanic and Native populations in that region granted me greater understanding in the diversity within my own country of origin. I realized that, although I love travel, I need not go abroad in order to consider the implications of community and culture on the individuals with whom I was working. I was reminded time and time again about the diversity in my "backyard." Yet, I still longed to see more of the world. I completed my Ph.D. and began to look for positions that would allow me to travel and study Deafness in various regions, as well as utilize my acquired skills to serve the Deaf communities with which I came in contact.

Currently, I serve on the faculty of Comparative Culture at Miyazaki International College in Miyazaki, Japan. I am teaching psychology courses and working with the teacher-training students regarding educating children with disabilities. I remain highly interested in international issues. Now, I am studying Japanese Sign Language (JSL) and becoming involved in the Japanese Deaf Community.

While I certainly cannot claim to know or fully comprehend the situation of Deaf people everywhere in the world, I hope that my training and experience has provided me a lens through which to look at these issues from a somewhat objective viewpoint. I welcome you to join me on this journey as we consider Deafness in the global context.

What Does it Mean to "Be Deaf?"

Ah, the age-old question. It is mentioned again here because the answer is not a simple one. Including *Deafness* and *disability* in the same chapter, I am quite aware, may prompt argument. From the perspective of leaders in the Deaf Culture movement, Deafness is about difference, and Deaf people are a linguistic minority group (Skelton & Valentine, 2003). *The use of "Deaf" in this chapter, consistent with the form often used by academics and researchers in the area, refers to individuals who identify with Deaf culture. The use of "deaf" is also used, in the context of referring to those with hearing loss, who do not define themselves as members of Deaf communities.* For some, Deafness is a social construction of identity involving the use of Sign Language, understanding the Deaf Culture of one's country or place of origin, and being involved in the Deaf community. Deaf people who adopt this identity are likely to be against the inclusion of Deafness in this discourse about disabilities.

I strongly support the actions of Deaf leaders in adopting this stance and shifting the focus from the medical view of "hearing loss" to that of understanding the oppression that has existed against Deaf people and to celebrating the uniqueness of their culture. However, I maintain that, in the global perspective, we are not yet at a place where deafness and disability can be discussed in separate terms. Many Deaf people around the world are unaware of this movement, either because they have not been exposed to the ideas of empowerment or because they are, as a collective, more concerned with imminent issues of survival, and the work taking place within the disability movements are providing them with services to meet their needs. In a personal conversation with a Deaf woman in Cambodia, for example, she mentioned that the National Center for Disabled Persons had been a lifeline for her (personal communication, March 11, 2005). When asked about her perspective on Deafness as a disability, she stated, "Of course, deafness is a disability, just like being blind, or being in a wheelchair. If it were not a disability, I would not get the help that I need. I am a Khmer, that is my culture. Deafness is not my culture, it is my disability."

This chapter will attempt to discuss Deaf communities and the situation of persons who consider themselves *Deaf*, as well as those who call themselves *deaf*, and identify themselves as persons with a disability. Both realities are important and justified in the world as it is today.

What are Some Common Experiences of Deaf People Internationally? What are Some Differences?

A full account of international perspectives is not possible within this chapter. However, an overview of some selected research from various parts of the world will highlight some of the cultural differences in perceptions of Deafness. Although the list is not exhaustive by any means, it will attempt to point out some differences that may be of interest to art therapists working in different parts of the world. Regardless of the culture and location where the therapy is taking place, the art therapists need to be informed of the perceptions of Deafness and of disability that are commonly held by the general population in their area.

The research below highlights some important aspects to consider when working with Deaf clients, including their self-perception and identity, as either Deaf, deaf, hard-of-hearing, or something else. It is also important to consider the historical context of deafness within a particular country, to better understand how Deaf people perceive of themselves, either as a community, a culture, or a group of individuals. The experiences of the families and parents of Deaf children can offer important information for understanding young Deaf clients as well. By gaining knowledge about the opportunities for employment and the laws in place to assist Deaf people, professionals can better understand the potentials that likely exist within a culture to help Deaf clients maximize their potential. Similarly, information about the social movements within a particular culture can inform the therapist about the collective consciousness of that culture regarding Deafness and/or disabilities. Lastly, by considering the disability perspective of various regions, art therapists can place their work with clients within a frame of reference that will be helpful to both the therapist, in understanding the client, and to the client, in understanding him or herself.

Britain

A study conducted in Britain looked at the identities and self-descriptions of young Deaf people (Skelton & Valentine, 2003). The researchers interviewed 20 young people to assess their self-identification as *Deaf* or *deaf,* in accord with the definitions of such described above. They found that the identities of the young people they interviewed were hybrid and dynamic. The majority of the teens considered themselves bilingual (English and British Sign Language). They spoke at length of their initial rejection of the idea of being *deaf,* and their growing acceptance of themselves as *Deaf* people. Nearly all of the participants described a love of sign language and an appreciation of being able to fully express themselves. They indicated that they were comfortable with their Deaf peers, though they admitted frustration with the lack of social opportunities for interaction in the Deaf clubs, reportedly utilized by the older generation in Britain. However, nearly all of the young people also expressed resignation at being Deaf, and shared with the researchers their varying degrees of desire to be a part of the larger hearing community. Skelton and Valentine (2003) reported an overall optimism regarding the future, which they perceived as a positive indication that these young people would adopt a "healthy" Deaf identity.

The young people interviewed in the British study expressed confusion about the definitions of *D/deaf* and *disability* (Skelton & Valentine, 2003). It was common for the participants to state that they did not perceive themselves as disabled, yet they acknowledged the need for Disabled Student Support grants to further their education. The participants spoke in terms consistent with the "social model" of Deafness, which recognizes that Deaf people are excluded by the hearing world (Tregaskis, 2004). This model does not deny the existence of a bodily impairment, but rather stresses that "disability" is perceived by the society, secondary to the social attitudes of the nondisabled and practices of the "able-bodied" against those with physical limitations. The "identity searching" found via the interviews with these young people seems to be par for the course for young people at this stage in life, at least in Western cultures (Skelton & Valentine, 2003). Yet, added to the typical self-questioning of "Who am I?" these young people also ask themselves, "What does it mean to be deaf?" Their answers vary depending on the circumstances. The research suggests that, when accompanied by other Deaf people and using British Sign Language (BSL), they are comfortable defining themselves as Deaf. In other situations, particularly when they are not with any other people with a hearing loss, they identify themselves as Deaf, and downplay their Deaf identities. This research did not include Deaf people who utilize oral methods. It could be speculated that a group of young Deaf people who communicate via oral methods would have a different outlook on being Deaf.

It is likely that the self-perceptions of deaf people are correlated with the acceptance of deafness in the society. In the United Kingdom, legislation for the Disability Discrimination Act was passed in 1995, which served as a stepping-stone to ensuring rights for people with disabilities. Rights to equal access and education were addressed as a section of that Act, though this section was not implemented until 2002. By the end of 2006, the Special Education Needs Disability Act is to be fully implemented. The inclusion of interpreter services for all Deaf students who attend higher education is likely to impact the number of students who attend college, and their experiences at college as well.

Russia

A look at the Deaf culture in Russia provides a different perspective to the typical ideas of formation of Deaf identity provided by many Western European scholars (Burch, 2000). Whereas Deaf culture is often defined in those places in terms of being linguistic minorities who experienced oppression, Burch (2002) argues that the situation for Deaf Russians has historically been quite different. Deaf culture began in Russian with the establishment of Deaf residential schools, as it did in many other places. Also similar to other Deaf cultures, members of the Russian Deaf Culture share a common sign language, have their own folklore, socialize with other Deaf people and are involved in Deaf community events. In contrast to other Deaf cultures, however, Russian Deaf Culture differs in important ways, such as its employment and economic status, the social characteristics of the Russian Deaf people, their education and the relationship between the community and the government.

The first school for the Deaf in Russia was founded in 1807 (Burch, 2000). It was moved to St. Petersburg in 1809, and other schools soon followed in other capital cities within Russia. These schools sanctioned the use of sign language and were recognized by the Imperial government. Whereas Deaf schools in the West were often begun by Christian churches, in Russia, secular philosophy and educational training informed Deaf education.

Historical accounts of Deaf education in Western literature often describe the oralist movement, whereby Deaf education went from being taught with sign language to utilizing oral methods (Burch, 2000). Members of Deaf culture describe the movement back to using sign language as important and freeing for the advancement of Deaf communities. However, in Russia, there existed a pluralistic view of Deafness. While they preferred sign communication with their peers, they viewed oralism as a means that met a crucial need to work with the larger society. During the height of the oralist movement, the teachers of the Deaf in Russia were largely Deaf themselves. The Deaf schools were under the educational system and did not rely on charities to support them (in contrast to the early schools for the Deaf in the West), so they could not be "told what to do" in the same way that a school whose direct funding relies on a single source might need to cow to the demands of the funding agency. Thus, the perception by much of the Deaf population was that oral methods were an additional tool for them, rather than oppression of their existing communication methods. Indeed, one of the most well-known and well-loved leaders in Russian Deaf Culture was Feodor Andreevich Rau, a strong proponent of oralism. He is known for his love of Deaf people, as well as his assistance in helping them obtain work and living spaces. He fought for the protection of legal rights for Deaf people and worked to expand the educational opportunities afforded them.

In 1926, the Russian government granted Deaf people their own constitutive congress, the All-Russian Organization for the Deaf, or VOG (Burch, 2000). Deaf people were hired to work in Rabfaks, which served as factory-educational facilities. Lenin's wife, Nadezhda Krupskaja, interceded with the VOG on behalf of the Deaf workers and students. Whereas elsewhere, Deaf people at that time had difficulty finding employment, Russia's need for able-bodied workers meant that Deaf people were welcome. They were not classified as disabled in any way, unlike other persons with disabilities, because they were seen as being able to benefit the larger society. The availability of work in the factories improved the economic standing of Deaf people in Russia and provided a means for transmitting Deaf culture. To date, Russian Deaf people are granted privilege in comparison with other disability and minority groups in that nation.

Germany

In his exploration of the experiences of parents of children with hearing impairments (sic), Hintermair describes the situation in Germany as the government having paid little attention to the families, and much attention to the education of Deaf children (2000). He indicates that Germany is struggling to find the "right way" to educate Deaf children, and states that most services for the Deaf center around educational issues.

Using a German translation of the Parenting Stress Index created by Abidin (as cited in Hintermair, 2000), the experiences of families with Deaf children were considered. The findings suggest that, in Germany, parents of Deaf children with additional disabilities express a higher level of stress than parents of Deaf children with no additional abilities. Adaptability, acceptability and demandingness are areas that parents reported being most stressful in their lives.

Hintermair (2000) posits that parents need to be asked about their real problems in everyday life with their children. Their feedback should be included and considered by the professionals from whom they seek guidance. Additionally, parent support groups for hearing parents of Deaf children have been found to be beneficial to the parents. A consideration of the impact of Deafness on the family is suggested, in addition to the emphasis on education. One might infer from this research that the perspective of deafness within the larger German community is one of "differences" between hearing and Deaf, with Deaf education being the focus of how to make the lives of Deaf and hearing more equitable.

United States

In the U.S., access to employment and education is perceived as the "equalizer," which guarantees rights to everyone, regardless of background (Smits, 2004). In 1990, the Americans with Disabilities Act was passed, providing legal ramifications for employers who discriminate against hiring persons with disabilities, as well as builders who create buildings that are not fully accessible to all. Additionally, the Individuals with Disabilities Education Act (IDEA) and the Workforce Investment Act collectively opened the doors for those with disabilities to engage more fully in society.

Traditionally in American society, individuals with disabilities were treated rather poorly (Smits, 2004). Following World War I, when numerous veterans returned with injuries from the war, legislation was initiated that would ensure they would be able to participate in society. President Eisenhower and his administration developed the Office of Vocational Rehabilitation (VR) in the Department of Health, Education, and Welfare. Since that time, VR has played a significant role in determining services provided to those with disabilities and has advocated for changes to public policy for better treatment and services.

Deaf Culture in the U.S. is widely seen as a community of individuals who communicate via American Sign Language, are involved in the Deaf community, and perceive of themselves as a linguistic minority (Woll & Ladd, 2003). A well-known Deaf leader, MJ Bienvenu, identified the four categories that she believes reflect the norms, beliefs, and values of American Deaf Culture. In her plenary address at the Deaf Way conference (1989), Bienvenu presented concepts of Deaf humor, indicating that Deaf humor is a shared language about Deaf experiences that are often not funny or are unknown to outsiders of Deaf Culture. She claims that Deaf jokes are visual and often include mimicking others. They laugh at situations when hearing people are the objects of jokes, and they alter signs and "play" with the linguistic aspects of ASL. Additionally, members of Deaf Culture in the U.S. often joke about and refer to their shared experiences of oppression.

American Deaf Culture is not a homogeneous group. Given the ethnic diversity in the U.S., there are many subgroups of Deaf people who also seek to have their identities recognized (Sedano, 1997). Deaf Hispanic people, largely located in the Southwestern U.S., face a situation of needing to be trilingual, often because their parents are Spanish-speaking, they are taught English in school, and they use ASL to communicate. Interpreters trained in New Mexico require education about Spanish, Mexican, and Chicano traditions. In the Southeastern U.S., African American Deaf people exhibit signs that are unknown to others outside the region, such as the sign for "cornbread" (Hairston & Smith, 1980), though there is concern that some of those signs are being lost as more Deaf people adopt the most common ASL expressions.

In addition to the differences of opinions and ideology within Deaf Culture, there are many others among Americans whose preferences are to not be involved with Deaf Culture or to use ASL. The Alexander Graham Bell Association for Deaf and Hard of Hearing, focuses on oral education and has been highly involved in promoting research on cochlear implants (A. G. Bell Association, 2005). As opposed to having "one movement" in education or services, it seems as though the movement afoot in America is to provide choices for Deaf individuals (Calderon & Greenberg, 2003). Bilingual-Bicultural programs exist and early intervention programs are gaining ground in working with parents soon after the child is diagnosed as Deaf. The focus seems to be less on finding "the right way" than on finding "the right combination of methods" that will work for a given family. In addition to education, the socio-emotional development of Deaf children has taken on a great deal of importance. Parent-child interactions, and the understanding of contextual factors in Deaf children's development have been of significance in recent years (Traci & Koester, 2003). Collectively, these findings suggest that "being Deaf" in American means being faced with many oftentimes difficult choices, in communication modes, types of intervention to implement, and educational systems. Yet, the plethora of options allows for parents to create programs that appears to best suit their children. The laws in place are not perfect, though they have set the tone in the U.S. that Deaf individuals have rights that need to be respected.

Japan

In Japan, much of the work being done by the Japanese Federation of the Deaf is on the implementation of legislation that would ensure that Deaf people achieve full participation and equality (Takada, 2003). Deaf people in Japan are, in recent years, becoming significantly more involved in policy-making.

A number of laws were changed or abolished in 2002, which had previously kept Deaf people from participation in the greater community (Japanese Federation of the Deaf, 2005; Takada, 2003). Previously, Japan had laws stating that Deaf people could not become pharmacists or medical practitioners. Deaf people in Japan were also prohibited from obtaining a driver's license. Underway in that year was the "Barrier-Free" movement, which has had significant impact on the awareness of the general public regarding Deafness and disability issues. At the present time, however, of great concern to leaders in the Deaf community is the way in which these laws can be implemented (Japanese Federation of the Deaf, 2005). As an example, the "Law for the Welfare of Physically Disabled Persons" guarantees sign language interpretation, but does not illustrate how this law is to be enacted. Similarly, the "Fundamental Law for Disabled Persons" was established to protect the rights of persons with disabilities, yet it lacks any regulations for penalizing individuals or companies who are not in compliance.

Japan largely looks to the Scandinavian countries as models for developing and implementing laws and policies with regard to Deaf people (Takada, 2003). Often, when they are offering assistance elsewhere in the world, Scandinavian countries send Deaf people themselves to help establish organizations. Although the Japanese Federation of the Deaf acknowledges that there remain problems to be solved in ensuring equality for Deaf people in Japan, they view themselves as having international influence, particularly in Asia. While continuing to address issues within their own system, Japanese Deaf groups are also highly invested in assisting Deaf people in other nations as well, as evinced by their involvement with Deaf development programs in Cambodia, Thailand and Vietnam (Japanese Federation of the Deaf, 2004).

Research currently underway with Deaf Japanese individuals suggests that many of them perceive of the situation as getting better, but not there yet. They are aware of the changes in laws and the increasing awareness of the public regarding disability issues. A recent television drama that depicted a Deaf character has been influential as well, with the number of students enrolled in Japanese Sign Language classes more than doubling following the airing of that series (Japanese Federation of the Deaf, 2004). Deaf people in Japan continue to express concerns about employment opportunities and educational limitations.

Micronesia

The work completed by Mac Marshall (1996) in the Carolina Island atoll of Micronesia provides an interesting frame against which to compare perspectives of disability. In addition to his work on this particular island, Marshall also draws on the work of other researchers who have studied various Micronesian and Polynesian island cultures. Collectively, their work suggests that these communities are group-centered and that communication among community members is of vital importance. They found that the most important defining characteristic of disability in these islands is the inability to connect with the community and share their own thoughts. Thus, individuals with physical limitations, even those who are blind or deaf, are not considered "disabled" so long as they can participate in community life.

In this view of disability reported by the Namoluk people on the Carolina Island, individuals should participate in the community to whatever extent they are able (Marshall, 1996). Individuals on the island who had congenital afflictions, crippling diseases and physical impairments were not treated differently from the others in society. However, when a person displays bizarre behavior or behavior that is deviant from the norm in that culture, then they are labeled "bush" which roughly translates to social incompetence. In the Namoluk culture, young children who are not yet able to express themselves verbally and participate in communication are also perceived as being "disabled."

Research cited by Marshall (1996) indicates the theory held by the people in these islands is that wisdom, knowledge and intelligence are grounded in the ability to speak and hear. They believe that competent people are able to listen and understand, and then to be able to speak their thoughts. In this culture, the "feelings area" is believed to be in the body center, above the navel. The mind is below the navel in the lower part of the body core. The two kinds of knowledge overlap. Namoluk people believe that expressing one's feelings and thoughts is the sign of maturity. Blind people, for instance, in these communities were assisted in navigation when needed, but were treated normally in all other respects. They are not considered disabled.

What, then, does this mean for Deaf people in these islands? At the time of the research by Marshall, there were two Deaf children on the island. Both made sounds, though neither had acquired speech. One reportedly developed a "system of gestures" for use with her family and both were labeled "highly expressive" with the gestures and facial expressions. Given the impact of their Deafness on their ability to "share their mind," an important aspect of this culture, the Deaf children were considered quasi-disabled. Yet, they were well socialized and participated in the productive tasks of the community. The truly disabled in the Namoluk community tended to have chronic psychological problems, which isolate them from one another. Taken together with other research on the Micronesian islands, it can be said that disability is perceived in a way different from the medical model or that proposed by the World Health Organization (as cited in Marshall, 1996), which defines disabilities as a restriction or lack of ability to perform an activity within a normal range. Clearly, the situation in the Carolines provides at least one alternative to perceiving of disability in such a way.

Nigeria

Woll and Ladd (2003) described a variety of Deaf Communities; among them was the Hausa tribe in northern Nigeria. The Hausa society is said to have a "chief of the deaf" (Schmaling, 2000, as cited in Woll & Ladd, 2003, p. 159). The Deaf members of the tribe communicate via sign language. The hearing members of the tribe are able to converse with the Deaf members of the tribe, and willingly use signs and gestures to communicate. The relatively high incidence of Deafness and of disability may be a contributing factor in the high involvement of the Deaf members of the tribe in the society. The Deaf Hausa are said to have a high level of Deaf consciousness and seem to take pride in their communication abilities and their membership in their Deaf cohort.

Based on the definition of Deaf Community, as defined by shared Deafness, communication and mutual support (Woll & Ladd, 2003), the Hausa of Nigeria depict a strong Deaf community. The issues of legislation for employment and access are not immediately relevant for the members of this Deaf group. However, the changes in the tribes in Nigeria as a result of governmental conflict, and the introduction of individualization in traditional collectivist cultures, may have an impact on this Deaf community in the near future.

Disability Models

The framework for thinking of disabilities has changed over time. What started as a medical model of disability, focusing on impairment, such as the definition by the World Health Organization (Marshall, 1996) later moved to a focus on how individuals with disabilities were treated in their respective societies. In her review of disability models, Carol Thomas (2004) recognizes Oliver and Finkelstein for the establishment of the social model of disability, which was at the forefront of disability studies in the 1970s. This theoretical model had impressive implications for many nations, over the course of many years. Although the original authors of this model subsequently wrote of their misgiving with this paradigm, it remained, and remains, an influence way of thinking about disability. Indeed, as late as 2004, scholars continued to write about the importance of the social model of disability and the importance of holding societal structures accountable for their actions against persons with disabilities (Tregaskis, 2004). Proponents of the social model argue that it encourages a pragmatic means for addressing oppressive situations and encourages the involvement of persons with disabilities in creating or changing policies and legislation. They argue that the usefulness in the social model stems from the focus on removing the barriers that prevent people from fully contributing and participating in society.

In 2001, Shakespeare and Watson (2001) took issue with the limitations they perceived with the social model of disability. They claimed that studies in disability need to address impairments as well as societal oppression. "Disability is a complex dialectic of biological, psychological, cultural, and socio-political factors . . ." (Shakespeare & Watson, 2001, p. 22). Others who consider both physical impairments and society oppression of persons with disabilities are Bury and William (Thomas, 2004). Michael Bury and Simon Williams are medical sociologists. They focus on the interplay of the physiological impairment, the structural conditions in the immediate environment and the socio-cultural interaction. An additional perspective is the one provided by the resistance theory of disability, wherein people are believed to be going against societal authority, against "the system" and against dehumanizing instances has also taken hold in some parts of the world (Gabel & Peters, 2004).

The emerging paradigm of disability, proposed by Schalock (2004), states that there are four realms in which disability must focus. The first is functional limitations, with acknowledgement on the need to address medical concerns or issues for a person with a disability. Secondly, the emerging paradigm considers the personal well-being of persons with disabilities, including the utilization of their strengths (drawing from Positive Psychology) and addressing their quality of life. The third branch of this model is individual supports needed by persons with disabilities. The need for understanding of the ecological situation, and the factors that support or prohibit persons with disabilities from full participation in society should be considered and understood. Lastly, this model considers adaptation and competence. Conceptual, social and practical knowledge are important to living a full life and this model suggests thinking of adaptive skills in each realm to better understand the lived experience of each individual with a disability. Schalock (2004) argues that adoption of this model will allow for movement from perceiving of disability as a personal trait to understanding it as a functional limitation.

How do these disability paradigms relate to Deafness? Some members of the Deaf community might argue that they are not, in fact, applicable at all. Other Deaf people might think of themselves within one of the frameworks presented, such as the social model of disability, for example. That model might, for some, allow for a self-conceptualization that is free of self-blame and urges the larger community/society to take action. Regardless of the perspective of individual Deaf people, each of those people is a part of, and interacts with their environment. Their experience as a *Deaf* or *deaf* person is largely influenced by those contextual factors and the interaction between themselves and those in their communities. Understanding the major disability and Deafness models allows art therapists working with Deaf people greater understanding and awareness.

Positive Perspective

While global trends can be difficult to recognize and label, I propose that there is a change toward perceiving Deafness specifically and disability more generally in an increasingly positive light. A recent edition of *The Journal of Rehabilitation* was dedicated to the positive approach to rehabilitation practice and research (2005). There is movement afoot to incorporate some of the principles of Positive Psychology, such as optimism, resilience, coping, subjective-well-being, sense of coherence and self-efficacy, into rehabilitation work by focusing on human strengths rather than on individual deficits (Wright & Lopez, 2002). The American Psychologist also dedicated an issue to topics related to Positive Psychology (APA, 2001). While the global community does not have agreement on definitions of disability nor does it share common views on deafness, the recent emphasis on human strengths seems to be moving the global community in a more positive direction with regard to its perceptions of Deaf individuals.

Other evidence of an overall shift in the global zeitgeist was the "United Nations Decade of Disabled Persons, 1983–1992," suggesting that the world was ready to begin thinking about issues pertaining to disabled persons (Takada, 2003). For developed countries and those with progressive social agendas, this decade allowed for greater expansion of legal rights and programs to address the needs in their respective countries. For developing countries, this emphasis by the UN on persons with disabilities was, in some cases, the first time that disability issues had been introduced formally into legislation and policymaking. These initial efforts by the UN have been carried further in some areas by programs such as the "Asian and Pacific Decade of Disabled Persons, 1993–2002." Although significant progress has been made in much of Asia and the Pacific, more remains to be done. This has led to the "Second Asian and Pacific Decade of Disabled Persons, 2003–2012." Whereas, the first decade of emphasis on disabled persons in this region was largely focused on the legal ramifications of providing services and ensuring access, the current focus is on the improvement and enjoyment of life by those with disabilities. This paradigmatical shift in the collective consciousness of individuals in this region has seemingly resulted in a more positive perception of disability and Deafness.

Several studies have demonstrated that exposure to Deaf people and to Deaf Culture have a significant positive impact on the attitudes that people have toward the Deaf (Hahn & Beaulaurier, 2001; Nikolaraizi & Makri, 2004/2005). A study conducted in Greece, for example, found that hearing people taking courses in Greek Sign Language (GSL) had significantly better opinions about Deaf people than did other Greeks with no relationship with deafness (Nikolaraizi & Makri, 2004/2005). The authors of that study cite the changing perceptions in Greece as a whole regarding Deafness, which also may have "primed" those in the GSL class, or indeed have influenced their decision to participate in the course.

International Implications for Art Therapists Working with the Deaf

Art therapists are in a unique position to be able to assist Deaf individuals in accessing and expressing their thoughts and emotions related to events they have experienced in their lives. Frost (2005) cited examples of children who expressed themselves through play and creative art, even in harsh conditions. Children of the Holocaust, for example, did more than merely survive; they demonstrated resilience and a will to live through their artwork and poetry.

Children who have experienced war and genocide, such as in the conflicts in Niger, Rwanda, and the Sudan, in Africa, use art to express their emotions and make sense of their worlds (Frost, 2005). Initially, the children often draw pictures of violence, although after they are out of harms' way, they create landscapes and scenes of happy times they shared with loved ones. Frost (2005) argues that play and creative expression are natural for children, allowing them to express feelings and thoughts that they might not have the words to describe. This release can be cathartic and can allow art therapists to help them and address their needs. In his suggestions for helping children recover from disasters and trauma, Frost (2005) suggests that art therapists encourage children to use make-believe play and act out feelings, particularly if they do not seem to understand their own feelings. Using creative arts, through painting or drawing, or even music, drama or storytelling, can help children to heal.

Deaf children and adults seem especially likely to benefit from the use of art therapy techniques in dealing with mental health issues or trauma, since it provides a "natural method of expression" that is not dependent upon oral abilities. By understanding the cultural context from which the Deaf person originates, and the cultural context in which the work is taking place, art therapists can better understand the contextual issues that are likely influencing the person. In societies where Deaf people have near-equal access to employment, for example, they may experience less job-related anxiety. In cultures where being Deaf is not considered a disability, but rather a linguistic minority, those individuals are likely to perceive of themselves in a different way than Deaf individuals in cultures with more open oppression and negative images of Deafness.

There are many ways of conceptualizing Deafness. There appear to be global trends in the treatment of Deaf individuals, moving from a medical view that focuses on "impairments" to a social model that recognizes the role that society plays in determining the perception of Deaf people, to an emerging paradigm that includes multiple layers and acknowledgment of different ways of thinking about Deafness. Globally, it can likely be said that there has been an increase in acceptance of signed languages and an increase in access to services and rights for Deaf people. However, in some places, acceptance has not been a significant problem. In other parts of the world, in areas struggling against severe poverty, for example, Deafness issues are of lower priority. Thus, although collectively strides have been made to improve the lives of Deaf people, more remains to be done. Art therapists can assist clients in understanding their situations within a global context, and explore with clients the impact on them of their surroundings and the societies in which they live.

REFERENCES

A. G. Bell Association (2005). [Organizational website] Retrieved January 28, 2006 from http://www.agbell.org/DesktopDefault.aspx

American Psychologist (2001). *Positive psychology.* Washington, D.C.: American Psychological Association.

A positive approach to rehabilitation research and practice. (2005). *The Journal of Rehabilitation, 71* (2), 3.

Bienvenu, M. J. (1989). Reflections of American Deaf Culture in Deaf humor. Plenary address at The Deaf Way Conference in Washington, D.C., 2000. In Lois Bragg (Ed.), *Deaf world: A historical reader and primary sourcebook,* (pp. 99–103). New York: New York University Press.

Burch, S. (2000). Transcending revolutions: The Tsars, the Soviets, and Deaf Culture. *Journal of Social History, 34* (2), 393–400.

Calderon, R., & Greenberg, M. (2003). Social and emotional development of deaf children: Family, school and program effects. In M. Marschark & P. E. Spencer, (Eds.). *Oxford handbook of deaf studies, language, and education,* (pp. 177–189). Oxford, England: Oxford University Press.

Frost, J. L. (2005). Lessons from disasters: Play, work and the creative arts. *Childhood Education, 82* (1), 2–11.

Gabel, S., & Peters, S. (2004). Presage of a paradigm shift? Beyond the social model of disability toward resistance theories of disability. *Disability & Society, 19* (6), 585–600.

Hahn, H., & Beaulaurier, R. L. (2001). Attitudes toward disabilities: A research note on activists with disabilities. *Journal of Disability Policy Studies, 12* (1), 40–46.

Hairston, E., & Smith, L. (1980). Black signs: Whatever happened to the sign for "cornbread?" In L. Bragg (Ed.), *Deaf world: A historical reader and primary sourcebook,* (pp. 97–98). New York: New York University Press.

Hintermair, M. (2000). Children who are hearing impaired with additional disabilities and related aspects of parental stress. *Exceptional Children, 66* (3), 327–334.

Japanese Federation of the Deaf. (2004). Asian Deaf Friendship Fund. *Japanese Deaf News,* May 2004 issue. Retrieved July 12, 2005 from http://www.jdf.or.jp/en/news/2004-05b.html

Japanese Federation of the Deaf. (2005). And now . . . 4 years from the Elimination of Disqualification Clauses . . . *Japanese Deaf News,* May 2005 issue. Retrieved February 14, 2006 from http://www.jdf.or.jp/en/news/2005-05.html

Marshall, M. (1996). Problematizing impairment: Cultural competence in the Carolines. *Ethnology, 35* (4), 249–261.

Nikolaraizi, M., & Makri, M. (2004/2005). Deaf and hearing individuals' beliefs about the capabilities of deaf people. *American Annals of the Deaf, 149* (5), 404–414.

Schalock, R. L. (2004). The emerging disability paradigm and implications for policy and practice. *Journal of Disability Policy Studies, 14* (4), 204–217.

Sedano, R. (1997). Traditions: Hispanic, American, Deaf culture: Which takes precedence in trilingual interpreter training? In Anita B. Fard (Ed.), *Who Speaks for the Deaf Community? A Deaf American Monograph,* p. 47. Silver Spring, MD: National Association for the Deaf.

Shakespeare, T., & Watson, N. (2001). The social model of disability: An outdated ideology? In *Research in social science and disability,* Vol 2: *Exploring theories and expanding methodologies,* (pp. 9–28). London: Elsevier Science Ltd.

Skelton, T., & Valentine, G. (2003). 'It feels like Being Deaf is Normal': An exploration into the complexities of defining D/deafness and young D/deaf people's identities. *The Canadian Geographer, 47* (4), 451–467.

Smits, S. J. (2004). Disability and employment in the USA: The quest for best practices. *Disability & Society, 19* (6), 647–662.

Takada, E. (2003). Report for Japan for the Expert Group Meeting and Seminar on the International Convention to Protect and Promote the Rights and Dignity of Persons with Disabilities. Bangkok, Thailand, 2–4 June 2003. Retrieved July 25, 2004 from http://www.jfd.or.jp/en/doc/bangkok2003-jpcr.html

Thomas, C. (2004). How is disability understood? An examination of sociological approaches. *Disability & Society, 19* (6), 569–583.

Traci, M., & Koester, L. S. (2003). Parent-Infant Interactions: A transactional approach to understanding the development of Deaf infants. In M. Marschark & P. E. Spencer (Eds.), *Oxford handbook of deaf studies, language, and education,* (pp. 190–202). Oxford, England: Oxford University Press.

Tregaskis, C. (2004). Applying the social model in practice: Some lessons from countryside recreation. *Disability & Society, 19* (6), 601–611.

Woll, B., & Ladd, P. (2003). Deaf Communities. In M. Marschark and P. E. Spencer (Eds.), *Oxford handbook of deaf studies, language, and education,* (pp. 151–163). Oxford, England: Oxford University Press.

Wright, B. A., & Lopez, S. J. (2002). Widening the diagnostic focus: A case for including human strengths and environmental resources. In C. R. Snyder & S. J. Lopez (Eds.), *Handbook of positive psychology,* (pp. 26–44). New York: Oxford University Press.

Chapter 8

COMPUTERS, EVOLUTION AND CULTURE: ART THERAPY POTENTIALITIES FOR THE DEAF

ELLEN G. HOROVITZ

The Internet remains an untamed frontier. Its rules and etiquette have evolved, and continue to evolve, from its participants. You can find unparalleled richness in human expression; the principles of mass publication are no longer the property of the elite. You can also find unconscionable mean-spiritedness, the darker side of faceless, facile communications. As a member in the electronic community, you might ask yourself how you'd like to contribute.

Netscape Navigator Handbook (1995)

ABSTRACT

People are transmitting signals via e-mail, IRC (chat rooms), IM (instant messaging), blogging, virtual reality (via video and software hookups such as invented originally by Cornell University's CUSeeMe), IPhone, IChat, ISight, SightSpeed and WebPhone, just to mention a few. Accessing and downloading information from the super highway known as WWW (World Wide Web) has become a culture in which society now processes information. This form of communication is immediate, comprehensive, and available to anyone with transport to a computer. While the FAQ's (frequently asked questions) are in, the facts aren't even out: electronic communication is here to stay. The unknown is its long-term impact on the user.

The possibilities and advantages of computers and culture coupled with hypermedia and computer animation will be explored as a specific educational tool in which these resources are applied to the teaching-learning process when working with emotionally disturbed Deaf/hearing-impaired clients. Moreover, it is proffered that a methodology, which incorporates these features, could foster improved spoken and written communication skills of the hearing-impaired. Current research will be examined regarding aspects of language systems (speech, linguistic structure, writing, etc.) and the different communication codes employed when working with this population. Art therapy coupled with hypermedia applications will also be investigated as a means toward fostering educational and therapeutic learning. Improving attention span, the development of visual expression, increased self-confidence, creativity and enhanced communicative skills will be reviewed as by-products of computer-assisted learning (CAL).

Language Acquisitions Systems

Human communication codes, complex and mysterious, are normally based on a combination of signals that can be picked up by several senses (Chomsky, 1965). Nevertheless, the Deaf/hearing-impaired person does not have access to the communication code used by aural/oral persons: that is those who can hear the spoken language. Deprived access to this operational code leads to difficulty in interaction and understanding of one's environment as well as affliction with appropriate thought structures for each stage of development (Carretero & Garcia, 1984; Fourcin, 1982; Meadow, 1980; Rodriquez, 1990; Sieflbuch, 1980; Vygotsky, 1962).

For the Deaf person, visual information constitutes inner language. Without expression or a way to communicate this language, the individual can become isolated within his environment, community, and his world (Horovitz-Darby, 1991). Analyzing an individual's mode of communication is critical when working with the Deaf/hearing-impaired population. For example, modes of communication employed by family members may vary and the range of language systems may be expansive, circumscribed, bimodal, or virtually absent.

Meadow (1980) reviewed language acquisition for these three categories of Deaf children whose linguistic environments and socialization inputs differed according to the communication modes of their parents: (a) Deaf children of Deaf parents who use only Ameslan (American Sign Language); (b) Deaf children whose hearing or Deaf parents use a simultaneous communication of spoken and/or signed English; and (c) Deaf children whose hearing parents speak only English. Harvey (1982) found most Deaf children and their hearing parents unable to communicate in the primary language system of Ameslan. This language is linguistically distinct from signed English even though both are considered manual communication. Ameslan has its own syntax and is therefore not derived from English grammatical structure, whereas signed English follows the same syntax as spoken English.

Whereas Deaf children whose parents expose them to a simultaneous combination of signed and spoken English develop bimodal expressive language, the children, whose parents use the strict oral English approach acquire language at a "painfully slower" rate. Moreover, Moores' (1982) research indicated that children of Deaf parents are superior to Deaf children of hearing parents in academic achievement and English language abilities. Since 90 percent of hearing parents do not speak sign language (Schein & Delk, 1974), two distinct languages can be represented in families with both Deaf and hearing members and as a result, educators and therapists alike are commonly faced with members who do not speak the same language. This finding cannot be underestimated in treatment and education. Two distinct cultures and languages are represented. Thus, therapists and educators alike confront a cross-cultural and bilingual phenomenon (Horovitz-Darby, 1991).

Difficulties in gaining access to this aural/oral code used by hearing people require the Deaf/hearing-impaired person to be provided with an alternative code to develop communication and thought structures normally, thus facilitating spoken and written language learning. Experience has demonstrated that the most appropriate code for this task is sign language, whether bilingual or bimodal. Bilingual sign language implies acquiring competency in the mother tongue's sign language and then employing that as a basis for acquiring oral language as a skill as a "second" language. Bimodal sign language is based in the structures of the primary language; grammatical context of sentences and morphosyntactic elements of the spoken language are maintained.

Difficulties in Linguistic Translation

As stated earlier, hearing impairment affects the transmission of aural/oral humans' most commonly used operational code: spoken language (Crystal, Fletcher, and Garman, 1976). This impairs the Deaf/hearing-impaired person's ability to receive and transmit aural/oral messages and therefore hampers interaction in a "hearing" environment. For a Deaf person, learning spoken language is an arduous and laborious process. Voice control and articulation training sessions are integral parts of speech comprehension that can aid the Deaf person to acquire adequate speech registration for enabling communication with hearing people.

Two channels currently exist to aid the Deaf person in accessing spoken language: (a) the hearing channel: whether functional or not, due to decibel loss its use depends on the auditive remains; and (b) lip-reading. Either conduit is limited and communication exclusively directed through one or the other compromises comprehension. This is due to two factors: (a) grammatical elements are lost without contextual references to increase the semantic contents of the message; and (b) solid thought structures normally reinforced through spoken language are shunted and do not simultaneously develop with the cognitive processes. These limitations do not necessitate abandoning training but rather augmenting it with existing improvements in technology (such as hypermedia assistance).

Additionally, previous research has indicated that art therapy techniques concurrently lead to unlocking cognitive delays with emotionally disturbed Deaf populations when development has been arrested due to emotional maladjustment and trauma (see Horovitz, 1981, 1983, 1999, 2004, 2005a; Silver, 1970, 1976, 1978, 1996). Moreover, it has been concluded that art therapy techniques coupled with exploration of emotionally-laden experiences leads to improved self-esteem, social adjustment, and cognitive gains (Horovitz, 1981, 1983, 1999, 2004, 2005a; McNiff, 1995; Moon, 1996). In fact, Moon (1996) purported the efficacy of utilizing art materials for concomitant gain both emotionally and cognitively in the work of his clients. In one vignette, he cited a case of a woman who had been referred by her primary therapist in order to increase her ability to "talk about her post-traumatic stress disorder (PTSD)." While Moon (1996) pooh-poohed the idea of using art materials to elicit verbalization, nevertheless, the client's capacity for increased communication was enhanced and the referring physician was pleased. Moon (1996), of course, reiterated, "All we are doing is painting." Nevertheless, while her cognitive skills were increasing in the studio, her ability to communicate and verbalize her (formerly) repressed issues was mended, presumably by using the art as a conduit to unlock the client's potential. Furthermore, McNiff (1995) also stated that art's medicine always "flows from the studio" and has been quite clear about its inability to fit "the linear language and concepts of behavioral science" (p. 183).

On the contrary, this writer both agrees and disagrees since art informs behavioral change. As suggested by the foremost researcher in Evolutionary Psychology, Buss contends:

> . . . the other arts do have an adaptive function. I argue that they fulfill the specifically and uniquely human need to produce an emotionally and aesthetically saturated cognitive order. The need to produce that order is a major component in the model of human nature. . . . (2005, p. 938)

Moreover, Dissanayake (1992) talked about art as "making special" and aligned it to an important cultural activity:

> . . . making important activities special has been basic and fundamental to human evolution and existence, and . . . while making special is not strictly speaking in all cases art, it is true that art is *always* an instance of making spe-

cial. To understand art in the broadest sense, then, as a human proclivity, is to trace its origin to making special, and I will argue that making special was often inseparable from and intrinsically necessary to the control of the material conditions of subsistence that allowed humans to survive. (1992, p. 92)

Furthermore, Buss articulates that art has adaptive values in the following venues:

(1) it is a human universal language that seems to develop in all cultures . . . (2) it is expensive . . . *(Editor's note: thereby suggesting value and worth)* . . . (3) it involves highly structured processes . . . *(Editor's note: involving plaited hemispheric thinking—right brain/left brain lateral cross over)* and finally . . . (4) it is indeed necessary to personal and cultural identification. (2005, p. 940)

Naturally, the result of artistic inquiry requires a review of mirror cells and the neuronal connections as it informs social learning and cultural proclivity.

Mirror Neurons, Social Learning and Cultural Implications

A recent definition from Wikipedia describes mirror cells as:

. . . a neuron which fires both when . . . perform(ing) an action (or when) observ(ing) the same action performed by another (especially conspecific). . . . Thus, the neuron "mirrors" the behavior of another . . . as though the observer were himself performing the action. These neurons have been observed in primates, in some birds, and in humans. In humans, they have been found in Broca's area and the inferior parietal cortex* of the brain. Some scientists consider mirror neurons one of the most important findings of neuroscience in the last decade.

– http://en.wikipedia.org/wiki/Mirror_cells

In a more recent account Dobbs (2006) writes of how the hominid brain acquires information. There has been much discussion about:

mirror neurons, which are scattered throughout the key parts of the human brain—the premotor cortex and centers for language, empathy and pain—fire not only as we perform a certain action but also when we watch someone else perform that action. (p. 22)

This concept has enormous implications when viewing this from the perspective of the Deaf person. Given that the Deaf person learns information from a visual rather than an aural platform, learning by "copying" or "mirroring" another person's action is really quite pivotal, especially since numerous signs are based on exactly this concept. This not only has language

---

* *Editor's note:* the inferior parietal cortex is that section of the brain, which simply put, involves vision; therefore this area has major application to sign language system and art therapy. (See illustration by Horovitz):

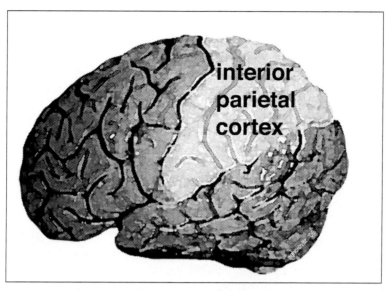

Figure 8–1. (Illustration–E.G. Horovitz-2006).

acquisition implication but also translates into culture, sociological learning and indeed intelligence. Van Schaik (2006) goes on to purport that "animals that are intelligent are the ones that are cultural: they learn from one another innovative solutions to ecological or social problems" (p. 66). More importantly, Van Schaik (2006) goes on to reason that the analyses of orangutans suggests that "not only does culture-social learning of special skills promote intelligence" but more precisely "favors the evolution of greater and greater intelligence over time" (p. 69). In this article, Van Schaik (2006) pointed out that this increased acumen was the direct result of utilizing tools. But it was beyond the fashioning of these implements that harbored brainpower: it was the transmission of this skill handed down from generation to generation. The observing scientists noticed a patterning of information that indeed was akin to "collective archetypal unconscious." It was herein that made the difference. The very act of mirror cell learning replicated the ability to survive and carry on genes but more importantly this gave rise to culture (social learning of special skills). This might indeed be considered spiritual, an expression for life perceived as higher, more complex or more integrated as contrasted with the merely sensual or in this case, survival instinct.

The theory of mirror cell exchange quite exactly dovetails with sign language, meaning, and cultural acquisition as described above by Van Schaik (2006). It is quite clear that the sign-based language of Ameslan is indeed based in visual exchange. One need only look at some of the most basic signs such as the sign for a "book" to see how aptly this sign actually replicates the image of the book: hands together are dropped with palms facing up (if indicating an open book) or closed palms (to indicate a closed book). Moreover, sign language is clearly a visual language, where the signer communicates past, present and future just by mere body posture. In that respect it clearly is the closest language for mirror cell replication and learning. Indeed, this writer would go one step further to suggest that teaching this language could indeed foster learning in the interior parietal lobe and promote aptitude. Since learning signs requires copying on a visual level, it is indeed the closest language that we have to stimulate mirror cell functioning.

Computer-Based Learning as an Acquisition Tool

While the Deaf/hearing-impaired person acquires the skill to read in the same way as hearing people do, difficulties related to the process (particularly graph-phonene transformation and acquisition of correct pace, intonation and speed) create difficulties which last longer among the Deaf. The problems of voice, articulation, phono-respiratory coordination and the like are severely compromised by Deafness due to the lack of a model and auditory feedback. Thus, reading by the Deaf/hearing-impaired person is generally arrhythmic, monotonous and often unintelligible for the listener. Yet transmission of the messages received is undoubtedly even more significant. These problems can take form in two ways: those that arise from lack of auditory feedback and those that arise from linguistic deficiencies. Since reading analysis is made in reference to the interlocutor, analysis of reading articulation and association to its meaning in context as well as enunciation is severely compromised. The linguistic deficiencies result in lack of vocabulary and jeopardized syntactic structures, semantic values (derived from morphological aspects of language), and linguistic contextual understanding.

If one wanted to generate the aforementioned learning processes in assisting cognitive development with this population, a computer system incorporating a hyper/multimedia environment would have to be composed of various hardware and software resources: (a) a voice card centered on correction of different speech parameters within a meaningful context; (b) iconographic and sound-animated supports to enable the introduction of situations animated through sign language, a sign language dictionary, and dactylogical and visual-phonetic supports for creating emission; (c) computer video for incorporating training exercises to correct lip configuration for improved lip-reading; (d) vibratile-tactile output offering the possibility of incorporating the rhythmic aspect of musical structures and adapting them to speech emission programs; and (e) digital imaging capabilities with various software programs in order to animate drawings and dovetail with existing software programs such as: ALLALO (exercises and evaluation tests that deal with visual perception, lip movement, and vocabulary access), VISHA (voice board-based system that trains students in sound presence/ absence, tone, intensity, while simultaneously analyzing sound emissions), HANDS ON (laser disc technology to present a real person on the screen communicating in ASL (Ameslan)–texts stored in the computer combine on the screen with ASL videos), and LAO (Lenguaje Asistido por Ordenador/ Computer Assisted Language) incorporating a multimedia dictionary which presents not only a written definition or description of a word, but also images of its corresponding sign language equivalent as well as usage examples.

Art Therapy, Hypermedia and Computer Animation: Applications for the Emotionally Disturbed

The effects of art therapy techniques on all aged people with behavioral and emotional problems have long been documented (Kramer, 1975; Naumburg, 1980; Silver, 1989; Moon, 1990; Horovitz-Darby, 1994; Horovitz, 1999, 2004, 2005a) and specifically with the Deaf/hearing-impaired populations (Henley, 1992; Horovitz, 1988, 1999, 2004, 2005; Horovitz-Darby, 1988, 1991, 1994; and Silver, 1970, 1976). Coupling CAL (Computer Assisted Learning) with art therapy, however, is a relatively undeveloped potential.

As early as 1989, Canter experimented with creativity and software in art therapy sessions. Canter (1989) concluded that people who exhibited difficulty with fine motor coordination and/or impulsive or destructive personalities found computers to be constructive and beneficial tools due to calming effects in the stimulation of creative and intellectual challenges. Moreover, the results concluded after a three-month study that: (a) attention span was increased from 10 minutes to over an hour; (b) visual expression was enhanced via drawing and animation programs; (c) computerized musical expression was possible even if the client was unfamiliar with music or musical composition; (d) self-confidence, creativity, and problem-solving was developed due to the experience provided by the positive reward from others; and (e) clients cultivated communicative skills in an atmosphere without conflict due to a "user friendly environment." However, what was not researched was the power of the personal computer (PC) coupled with creative software as therapeutic tools and how this might impact more specific populations such as the emotionally disturbed Deaf/hearing-impaired.

Turkle (1984) concluded that computers change the way people think about themselves via computational metaphors. Hopkins (1991) researched implications of utilizing computer technology with emotionally and behaviorally disturbed children. In working with emotionally disturbed Deaf clients, both of the aforementioned researchers claimed that the use of computers were found to increase motivation, control pace of learning, improve self-image and self-esteem, minimize differences between able and less able subjects and improve overall concentration and attention span. Rutter (1967) determined that language skills, perceptual and perceptual-motor skills were often adversely affected in children with emotional behavioral difficulties.

Yet, computers have been linked to productivity because the monitor is like a TV screen and children who are accustomed to watching for long periods of time are able to focus attention longer because of its small, brightly lit areas. Informational technology has also been deemed user friendly in that it is a nonjudgmental teaching system and, therefore, emotionally disturbed students with behavioral difficulties tend to persevere in this environment. Being able to project problems onto characters on the screen enables them to work in a more detached, dispassionate and productive way than would otherwise be possible.

For example, Bailey and Weippert (1992) described a qualitative case-based study that assessed the effectiveness of computer-based learning in improving the linguistic and behavioral responses of two young aboriginal girls who had profound hearing impairment. Moreover, syntax errors were reduced from 45 percent to 25 percent. Worth noting is that despite the cultural differences, the aboriginal girls in the study were neither daunted nor confused by the technology, nor language used by the computer. It would seem that computer-based learning can thus improve the language competence, attending and concentrating behaviors of young Deaf, aboriginal children.

Deafness is not a problem of speech, but the frustration of missing concepts. Since art, as well as language, is a means of communicating concepts, and coupling CAL has already been documented to enhance self-esteem, communicative reasoning, and behavioral management, it would stand to reason that increased communication and behavioral management could be augmented with the use of the aforementioned software and hardware applications. As well, making movies with the use of digital equipment and simplistic editing tools such as Imovie could also play a role in unleashing creativity, cognitive development, and increased self-esteem. In fact, Horovitz (2002, 2003, 2005b) worked with the same child over a period of four years making movies and this led to enhanced cognition, behavioral change, improved prosody and articulation as well as maturation and increased cognitive development.

There are qualities of experience that cannot be put into words, but can be articulated in art. An uncaptioned cartoon may be eloquent. Even for the hearing in a literate society, verbal language is often not enough.

Art requires the exercise of many mental processes. It sharpens awareness and reinforces memory (Silver, 1970, 1976). Young, Deaf children often cannot verbalize imaginary or vicarious experiences, but they can draft them (Horovitz, 2004, 2005a). Many art therapists have claimed and proven that art develops reasoning power by requiring organization and the constant exercise of judgment. Art does more than reveal emotions. By providing release from emotional tension, art has proven to be both integrating and healing. Moreover, visual expression seems to be intensified for the Deaf. Perhaps Deaf people seize the opportunity of image-making because their channels for communication are already constricted and concentrated on the visual (interior parietal cortex). Paradoxically, since the Deaf may not know the pleasure of aural conversation, useless chatter also has not distracted them. By offering encouragement and opportunity for creative expression, perhaps the Deaf can create a speech to which the rest of us can listen with our eyes.

Language is not the only means of articulating thought. Whenever a symbol operates, there is meaning. Depictions, no less than words, are forms of symbolic expression. Since the beginning of time, art has served to communicate experiences and ideas, explicitly or implicitly, in form as well as content. Art meanings are so universal that they transcend languages and cultures. Just as the writer uses words, the artist uses the plastic elements of form, space, line, texture and color. Representation requires the review of experiences and clarification of impressions, which call memory into play. Like words, visual symbols preserve ideas that might otherwise vanish. According to Silver (1970, 1976), for the "linguistically challenged," pictures appear to be a way of depicting one's knowledge base while simultaneously sharing this with others.

It has been submitted that emotionally disturbed Deaf/hearing-impaired people may lack the opportunity for developing the capacity for abstraction; computer-assisted learning (CAL) coupled with hypermedia/computer animation techniques and moviemaking could foster such opportunities by exercising imagination, association, memory, perception, organization, and language acquisition. The function of the CAL equipment is merely to provide a computer interface, which allows for maximum creativity.

Hypotheses of Coupling Art Therapy and CAL

Conceivably increased communication, attention span, and positive self-worth are fostered vis a vis Computer Assisted Learning (CAL) coupled with art therapy techniques. Drawing or digital images could be scanned or linked into the computer and manipulated with existing software to offer the Deaf patient an opportunity to create visual, animated stories. These art products could foster integration of abstract thinking, spatial reasoning, and augment existing modes of communication. Additionally, the patient's ability to manipulate his/her work via hypermedia applications could be assessed for increased attention span and developmental gains using the Silver Drawing Test (Silver, revised 1996) as a pre-test/post-test measure.

This procedure would need to employ art therapy techniques, coupled with hypermedia and CAL applications on at least a twice-weekly basis in an open-studio format. Research indicates that a minimum of twice-weekly intervention accelerates the therapeutic process and anything less than that would compromise outcome-based assessment (Harvey, 1982; Henley, 1992). Moreover, the sessions should be no less than an hour in length and if possible should allow for interaction in three-hour blocks (Kramer, 1975). The reasons are multifold but in this specific instance are quite concrete. Initially, Deaf patients might need to be taught how to utilize the software applications, engage in digitally scanning existing artwork and begin to animate or film their art products. Because using existing programs would require extensive educating and trial and error applications, a certain degree of frustration is to be expected. Past research (previously noted) has indicated the advantage of employing CAL (a "user friendly tool") to verily reinforce the learning process with emotionally disturbed students. Additionally, providing an open-studio format, which would invite the element of play and experimentation, could perforce fortify the learning process. As a result, this research base should have structured open-studio times replicating the learning-based environments offered at higher education institutions. It is proposed that modeling the computer labs in this manner would instill responsible behavior and social interaction.

Additionally, all sessions could be monitored on videotape in order to assist in analyzing information that leads to frustration and communication breakdown as well as educational breakthroughs. (With very disturbed, dual-diagnosed clients, it is expected that frustration may lead to destructive behavior and require removal from the studio.) While rules would be posted and enforced regarding the care of computer equipment, the research has to build in factors to prevent such behavior. It has been proven by aforementioned researchers (Kramer, 1975; Henley, 1992; Allen, 1995; McGraw, 1995; McNiff, 1995) that the open studio space enhances physical relaxation, creativity and supports nonlinear communication. In the words of McNiff (1995, p. 183):

> We reframe the practice of art therapy by focusing on what the studio does, what the materials do, and how artworks created by ourselves and others affects us. When we look at art therapy through the eyes of the soul, we see an ecological field of forces, a total presence of creation that simply does not fit the linear language and concepts of behavioral science. The mainstream of art's medicine will always flow from the studio.

It has also been this writer's experience (of a little over 30 years) that offering art materials in fact reduces acting-out behavior rather than encouraging destructive demeanor. Therefore, by offering an open-studio format, subjects would be allowed to enter and exit at free will thus eliminating potentially restrictive environments that often result in exacerbating violent behavior. While it is expected that some frustration will occur, back-up personnel should be available should crisis intervention become necessary.

Outcome-based assessment could include the data results from videotape analysis, pre-test/post-test results from the Silver Drawing Test (designed to measure cognitive functioning over time that includes concepts of sequencing, conservation, language acquisition, spatial reasoning, and imaginary skill building), and the actual artistic products created through hypermedia applications and CAL structure.

Because the Deaf/hearing-impaired respond extremely well to nonverbal interventions and assessment batteries, a pre-test/post-test of the Silver Drawing Test of Cognition and Emotion (SDT) should be given to each subject (Silver, revised 1996). Drawings have been used to assess intelligence for over 50 years. While several tests including the Bender Visual-Motor Test (Bender, 1938), the Draw-A-Man Test (Goodenough-Harris, 1963), the Human Figure Drawing Test (Koppitz, 1968), and the Torrance Test of Creative Thinking (Torrance, 1984) measure fluency, flexibility, originality, and elaboration, they are <u>not</u> designed for assessing the ability to solve conceptual problems graphically.

In the SDT, drawing takes the place of language as the primary channel for receiving and expressing ideas. Stimulus drawings prompt response drawings that solve problems and represent concepts. The three subtests, Predictive Drawing, Drawing from Observation, and Drawing from Imagination, require cognitive and emotional replies. Moreover, Silver (revised, 1996) specifically developed this assessment with the Deaf population in mind. As a result, the results of this test correlate well with other more traditional methods of evaluation such as the WISC-R. Developmental techniques of the Silver Drawing Test are listed under the National Institute of Education Project #79-0081, which can be found under Appendix C of the Silver text (1996).

Information gleaned from the pre and post-test components of the Silver Drawing Test could underscore developmental and cognitive delays or achievement as directly related to the function of computer-based learning extracted from experimentation with hypermedia and computer animation. While research has already indicated that CAL combined with hypermedia effectively translates into cognitive and developmental acceleration (when working with the hearing population), the data extracted from the SDT could estimate the findings from a developmental vantage point as well as provide quantitative data that could be analyzed and calibrated.

Moreover, as previously described, all sessions could be videotaped and further analyzed in order to assess behavioral changes over time that might be linked to specific software and programmatic influences that led to increased language acquisition, communication, and developmental and behavioral changes.

It is proposed that art therapy applications coupled with the aforementioned software could, in fact, induce the learning process, bolster self-esteem and lead to improved communication and social interaction.

While computer technologies applicable for education have been myriad (intelligent tutoring systems, programmed learning systems, etc.), many researchers have concluded that hypermedia/multimedia techniques effectively facilitate learning. Its treatment of information, access, and structure resemble the mental processes and, in fact, corral and stimulate the investigative properties involved in the learning process (Jonassen, 1992).

Key changes in the hominid evolved when the early *Homo* collectively created tools and strategies in order to sustain existence. This fostered both interdependence and innovation. The result was the perpetuation of intelligence via cultural application. According to Van Schaik (2006), "The explosion of technology in the past 10,000 years shows that cultural inputs can unleash limitless accomplishments, all with Stone Age brains. Culture (Editor's note: social learning of special skills) can indeed build a new mind from an old brain" (p. 71).

The Deaf are informed by a visual culture that predisposes itself to learning via enlisting "mirror neuron" transmission. This has both informed the language of the Deaf as well as the culture that demands a capitalized "D" when describing Deaf individuals. Deaf culture goes beyond mere communication via sign language. It is indeed a culture that most aptly represents learning by mirror neuron transmission.

Both art and CAL-assisted materials feed directly into this type of learning since indeed they inform the same neural pathways. Understanding a future that is currently bootstrapped to computer technology requires cultural (global) exchange, computer understanding and meaning. According to Negroponte (1995), the guru and author of *Being Digital,* new ideas come from differences. Creativity, it seems, comes from these same "unlikely juxtapositions." Maximizing differences engages the imagination, fuels creativity and engages optimism and passion. May we all work towards that end.

REFERENCES

Allen, P. (1995). Coyote comes in from the cold: The evolution of the open-studio concept. *Arts in Psychotherapy, 12* (3), 161–166.

Bailey, J., & Weippert, H. (1992). Using computers to improve the language competence and attending behaviour of Deaf and aboriginal children. *Journal of Computer Assisted Learning, 8,* 118–127.

Bender, L. (1938). *The Bender visual motor integration test.* New York, NY: The American Orthopsychiatric Association, Inc.

Buss, D. (Ed.). (2005). *The handbook of evolutionary psychology.* Hoboken, NJ: John Wiley & Sons, Inc.

Canter, D. S. (1989). Art therapy and computers. *Advances in Art Therapy.* (Ed. Harriet Wadeson). New York, NY: Wiley & Sons, Inc.

Carretero, M., & Garcia, J. A. (1984). *Lecturas de Psicologia del Pensamiento.* Madrid, Spain: Alianza Editorial.

Chomsky, N. (1965). *Aspects of theory of syntax.* Cambridge, MA: MIT Press.

Crystal, D., Fletcher, P., & Garman, M. (1976). *The grammatical analysis of language disability.* London: Arnold.

Dissanayake, E. (1992). *Homo Aestheticus: Where art comes from and why.* New York, NY: The Free Press.

Dobbs, D. (2006). A revealing reflection. *Scientific American Mind.* April/May, 22–27.

Fourcin, A. J. (1982). Desarralo Linguistico en Ausencia de Lenguaie Expresivo. In E. Lennenberg (Ed.), *Fundamentos del Desarrollo del Lenguaje.* Madrid, Spain: Alianza.

Goodenough, F., & Harris, D. B. (1963). *Children's drawings as measures of mental maturity.* New York, NY: Harcourt, Brace, and World.

Harvey, M. A. (1982). The influence and use of an interpreter for the deaf in family therapy. *American Annals of the Deaf,* 819–827.

Henley, D. R. (1992). *Exceptional children, exceptional art: Teaching art to special needs.* Worcester, MA: Davis Publications, Inc.

Hopkins, M. (1991). The value of information technology for children with emotional and behavioural difficulties. *Maladjustment and Therapeutic Education,* Win, *9* (3), 143–151.

Horovitz, E. G. (1981). Art therapy in arrested development of a preschooler. *Arts in Psychotherapy, an International Journal, 8* (2), 119–126.

Horovitz, E. G. (1983). Preschool aged children: When art therapy becomes the modality of choice. *Arts in Psychotherapy, 10* (2), 23–32.

Horovitz, E. G. (1988). Short-term family art therapy: A case study. Chapter 11 in *Two decades of excellence: A foundation for the future.* (Eds. Watson, D., Long, D., Taff-Watson, and Harvey, M.), Little Rock, Arkansas: American Deafness and Rehabilitation Association (ADARA).

Horovitz-Darby, E. G. (1988). Art therapy assessment of a minimally language skilled Deaf child. Proceedings from the 1988 University of California's Center on Deafness Conference: *Mental Health Assessment of Deaf Clients: Special Conditions.* Little Rock, Arkansas: ADARA

Horovitz-Darby, E. G. (1991). Family art therapy within a deaf system. *Arts in Psychotherapy, 18,* 251–261.

Horovitz, E. G. (1999). *A leap of faith: The call to art.* Springfield, IL: Charles C Thomas.

Horovitz, E. G. (2002). *Art therapy and speech/language therapy: An interdisciplinary approach.* [DVD]. Rochester, NY: Julia Production, 16-minute film.

Horovitz, E. G. (2003). *Paddle to the sea: A psychopuppetry documentary.* [DVD]. Rochester, NY: Julia Production, 16-minute film.

Horovitz, E. G. (2004). *Spiritual art therapy: An alternate path.* Springfield, IL: Charles C Thomas.

Horovitz, E. G. (2005a). *Art therapy as witness: A sacred guide.* Springfield, IL: Charles C Thomas.

Horovitz, E. G. (2005b). *Yo-Yo Man.* [DVD]. Rochester, NY: Julia Production, 15-minute film.

Horovitz-Darby, E. G. (1991). Family art therapy within a deaf system. *Arts in Psychotherapy, 18,* 251–261.

Horovitz-Darby, E. G. (1994). *Spiritual art therapy: An alternate path.* Springfield, IL: Charles C Thomas.

Jonassen, D. H. (1992). Designing hypertext for learning. New directions in educational technology. *Proceedings of the NATO Advanced Research Workshop, I.*

Koppitz, E. M. (1968). *Psychological evaluation of children's human figure drawings.* New York, NY: Grune & Stratton.

Kramer, E. (1975). *Art as therapy with children.* New York, NY: Schocken Books.

Meadow, K. (1980). *Deafness and child development.* Berkeley, CA: University of California Press.

McGraw, M. (1995). The art studio: A studio based art therapy program. *Arts in Psychotherapy, 12* (3), 167–174.

McNiff, S. (1995). Keeping the studio. *Arts in Psychotherapy, 12* (3), 179–183.

Moon, B. L. (1996). *Existential art therapy: The canvas mirror.* Springfield, IL: Charles C Thomas.

Moores, E. (1982). *Educating the deaf: Psychology, principles and practices.* Boston: Houghton-Mifflin.

Naumburg, M. (1980). *Dynamically oriented art therapy: Its principles and practices: Illustrated with case studies.* Chicago, IL: Magnolia Street Publishers.

Negroponte, N. (1995). Being decimal. *Wired.* November, p. 252.

Rodriquez, J. M. (1990). La Deficiencia Auditiva: Un Enfoque Cognitivo. *Publicaciones de la Universidad Pontifica de Salamanca.* Salamanca.

Rutter, M. (1967). A children's questionnaire for completion by teachers. *Journal of Child Psychology and Psychiatry, 8,* 1–11.

Schein , J. D., & Delk, M. T. (1974). *The Deaf population of the United States.* Silver Spring, MD: National Association of the Deaf.

Sieflbuch, R. (1980). *Non-speech language and communication.* Baltimore, MD: University Park Press.

Silver, R. A. (1970) Art and the Deaf. *Bulletin of Art Therapy.* Washington, D.C.: Ulman.

Silver, R. D. (1976). *Shout in silence, visual arts and the Deaf.* Rye, NY: Silver Publications.

Silver, R. A. (1978). *Developing cognitive and creative skills through art.* Baltimore, MD: University Park Press.

Silver, R. (1989). *Developing cognitive and creative skills in art through art programs for children with communication disorders.* Baltimore: University Park Press.

Silver, R. A. (1996). *The silver drawing test of cognition and emotion.* Sarasota, FL: Ablin Press.

Torrance, E. P. (1984). *The Torrance test of creative thinking, figural form.* Bensenville, IL: Scholastic Testing Service, Inc.

Turkle, S. (1984). The second self. *Computer and the human spirit.* New York, NY: Simon & Schuster.

Van Schaik, C. (2006). Why are some animals so smart? *Scientific American,* April, 64–71.

Vygotsky, L. S. (1962). *Thought and language.* Cambridge, MA: MIT Press.

Chapter 9

CLINICAL AND LOGISTICAL ISSUES IN CREATING AN ART THERAPY PROGRAM IN A RESIDENTIAL SCHOOL FOR THE DEAF

CAROLE KUNKLE-MILLER

INTRODUCTION

Deaf individuals live in a world in which the vital skill of communication is impaired. This impairment often results in delayed development of speech and language; therefore, attempts at expression of simple thoughts and feelings may frequently be met with frustration. Given time, these negative feelings can build and lead to difficulties with self-confidence and emotional stability. Robinson (1978, p. 5) states that, "Deaf people experience one or more of a variety of situations which are stressful, for example, communication problems . . . which usually begin in infancy; separation from family at an early age; job discrimination; prejudice, ridicule, and social isolation from the mainstream of society." Brauer (1981) has described general characteristics of hearing-impaired individuals and their potential for developing mental health problems, he states:

> Probably many of us would be in agreement on the following points: that a large number of deaf individuals do not have effective ways of coping with life problems; that a large number of deaf persons have learned to be helpless; that because of the experience of deaf people is that the world is often a place where events happened without explanation, that have therefore developed external loci of control—in other words, they have developed a passive and extreme expectation of the "dominant other" to solve all problems as if by magic; and, finally, that several social environmental factors may act to produce stress, anxiety, and abnormal states for deaf individuals. (p. 7)

163

Emotional adjustment problems in hearing-impaired children are likely to develop due to difficulties with language and communication, which inhibits "normal social interaction," combined with the normal stressors of childhood (Warren & Hasenstab, 1986, p. 289). Schlesinger and Meadow (1972) studied the incidence of emotional disturbance in a residential school for the Deaf. They found that over 10 percent of the children were "severely emotionally disturbed," which approximately 20 percent has less severe emotional problems. The results of a similar study conducted in the state of Pennsylvania were reported by Forquer and Gibney (1984); they also found that over 10 percent of the hearing-impaired school-age population exhibited emotional and/or behavioral problems. The investigators reported that 71 percent of these students were in need of immediate services, with 67 percent being recommended for outpatient services and four percent in need of inpatient treatment services.

Appropriate mental health services are often not provided due to a lack of trained staff and/or funds for hearing impaired persons (Forquer & Gibney, 1984). In a 1978 report to the President's Commission on Mental Health, it was stated: "85 percent of Deaf people needing such services are not receiving them because they are not available" (Sachs, Robinson, & Sloan, 1978, p. 1001). In an elementary school for the hearing children, the school psychologist and guidance counselor generally have resources for referring more severe emotional or behavioral problems to mental health experts outside the school system. In a residential school for the Deaf, this network of referral sources may not exist, unless located in a city with a large hearing-impaired population (i.e., Washington, D.C. or Rochester, New York). If a hearing-impaired child is in need of psychotherapy, and it is not provided by the school, then the changes are good that it will not be provided at all. Therefore, children attending a residential school for the Deaf are clearly in need of a comprehensive mental health program which offers nonverbal psychotherapies, such as expressive arts therapies, in addition to the guidance and adjustment counseling programs which are typically offered by the residential school.

Therapeutic modalities, which offer nonverbal communication, help hearing-impaired persons overcome some of the difficulties inherent in living with a communication impairment. The nonverbal communication and expression, which are available through the arts, builds upon the assets of hearing-impaired children and adolescents. This discussion describes a full range of therapeutic techniques found effective with this population, including illustrations of the application of such techniques with clinical data.

Review of Literature

The presence of Deafness, although a disabling condition, should not adversely affect a child's capabilities in creativity and art. The artistic abilities of hearing-impaired children can be expected to be similar to those of normal children of an equivalent age and grade level (Anderson, 1978). Divergent or creative abilities of the Deaf have been found to be similar to the capabilities of nonhearing-impaired children when nonverbal or no linguistic testing measures are used (Laughton, 1979; Pang & Horrocks, 1968).

While the potential for creative expression with the Deaf is obvious, the provision of creative arts experiences are not offered frequently enough. Many art programs for the Deaf tend to emphasize imitation rather than expression, based upon a widely-held belief that individuals with hearing impairments lack abilities for abstract thinking and imagination. Harrington and Silver (1968, p. 477) dispute this notion: "it would be more accurate to say that the Deaf child lacks opportunities to use his imagination." Research on imagination, conducted by Singer and Lenahan (1976), found that Deaf children's dreams, play and story content are more concrete and less original than those of hearing children. They suggest that this difficulty with abstraction and imagination is related to the language limitation. Singer and Lenahan (1976) recommend that Deaf children be taught to explore inner feelings and fantasy as a means of developing their potential for imagination.

Creative art experiences have both educational values, which have been noted by many authors. Art with the Deaf has been reported to enrich language as early as 1959 (Jenson, 1959). Research results indicate that art experiences can develop abstract thinking abilities by teaching such concepts as conservation, sequential ordering, grouping of objects, and spatial relationships (Silver, 1976, 1977). Bell (1971) suggested that the art technique of montage or collage, reinforces the same process of combining words to form sentences, which is used to developing language.

Therapeutically, the arts have great potential as communication tools, as they improve possibilities for the Deaf person to experience self-expression and interaction with others. Art can also provide important emotional gains for persons with hearing impairments, because art experiences create a feeling of control over the environment through the process of controlling art media and content (Harrington & Silver, 1968). A Deaf person can learn to express unacceptable, negative feelings in a nonjudgmental atmosphere, obtaining "relief from tensions, confusions, loneliness, and fear" (op cit, p. 477).

Given the educational and therapeutic potential of art, combined with the unmet emotional needs of many Deaf individuals, it seems appropriate that art therapy would be included in a total treatment approach. Henley (1987) describes a therapeutic art program developed in a residential school for the Deaf. He uses art therapy as a means of helping hearing-impaired students "develop more effective defenses" (Henley, 1987, p. 82) and to explore emotional responses to the disability.

This chapter will describe the potential for emotional growth possible through an art therapy program, as well as the difficulties encountered in developing a therapeutic program for hearing-impaired children in a residential, private school system. The children treated exhibited such difficulties as destructive and aggressive behaviors, impulsivity, poor peer relationships, sexual maladjustment, depression, withdrawal, anxiety, and in some cases, poor contact with reality. Hearing-impaired children and adolescents were selected to participate in individual, group, and/or family art therapy as a means of improving their overall emotional functioning so that they could benefit more fully from their educational programming, and as a method of helping these children (and family members) adjust to the disability.

In traditional verbal therapy, problems in living are expressed and eventually resolved through the use of words. For many individuals with disabilities, such as those with communication disorders, the verbalization and comprehension of significant feelings may be difficult or impossible. Using the traditional verbal approach to counseling, many hearing-impaired students at the Western Pennsylvania School for the Deaf have difficulty with affective questions, such as "How do you feel about that?" The response generally received could be placed in one of three categories: (a) no response–a blank stare; (b) avoidance–changing the subject or avoiding eye contact; or (c) denial–the "Fine, I'm happy" response. One might be inclined to think that this child has no problem; therefore, it is wise not to create problems where there are none. However, an experienced counselor or therapist has only to look and listen to the child's behavior, the nonverbal cues, to know that the feelings are there but the child lacks the means or the vehicle to express those feelings. For these individuals with hearing impairments, words or language represent a sense of frustration due to repeated attempts and some failures to communicate. For hearing-impaired children, the task of communication is even more challenging as they are new to the process of learning a language, which is different from that spoken by the hearing world.

Dr. Thomas Goulder (1985) stated that–"words are in time and space," therefore words are abstractions, which are, limited in their ability to fully express the meaning of ideas or feelings. Words alone (whether communicated in American Sign Language or written English) may not be powerful enough to help hearing-impaired children express the complexities of their inner thoughts and feelings. Hearing-impaired children under the age of ten are still struggling with the process of learning appropriate words and signs to communicate their thoughts and feelings.

Expressive Arts Therapies

Traditional verbal therapy has sometimes been described as "healing by conversation," while Expressive Arts therapies could be called "healing by action." The term, expressive art therapies, is rather broad–including art therapy, music therapy, dance/movement therapy, drama therapy, poetry therapy, and more recently the inclusion of photo/video therapy. In expressive arts therapies, individuals give form to their feelings, transforming impulses, thoughts and affect into creative symbols. The symbol is a substitute for significant feelings and may include a drawing, a song, a dance, a puppet story, a poem, or a self-designed film. The expressive art therapies–art, drama, and music–are nonverbal; therefore, they focus on the nonverbal strengths of the hearing-impaired person and minimize the verbal weaknesses. Expressive arts therapies help to make real those feelings which are confusing, to make tangible and concrete that which is abstract. Words are symbols for thoughts and feelings. Art, play, and drama utilize symbols–or could be thought of as symbolic substitutes for thoughts and feelings. Words may vanish into thin air when they are spoken, but an art form is permanent. A person cannot easily deny a feeling that has been vividly illustrated through a painting or sculpture.

The arts provide symbols, which offer a common language. When a child draws or acts out a dramatic story about a "dragon," it conveys an image or feeling of evil, anger, aggression, and power. It expresses that feeling safely, as it provides a means of distance from powerful feelings. For an abused child, it is much easier to imagine that a witch bites a bad child, than for the child to admit verbally that he/she is beaten. The expressive arts allow individuals opportunities for creative expression–without reliance on words. Expressive arts therapies help to make clear those feelings which are confusing, to make concrete that which is abstract. The expressive arts therapies focus on the nonverbal strengths of the hearing-impaired person and minimize the verbal weaknesses.

Therapeutic Approach

The therapeutic style, which I developed, is a nondirective art and play interview, based upon the psychoanalytic approach to art therapy described by Naumburg (1947, 1966) and Rubin (1978, 1984), and upon the nondirective play therapy approach described by Axline (1947). This nondirective approach to child therapy was based upon the assumptions (a) many hearing-impaired children are capable of basic symbolic processes; and (b) unconscious feelings and desires are more readily revealed through an open-ended situation where projection can occur. In these expressive arts sessions, clients are offered a broad range of expressive arts media and told that they may create whatever they wish. The available materials include such art media as clay, paint, markers, chalk, collage materials, as well as such play equipment as puppets, dolls, dollhouses, cars, trucks, sand table, dress-up clothes, baby toys, blocks, and play doctor equipment. I have found that dramatic play often emerged spontaneously from the art experience; therefore, having a section of play materials available promoted communication between the hearing-impaired children and therapist.

My colleagues at the Western Pennsylvania School for the Deaf advised me that these children were limited in their abstract thinking abilities; therefore, the students would not be able to function in a setting that did not provide clear structure and direction. I was also advised that those children, who were capable of symbolic processing, had such limited experiences in decision-making, that they would have great difficulty being able to handle the freedom of choice in therapy sessions. Given these precautions, I expected to offer educational assistance with art media and possibly offer thematic suggestions; however, most of the time that assistance was not needed. During some initial sessions, students looked at me in shock when I described that the therapy time was for them to develop their own ideas, and unlike an art class, creations were not to be graded. After some initial exploration of the available materials, students felt comfortable indicating what they wished to use during a given session. Some art products were representational, some were not; some stories had a plot with beginning, middle, and end, but many did not. Whatever the level of expressive ability possessed by the child, strong feelings and conflicts were communicated in simple and sometimes complex levels of communication. Children became accustomed to the nondirective style in therapy, as therapy was one of the few places where they could do as they pleased.

In any residential school, the children's time is highly structured, with rules regarding aberrant behavior. Many of the children struggled with the feeling that being "angry" was equated with being "bad" or "out of control." Children in a residential placement were not given the opportunities to freely express negative feelings, as perhaps they might in the more relaxed setting of the home. In the beginning, children in therapy had to learn that it was "OK" to say or do negative things, without fear of punishment. This learning about the limits of therapy took some time for the children to acquire.

I communicated with children using a total communication approach, combining sign language with verbal speech. When the art therapy program first began, I was told that I would not need to learn sign language as the children could read lips, and because we could communicate through gesture, mime, and writing. It is true that some basic communication occurred without sign language. For example, I could determine from the artwork and nonverbal behavior of a child that he/she was angry. However, the significant details surrounding the child's feelings were lost unless I was capable of expressing and receiving sign language.

From the child's perspective, the focus of the sessions became the art and the play. Yet, verbal communication about feelings revealed through the stories and art products also became important. After the production of a story or art product, I ended each session with a "talk" time, where I would connect the feelings expressed through art and play with actual feelings the child was experiencing. When possible, a child is helped to develop insight into his/her behavior. If the child could not comprehend words, I would discuss alternatives to negative behaviors.

If the child could not understand or refused to use words, the art form was relied upon as a symbolic substitute to communicate therapeutic messages from the therapists. The meaning of the child's feelings and problems were thus translated into the art form.

For example, if a child perseveratively expresses themes where he or she is a victim, perhaps powerlessly stranded on a mountain, buried under sand, or caught in fires, I might offer a solution to these problems by introducing a helping character to the situation. I would work within the metaphorical context presented by the child to offer realistic solutions to problems. Therefore, if the child creates a story about a person trapped in a fire, I might offer a fire truck with several firefighters to help put out the blaze. Perhaps, a drawing or an actual puppet representing a helping person (i.e., police officer, doctor) might be introduced to the story and brought to the rescue. Through these therapeutic interventions I attempt to communicate the message that "someone cares about you and will help you." In this manner, the arts are used to stimulate the therapeutic process, to resolve emotional conflicts and to bring closure to an issue.

Adaptation of Therapeutic Environment and Materials

When working therapeutically or educationally with a child having any type of disability, it is the job of the professional to creatively adapt materials, ideas, and techniques for optimal use by the child. At first thought, a hearing-impaired child does not require the same technical adaptations as perhaps a physically impaired child. However, thoughtful consideration of the adaptation of some techniques may be useful.

Descriptions of appropriate therapeutic environments for individual children and groups have been described by Axline (1947) and Ginott (1961) in play therapy, and Rubin (1984) in art therapy. The general premise in these theories is that a variety of expressive arts media and play materials are provided within a nondirective context, in order to facilitate the spontaneous projection of material from the unconscious. Generally, the standards for the setup of a child therapy room for hearing-impaired children are the same as that for hearing children, with some additional considerations. The setup of the room and furniture within the therapy room involves some special brainstorming due to the importance of being able to clearly see all communications of persons with hearing impairments. For example, a colleague and I had a table specially designed for use with a group of adolescents. Previous attempts at providing group therapy at a table, which was rectangular in shape, were somewhat frustrating, due to difficulties in seeing the manual communication of all group members. Instructors at the school woodshop were asked to create a round table (72" in diameter), with a dark brown laminate top. The round table was intended to give ample space for all to see the group communication, and the dark color was intended to provide contrast so that manual signs could be seen more easily. Such a table was also extremely useful for group art projects, as it provided the needed space and an impervious table surface. Interestingly enough, it also became an instant play space (i.e., a cave or crawling space) during individual therapy sessions.

Another consideration in the therapy rooms was the presence of adequate lighting, so that manual communications could be seen with ease. At times, individual children enjoyed turning off the overhead lighting in order to create a special effect for a story or dramatic play. When this happened, a flashlight became available or a light sword (generally purchased at Halloween, as a costume accessory). If funding is available, spotlighting or track lighting may be very useful for psychodrama work or individual play therapy.

I found the presence of a sink in the therapy room to be very beneficial. Not only was the clean-up after art experiences more convenient, but the availability of water frequently led to spontaneous water play. The development of play skills were frequently delayed in the hearing-impaired children and adolescents referred for therapy. It was not uncommon for a ten-year-old child to choose water or sand play during the therapeutic session. One fifteen-year-old consistently indulged in the production of finger paintings. These children were aware that their choices of activities were below age level; therefore, they enjoyed the privacy allowed them by having the sink within the room, rather than down the hallway.

As the therapy was focused on art therapy, a wide variety of expressive arts materials were available. Crayons, craypas, markers, chalk, pastels, watercolors, finger paints, tempera paints, acrylic paints, ceramic clay, oil-based clay, wood scraps, and collage materials were only some of the choices made available to the children. Choices with regard to places to work were also made available, including an easel, tables, walls, and floor space.

Children were asked to create wherever they felt most comfortable. Through the course of the five years as a child therapist, I observed that certain materials appealed more to children with hearing impairments, than to children without language and communication disabilities.

Many of the hearing-impaired children preferred to create with three-dimensional materials. As gesture and movement are important aspects of the hearing-impaired child's communication system, they seemed to prefer art materials, which were three-dimensional and therefore, could be easily used in a dramatic manner. Often, the artwork stimulated dramatic play, spontaneously becoming a prop for a dramatic scenario. I observed this happening more frequently with hearing-impaired children, than with hearing children. For example, one child created a cake made of clay, which became the center of a story about a birthday party where the child was the only hearing-impaired child invited to the party.

The availability of a range of three-dimensional materials was useful in stimulating a full range of expression. Pleistocene clay in various colors was clearly preferred to ceramic clay. While ceramic clay was useful in providing an appropriate outlet for direct expression of anger and aggression, it made the hands of children feel or look "dirty." For many children, the messy aspect of ceramic clay is a valid reason for attraction to the material. However, for some children with hearing impairments, the slip for the ceramic clay impairs their ability to sign during the creation of the art product. Therefore, Pleistocene clay satisfied the need to create with a pliable material, while leaving hands free to communicate manually. Other three-dimensional materials which were popular were wood scraps and collage materials.

A sand table also presented children with multiple options regarding the expression of "messy" feelings, using materials, which were clean to the touch. Surprisingly, many children found exploration with water and toys at the sand table to be more appealing than the creation of art products. This attraction to water and sand play by latency age hearing-impaired children of all ages reflected the importance of presenting a full range of media options. The water and sand experiences available at the sand table provided them with safe alternatives to aggressive behavior, resulting in a positive experience.

A two-dimensional material, which was very attractive to children, was face paint. The use of washable paints intended for use on the face appealed to children's needs for self-expression while loosening inhibitions. Even shy and quiet children felt comfortable transforming themselves into a vampire, clown, werewolf, lion, or any character from their imagination as the paints allowed them to hide their own personality and unknowingly project the persona of another character. A significant aspect of the hearing-impaired child's total communication depends upon gesture and nonverbal body language; therefore, the dramatic element of face paints is an especially appropriate material to make available in a therapy room for Deaf children. Puppets were also found interesting by the children; however, they provided technical difficulties when the children attempted signed communication. When puppets were placed over top of quart jars, children could sign over the head of the characters speaking. This worked well, and children enjoyed the range of communication available through the puppets.

Art therapist, Edith Kramer (1979) supports the value of art as being "closer to reality than is play" (p. 64), arguing that art also provides more opportunities for extensive sublimation. As an artist and art therapist, Kramer prefers her creative modality of expression, and for many clients her approach is most appropriate. However, play is a primary language for children with language and communication disorders, which provides more detail and effect than art alone. Some children seemed more comfortable with expressions of aggression through play than through art, as the play provided no lasting record of "bad" feelings. I sensed that many children receiving therapy in a school setting were reluctant to express negative feelings, for fear of punishment by the school authorities. If a negative feeling were expressed through play, it could be easily forgotten but art provided a tangible reminder. Children who had been sexually abused disclosed much more detail of the abuse and resulting feelings through play, than through art. Again, the play provided more privacy.

I also discovered that the provision of specific toys elicited more self-expression in some children, than did the art materials. Certain toys became well-used favorites by the hearing-impaired children who received therapy in the art therapy room. Specific toys seemed to symbolize feelings about hearing and hearing loss; therefore, the availability of these toys promoted the expression of key emotional issues.

Pretend handcuffs, which actually locked and unlocked were very helpful for children dealing with feelings about having a hearing impairment and having a hearing therapist. On many occasions, children locked the therapist's hands behind her back, signing that she was a "bad guy." This type of power conflict between good versus bad is commonly seen in the play of hearing, as well as hearing-impaired children. However, with hands locked behind the back, manual communication became impossible. After this type of play, the child and I would discuss how it felt to be unable to communicate with another or control another's ability to communicate, and whether the child shared any feelings with the characters in the story.

Frequently, themes of frustrated communications arose, where I explained how it felt to play without being able to sign. Deaf children of hearing families sometimes admitted that they wished the therapist were

Deaf, as well as frequently wishing that family members were Deaf. Another aspect of this same scenario with handcuffs was the emergence of the issue of power. Children who were resistant to therapy and felt uncomfortable with questions from the therapist also used the handcuffs to gain superiority over the therapist and enforce silence.

For similar reasons, the therapist intentionally provided pretend and real medical equipment. Most of the children were hearing impaired due to a congenital complication or defect. Therefore, these children had experienced a wide range of medical situations (both situations typical of childhood and some traumatic) related to doctors, nurses, and hospitals. A doctor's kit, including syringes, a stethoscope, oxygen tubing, mask, and patient gown were available to children at every therapeutic session. Many children needed the opportunity to work through feelings about being hurt, about being powerless, and about having a disability that could not be "fixed." In particular, the stethoscope elicited feelings about the hearing impairment, as it is an instrument for the amplification of hearing (similar to a hearing aide). Children often assumed the doctor role, pretending that they could hear. The stethoscope was also used as an instrument of aggression, by yelling or making a loud sound in the end of the stethoscope, while the hearing ends were in the therapist's ears. Some children used their loud vocalizations as a means of expressing their anger in a harming way. When this was done during the therapeutic session, it was an excellent opportunity to discuss what it was about not being able to hear that made them so angry. In sessions involving the play doctor equipment, children often admitted their own wishes to have normal hearing. It is possible that the doctor/patient scenario brought up memories of previous visits to doctors where the child and/or parent wished for news of a cure.

Most play therapists provide a collection of dolls from which a child could chose during a therapy session. I found that having a wide assortment of dolls (multiracial, small and large, anatomically correct and neuter, infant and adult) provided children with multiple opportunities for projection. A special doll family for use with children who have been sexually abused had sexual parts, which actually "worked" (Friedemann & Morgan, 1985). This was useful for some children; however, these were kept in a private place to determine the children's need or readiness for such a toy that was certain to elicit strong emotions. One physically abused child chose to play out the scenes of domestic anger and violence with dolls of a race other than her own. This gave her the psychic distance that she needed, in order to feel comfortable enough to reveal the family secrets. I also provided a hearing aid to fit a large doll, which could be selected to add the characteristic of Deafness to the doll. Interestingly, this hearing aid was rarely selected for use, and dolls were rarely identified as having a hearing impairment. Art and play materials which were rejected were valued as indicators of projection, as much, if not more than the materials which were preferred.

One key adaptation was the timing of the therapeutic comments and questions. With hearing children, it is very common for a therapist to ask questions of the child during the art-making process and following the completion of the product. The therapist has to be very careful that the questions did not interfere with the creative process. When questioned, a hearing-impaired child has to stop working, look up from the artwork, and use his/her hands to respond to a comment. Some children became annoyed with this interruption. As a result, I generally waited until the end of the creative phase to ask questions or asked simple questions requiring a "yes" or "no" response. Several times, I used simple drawings of faces demonstrating different feeling states (happy, sad, angry). I could lay these out on the table near the child, and ask the child to merely point to indicate how they were feeling or how a character in their drawing might be feeling. Similar therapeutic interventions were used when children were playing. Again, too many therapeutic questions slowed down or interrupted the play process. The use of a psychodrama, called an "aside," was a useful way of asking children about the meaning of their play during the play process.

The Interfacing of School and Therapy

The presence of a therapeutic program in the school facility presents both advantages and disadvantages to therapy. The art therapy program was first placed in a classroom setting, and later placed in a special wing for mental health services. Due to the close proximately within the school building, children could easily be referred and seen for treatment. They did not have to wait through the red tape commonly associated with community mental health agencies, nor was transportation a problem. Communication with teachers, and coordination of school and therapeutic progress was easily achieved.

However, other unforeseen difficulties arose. An initial problem was the clarification of related roles. Since as an art therapist I worked in the school, there was some perceived overlap of job function with the art teachers and the guidance counselors. Description of role definitions eased this initial confusion. Frequent contact with these staff members, as well as in-service training about the nature of art therapy provided clarification regarding the need for all of these services, and the difference in the type of services provided.

Confidentiality became another difficult area of treatment. Because children were being seen in a school environment, there was a general reluctance to admit to negative feelings, or fear of getting in trouble. Dynamics in group art therapy was greatly affected because these children had a long history of both positive and negative contact with their classmates. Many of them had been taking classes together, and living in the residential setting since preschool. Therefore, the idea of confidentiality was difficult to maintain. Children in a residential school were accustomed to talking to each other or "gossiping" about their problems; therefore, they felt it was natural to share group therapy "process" material with their peers. Many children also resisted trusting the group with personal material, as they felt it would later be discussed in the dorm setting. Consequently, the creation of the cohesive therapy group within the microcosm of the residential school for the Deaf was difficult.

From the school's perspective, confidentiality was also an issue. Most of the issues discussed by children in therapy were kept as confidential information by the therapist. However, if a child was acting-out in school, the expectation from school officials was that relevant therapeutic material would be shared with all persons involved with the child. The standards for sharing privileged information are different in a school setting versus a therapeutic setting; therefore, these differences needed to be explained.

The final area of difficulty involved in the placement of a therapy program within the residential school system was the problem of maintaining contact with parents. Therapy was provided with parental consent; however, due to long distances between home and school, it was difficult to coordinate therapeutic gains and progress. Family art therapy was later initiated to resolve this treatment gap.

Clinical Data

Hearing-impaired children may discover that expression through art therapy and the related expressive art therapies is easier than counseling; the additional feature is that it is more fun. Art also stimulates the expression and recognition of feelings that are not in the child's awareness. The following information exemplifies how a very bright Deaf child perceived himself and his Deafness, as seen through his artwork. "A" was a 16-year-old, rubella child, with a gifted IQ. Peer relationships were difficult for him, as he was often the subject of teasing. Choosing Pleistocene clay, A created a multicolor image of a robot with two antennae. He developed the following story:

> It's a UFO, it would attack the art therapist. I was afraid of the UFO, it attacks men and women. He is 500 years old, they live to be 6 million years old. It is hungry, powerful, and dangerous. He eats all things, you cannot attack him. If he drinks acid, a nuclear missile cannot hurt him.

The symbolic messages revealed through this child's art and the related story are several. On a very basic level, the child is revealing his need to be powerful, aggressive, and invulnerable, implying that he feels the opposite.

Other Deaf children have revealed their feelings of vulnerability related to the hearing impairment (i.e., fear of fires, fear of traffic, and a general fear of harm coming their way without being able to hear the associated sounds). For A the feelings of vulnerability were enhanced by the fact that he was picked on by his own peer group. In addition to vulnerability, A was able to safely express feelings of aggression towards others, and in particular the art therapist. The art therapist is a safe target, who he knows will not retaliate nor punish him. The description of the UFO as "dangerous," is clearly a self-projection. This particular child passively withstood the teaching, until he reached an explosive point. Therefore, A may well perceive himself as being "dangerous," and out of control. The UFO is also something, which scares people away. Again, this metaphor fits A's situation, whereby he needs to keep people at a distance because they hurt him. The art therapist was aware of all the potential meanings of this art product, but chose to reflect only the most basic feelings of anger and power. A was able to discuss these feelings about the UFO, more readily than he could discuss his own feelings.

Art therapy is appropriate for intelligent Deaf children because they can benefit from the insight possible through symbolic imagery. However, the intellectually gifted Deaf child is not the typical client referred for treatment. Often, children who are low verbal, and even low functioning are referred, as art therapy treatment does not rely upon the use of words. A mentally retarded Deaf teenager, 16 years old, was experiencing difficulty adjusting to her foster home. When asked about her home, B would smile and respond that everything was fine. The art therapist asked her to draw a family portrait, in order to assess the family dynamics. She drew a basic picture of the family, but could not discuss it. In an attempt to make the technique more concrete and also to appeal to the intellectual level of the child, the therapist cut out the family figures and asked B to use them like paper dolls. Using the family figures in an interactive way, B created a distance between herself and the other family members. In this way, B was able to show that she felt isolated and different from the foster family, as they were not Deaf. B's drawn image was more primitively represented than the body images of other family members, also indicating poor feelings of self-worth. The art therapist asked B to show how the family felt towards each other, and then compare that to how she wished they felt. This self-designed technique was extremely useful as a means of helping B understand her present feelings about her foster family, as well as her wishes for more family closeness. These concepts of love, closeness, and conflict are abstract, yet can be made tangible and understandable to a Deaf retarded child through art experiences.

Sometimes, children began with an art image, which naturally evolved to dramatic play. One six-year-old Deaf child who had been physically abused early in life drew an image of a house surrounded by large clouds, rain and lightning bolts. He described the story, in sign language, stating: "Rain falls. Big clouds. Lightning. Wind blows hard. The roof of the house blows in. The mother is hurt. She dies." While this story was short and simple, it expressed very strong feelings for the child. The child lived at home with his mother, even though she continued to be emotionally unstable and erratic. Within the time period of one year, he and his mother have moved residences ten times. This particular child thrived on consistency, and unfortunately in his home life, there was none. The image expressed through his drawing correlated well with his strong feelings about instability in the home environment. The child was angry and felt powerless over his mother; therefore, this drawing was a concise way of describing complex feelings. To provide closure to these feelings, the therapist had the child rebuild the house from clay—a medium that could be destroyed, yet easily rebuilt.

Students were also involved in group art therapy, as a means of helping them learn improved socialization skills and learn how to express negative feelings more appropriately. In one group, a fifteen-year-old gifted Deaf student commented that his mother had just recently given birth to a baby girl the day before the group met. When asked how he felt about the family event, he denied any negative feelings. However, during the group art time, he created a series of weapons such as a land mine, an underwater mine, dynamite and a match to ignite all of them. Initially, D could see no connection between his artwork and his underlying feelings of anger towards mother for having another baby. Other group members helped him to acknowledge that the art images appeared to express anger; the group leaders then discussed the feelings of jealousy, which commonly occur when a new sibling is born. The art forms were tangible evidence of D's feelings, and therefore were more easily discussed by group members, without fear of hurting or upsetting D.

During another session of this same group, another hearing-impaired teenager appeared tired and depressed. He laid his head on the table, and refused to talk or participate in the art-making. Other students attempted to engage him in the group, but he was not interested. E grabbed a piece of clay and began to model it while he was sitting in the corner of the room, on a beanbag chair. E did not interact with the group at all, but by the end of the group time, he sat at the table with the group, with a more relaxed expression on his face. E showed what he had made, the head of a skeleton. He did not want to talk to the group about the content of the art product, but he later confided to one of the therapists that he became so angry at times that he wished he would die. This was the first clear image of suicide expressed by E. This incident alerted the group therapists to E's potential for violence, and prompted one therapist to see E for individual as well as group therapy.

One expressive arts technique, which worked very effectively with hearing-impaired students, was the creation of a film. The group collectively developed the characters and created the script for the film. Group members decided to create a story about adulthood. The plot revolved around a father who drank too much and his wife who spent too much money. Arguing and violence between the parents occurred. The group members revealed their fears and concerns about parental fights and possible divorce. The topics of alcohol abuse, money problems, domestic violence, and marital discord were emotionally-laden topics for the group members. As the film developed, the children relived issues of concern. At the end of the script, the group chose to end with a happy "wish" directing the father and mother to kiss and resolve their conflict. After enjoying themselves act in costume on film, the students discussed their serious feelings of fear about domestic violence and drinking at home. The students were also asked to creatively brainstorm solutions to the problems of the family (i.e., counseling). They recognized that the ending with a kiss was an unrealistic resolution, and further acknowledge that the real world consisted of difficult problems that did not have easy answers.

The use of video art has also proven to work very well with Deaf individuals, as it gives them the necessary psychic distance to view themselves and their problems. One eleven-year-old, hearing-impaired child who had been sexually abused dictated the following story for "TV."

QUEEN SISTERS: WHICH ONE?

Once upon a time, there was a queen who had a beautiful younger sister. The two sisters were very, very rich and had lots of lovely clothes. The younger sister was very kind and helped take care of the queen, hoping that someday she too would be a queen. However, the younger sister knew that there would be only ONE queen. This made her feel sad and sometimes mad. The queen became pregnant and had a baby boy. The younger sister wished that the child were hers, but it was not and she grew more sad and bitter. The younger sister also wished that she had a husband or boyfriend. One night, while the queen was sleeping, the younger sister stole the queen's magic shoes, and ran off to find a husband. This made the queen very sad, as her sister left without saying goodbye.

Many years later, there was a knock at the door, and it was the younger sister coming home to be queen. She was dressed in disguise and the queen did not know her. She rushed in the queen's home and acted bossy. She stole the queen's crown, and her clothes, her money and left the queen with nothing. She even wished to steal the queen's husband who had since divorced the unhappy queen.

This particular example indicates the child's conflicting feelings regarding normal competitive feelings resulting from the Oedipal phase, and feelings of jealous rivalry combined with wishes to replace mother, based on her feelings as a victim of sexual abuse. Feelings of anger and power also emerge in this drama. Unknowingly, this particular child told a great deal about herself and her situation through this dramatic enactment. By reviewing the videotape with the therapist, F was able to gain mastery over a situation, which had previously left her feeling victimized and powerless. As is apparent in this example, the layer of symbolic disguise is very thin. I have observed this to be the case with many Deaf children. Often Deaf children seem to adapt the characters enough, so that self-disclosure is not apparent to the ego. However, I have also observed that the story line and feelings underlying the story are most often a direct expression of the child's feelings at the present time.

Another variation of art therapy, which has proven to be very effective, is the use of phototherapy. During family art therapy sessions, various inappropriate behaviors were occurring between one parent and her Deaf child. The parent was unaware of these behaviors and not certain how they were affecting her child. The art therapists photographed several shots of the therapy session, including the child's demanding temper tantrums and the mother's response to these behaviors. When the child saw the finished photographs, he was aware these behaviors made him appear immature. His mother was equally surprised to see that her interventions were not age-appropriate. As a result of this type of intervention, the child was able to tell his mother that he did not want to be treated like a baby.

In a different case, Polaroid[8] photographs were used to educate a mentally retarded Deaf adolescent about different types of feelings and resulting behaviors. I asked the child to act out a variety of emotions, which were then photographed. I compiled a book of feelings for this child, which were referred to when the child was expressing a particular feeling through her art or play. The feelings book became an important reference point for this child, as she learned to discriminate between feelings and to judge appropriate and inappropriate behaviors. Children of low intelligence and with low verbal communication skills responded well to art therapy techniques, which were presented in a very concrete and visual manner, such as photo and video therapy.

CONCLUSION

In conclusion, this chapter has examined both the theoretical and the practical aspects of establishing an art therapy program within a residential school setting. There is no research on statistically preferred therapeutic modalities to lead the therapist treating hearing-impaired children in designing an effective treatment program. No one technique will work equally well with all Deaf children, as there exists such a diversity of functioning and communication levels. The "trial and error" method of experimenting with current art therapy techniques and brainstorming new techniques is the best method of approaching this population. As Rubin (1984) stated, the approach that is most effective with handicapped populations may be the "pragmatic" approach. In other words, the therapist uses what "works" best and adapts his/her style accordingly. Creative improvisation and flexibility are key therapeutic skills in working effectively with children having communication disorders. My therapeutic work with hearing-impaired children was not begun with set ideas of what was most effective, rather ideas, such as the photo therapy, evolved out of a need to more fully connect with the client's problems.

REFERENCES

Anderson, F. (1978). *Art for all the children.* Springfield, IL: Charles C Thomas.

Axline, V. (1947). *Play therapy.* New York: Ballentine Books.

Bell, J. (1971). Visual language. *Volta Review, 73* (3), 157–160.

Forquer, S., & Gibney, L. (1984). *Report on mental health needs of hearing impaired children and youth in Pennsylvania.* Submitted to: Office of Mental Health, Commonwealth of Pennsylvania.

Friedemann, V., & Morgan, M. (1985). *Interviewing sexual abuse victims using anatomical dolls: The professional guidebook.* Eugene, OR: Migima Designs.

Ginott, H. G. (1961). *Group Psychotherapy with children: The theory and practice of play therapy.* New York: McGraw-Hill.

Goulder, T. (1985). Pa. Speech and Hearing Association.

Harrington, J., & Silver, R. (1968). Art education and the education of deaf students. *Volta Review, 70* (3), 475–480.

Henley, D. (1987). An art therapy program for hearing impaired children with special needs. *American Journal of Art Therapy, 25* (3), 81–89.

Horovitz-Darby, E. G. (1988). Art therapy assessment of a minimally language skilled deaf child. Proceedings from the 1988 University of California's Center on Deafness Conference: *Mental Health Assessment of Deaf Clients: Special Conditions,* Little Rock, Arkansas: ADARA.

Jenson, P. (1959). Art helps the deaf to speak. *School Arts, 58* (9), 9–10.

Kramer, E. (1979). *Childhood and art therapy.* New York: Schocken Books.

Kunkle-Miller, C. (1985). *Competencies for Art Therapists whose clients have physical, cognitive or sensory disabilities.* University of Pittsburgh Dissertation.

Laughton, J. (1979). Non-linguistic creative abilities and expressive syntactic abilities of hearing-impaired children. *Voltra Review, 81* (6), 409–420.

Naumburg, M. (1947). Studies of the "Free" art expression of behavior problem children and adolescents as a means of diagnosis and therapy. *Nervous and Mental Disease Monograph,* No. 71.

Naumburg, M. (1966). *Dynamically oriented art therapy: Its principles and practices.* New York: Grune and Stratton.

Pang, H., & Horrocks, C. (1968). An exploratory study of creativity in deaf children. *Perceptual and Motor Skills, 27,* 844–846.

Robinson, L. (1978). *Sound minds in a soundless world.* Washington, D.C.: U.S. Department of HEW.

Rubin, J. A. (1984). *The art of art therapy.* New York: Brunner-Mazel.

Rubin, J. (2001). *Approaches to art therapy: Theory and techniques.* New York: Brunner-Routledge.

Sachs, B., Robinson, L., & Sloan, M. (1978). The mental health needs of deaf Americans: Report of the special populations subpanel on mental health of physically handicapped Americans. *Mental Health in Deafness, 2,* 6–13.

Schlesinger, H., & Meadow, K. (1972). *Sound and sign: Childhood deafness and mental health.* Berkeley: University of California Press.

Silver, R. (1976). Using art to evaluate and develop cognitive skills. *The American Journal of Art Therapy, 16,* 11–19.

Singer, D., & Lenahan, M. L. (1976). Imagination content in dreams of deaf children. *American Annals of the Deaf, 121,* 44–48.

Warren, C., & Hasenstab, S. (1986). Self-concept of severely to profoundly hearing-impaired children. *Volta Review, 88* (6), 289–295.

Chapter 10

ART THERAPY WITH EMOTIONALLY DISTURBED DEAF ADOLESCENTS

Ellen G. Horovitz

CASE 1: CG–INTRODUCTION

Because of the complexity of this case, a full medical and intake history will be presented on this adolescent male, CG, age 15, as he entered a residential treatment facility (RTF) for the Deaf, where this writer worked. The subsequent cases (presented herein) all took place in this RTF and the interdisciplinary work done with these adolescents was thorough, attentive and significant in aiding their recovery. In this case presented below, several factors influenced the dynamics beyond the secondary diagnosis of Profound Bilateral Sensory Hearing Loss Following Mumps: these were (a) complicated familial issues including loss, abandonment, and rejection at a very young age; (b) sexual molestation (victimization) and subsequent sexual abuse of others; (c) AWOL defiant and truant behavior at previous residential placements and psychiatric hospitalizations; and (d) identity disorder.

Presenting Problems

CG has been profoundly deaf since age 3, and was a student at St. Mary's School for the Deaf for many years.

CG had a history of stealing since age 7 (i.e., cigarettes, toys, diamond ring) and fire play since age 5. At age 11, he was placed on probation for setting a fire in the family's home. Reports also note CG setting himself on fire, but not being harmed. CG has been involved in numerous incidents of sexual acting-out (e.g., sexual play with other residents, attack of younger residents, molestation of his brother and a developmentally disabled adult (exposing himself).

CG was in a previous placement at Forest Hospital and Center for the Deaf in Des Plaines, Illinois at age 13 and 14. Parents reported that CG had a tendency to run away and was eventually discharged at his age 14. CG was at West Seneca Psychiatric Center prior to this placement and responded well to the intensive structure.

CG is in the superior intelligence range as indicated by his psychological evaluations (further on in this chapter). Mother reported CG being capable of excelling in school; however, described him as progressively resistant to school personnel and truanting on a regular basis.

CG and parents were motivated for placement at the time of this intake. Below see CG's genogram and timeline information followed by additional background information.

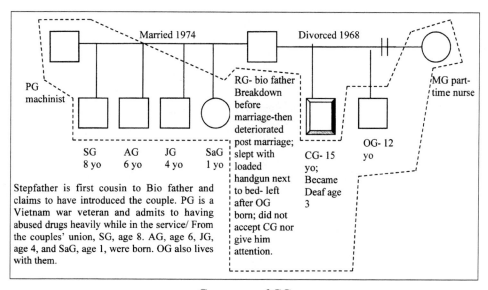

Genogram of CG

Timeline CG:

- CG born October 4, 1969 to MG and RG; MG (mother fingerspells and uses some sign—PG uses gesturing and home signing)
- born with pyloric stenosis, which was controlled by diet.
- CG was walking by 7 months and talked early also.
- Toilet training was accomplished without difficulty.
- At age 3, CG lost his hearing after having the mumps, and developed a

profound hearing loss due to bilateral nerve damage. Prior to this, CG had developed a good speaking vocabulary, according to mother.

- At age 3, tubes were placed in his ears after being taken to a hearing specialist.
- CG was hyperactive as a young child and medicated for brief periods with Mellaril and then Sylert. (Medication was eventually stopped due to CG's refusal to take pills).
- Age 3 years, OG born, biological father leaves family—does not visit or pay child support (Bio father had slept with loaded gun next to bed.)
- CG began attending St. Mary's School for the Deaf at age 4.
- PG and MG marry—CG's age 5; CG—fire play begins age 5.
- At age 5, CG severed the front tendon in his left leg.
- CG—history of stealing since age 7 (i.e., cigarettes, toys, diamond ring).
- Age 8, CG was forced into a sexual encounter with an older male resident, and after that began exploring sex with other male residents.
- PG (stepfather) described having a poor relationship with CG and being embarrassed by his behavior. In past years, PG said that he has displayed a violent temper and was hospitalized at CG's age 8 because of "nerves." Since that time, PG notes a more positive response toward CG. PG has reported that he is the disciplinarian, whereas MG (Mother) is inconsistent and gives up easily.
- Age 10, CG was kicked out of St. Mary's Residential Program because of his behavior. After commuting for two years from home, he was allowed back in. Within a year, he was again kicked out due to his involvement with another boy in an alleged rape of a younger boy. (Age 11).
- Age 10, CG's maternal grandfather (MGF) died, with whom he had a close and loving relationship.
- CG age 11—set self on fire, but unharmed.
- CG—11 on—involve in numerous incidents of sexual acting-out (e.g., sexual play with other residents, attack of younger residents, molestation of his brother and a retarded adult (exposing himself).
- CG—(age 13, 14)—in placement at Forest Hospital and Center for the Deaf in Des Plaines, Illinois. Parents report that CG had a tendency to run away and was eventually discharged age 14. CG at West Seneca Psychiatric Center since age 14 and has responded well to the intensive structure.
- CG—age 13—SG, half-brother reports that CG molested him but does not divulge frequency or type of molestation.
- CG (Age 14) raped his 12-year old cousin—no charges filed.
- PG is employed at Lapp Insulator as a machinist. MG works part-time as a nurse for quality care.
- CG in residential treatment again and begins art therapy.

Family Background

CG was born to MG (mother) and RG (biological father). Also born from this union was OG, now age 12. Biological parents RG & MG were divorced four years after marrying. Mother reports that RG experienced a nervous breakdown before their marriage. She noted deterioration in his behavior during the marriage, and incidences of him sleeping with a loaded shotgun next to the bed. Mother claimed that RG wanted girls, and did not accept CG or pay attention to him. When OG was born, (CG's age 3), RG left and the couple eventually divorced. RG has had minimal contact with the boys over the years. He never paid child support and mother believes that he is an alcoholic.

Mother married PG (stepfather) at CG's age 5. The couple had originally dated in high school. PG was RG 's cousin (and even sported the same last name); he claimed to have originally introduced the couple (RG & MG). PG was a Vietnam veteran and admitted to having abused drugs heavily while in the service. From the couple's union SG, age 8, AG, age 6, JG age 4, and SaG, age 1, were born.

PG (stepfather) described having a poor relationship with CG and being embarrassed by his behavior. In past years, PG stated that he displayed a violent temper and was hospitalized for three months (at CG's age 8) because of "nerves." Since that time, PG noted a more positive response toward CG. PG disclosed that he is the disciplinarian, whereas the mother is inconsistent and gives up easily.

The stepfather is currently employed as a machinist and the mother works part-time as a nurse for quality care.

Developmental Milestones

Mother reported that CG was a wanted and planned child, and that pregnancy and delivery were normal. CG was born with pyloric stenosis, which was controlled by diet.

> Pyloric stenosis is a narrowing of the pylorus, the lower part of the stomach through which food and other stomach contents pass to enter the small intestine. When an infant has pyloric stenosis, the muscles in the pylorus have become enlarged to the point where food is prevented from emptying out of the stomach. Also called infantile hypertrophic pyloric stenosis or gastric outlet obstruction, pyloric stenosis is fairly common–it affects about three out of 1,000 babies in the United States. Pyloric stenosis is about four times more likely to occur in firstborn male infants. It has also been shown to run in families–if a parent had pyloric stenosis, then an infant has up to a 20 percent risk of developing the condition. Pyloric stenosis occurs more

commonly in Caucasian infants than in babies of other ethnic backgrounds, and affected infants are more likely to have blood type B or O. Most infants who develop pyloric stenosis are usually between 2 weeks and 2 months of age–symptoms usually appear during or after the third week of life. It is one of the more common causes of intestinal obstruction during infancy that requires surgery.
(Source: http://kidshealth.org/parent/medical/digestive/pyloric_stenosis)

CG walked by 7 months and spoke early also. Toilet training was accomplished without difficulty. At age 3, CG lost his hearing after having the mumps, and developed a profound hearing loss due to bilateral nerve damage. Prior to this, CG had developed a good speaking vocabulary, according to mother.

CG was hyperactive as a young child and medicated for brief periods with Mellaril and then Sylert. (Medication was eventually stopped due to CG's refusal to take pills.)

At age 5, CG severed the front tendon in his left leg; as a result, that leg developed a bit smaller, but functioned well. At age 3, tubes were placed in his ears.

Education

CG began attending St. Mary's School for the Deaf at age 4. Mother reported that CG developed a pattern of picking on younger children while there. At about age 8, CG was coerced into a sexual encounter with an older male resident, and after that began exploring sex with other male residents. At age 10, CG was ousted from St. Mary's Residential Program because of behavioral problems. After commuting for two years from home, he was allowed re-entrance. Within a year, he was again expelled due to his involvement with another boy in an alleged rape of a younger boy.

Past school reports indicated that CG was able to work on a one-to-one basis. In a group, he was often found to be disruptive. He lacked respect for authority, refused to accept responsibility for his actions and did not improve when disciplinary action was taken.

Prior to his admission to Forest Hospital at age 13, mother reported that CG became discouraged with school; he often feigned illness or was truant. Nevertheless, at age 13, on the Standard Achievement Test, CG obtained a 3.0 GE in Math Computation.

Past Psychological Evaluation

At age 13.5, the school psychologist at St. Mary's School for the Deaf evaluated CG. On the WISC-R, he obtained a performance IQ of 121.

Nevertheless, the psychologist reported:

CG appears to be basically a normal deaf boy, but quite impulsive and lacks internalized inhibitions about his body. He does not show any sexual pre-occupations and appears prone to admit to dramatic things in order to get adult attention, especially from men. . . . It appears that CG is involved in these incidents out of impulsiveness, lack of inhibiting guilt, and in order to gain the protection/guidance from his stepfather.

On the TAT, major themes in CG's story indicated "sadness, a feeling of internal inadequacy and a hopelessness due to lack of support from the environment." On the Rorschach, CG offered more responses than the average hearing person of his chronological age, indicating good conceptualization and creativity. However, as the pictures increased in the degree of stimuli presented, CG's answers became less integrated. He indicated a tendency to distance himself from people with current relationships being at a very immature, surface, nongratifying level.

Previous Psychiatric Evaluation

Upon admission to Forest Hospital in December at his age 13, the preliminary diagnosis of Conduct Disorder, Undersocialized Aggressive was established. The diagnosis of Dysthymic Disorder was added one month later.

Recommendations were made for treatment in a locked facility as CG's past response to pressure was to run away. It was felt that the facility should also offer options of restraint techniques and a full understanding of deafness. Family's involvement in weekly therapy was felt to be necessary if CG was to return home.

Other Information

CG was admitted to Forest Hospital at his age 13.2. During the first few weeks of hospitalization, CG was willing to communicate in the systemic sessions, but during the remainder of the day he became increasingly hostile and aggressive. Throughout the day he participated in lying, cheating, stealing, verbally abusive, and physically aggressive behavior. His greatest frustration appeared to be his inability to run away as he perceived that as a weakness in himself that he could not "outsmart" the system.

After a few weeks of this behavior it was deemed appropriate to place CG in the intensive care unit where he received one-to-one attention and closer supervision. When placed in a less stimulating environment, CG became increasingly depressed and began to talk about his feelings of being unloved and psychologically abandoned. The therapeutic program designed for him was one of strict limit setting coupled with as much nurturance as possible. After being given smoking permission, CG began to cooperate stating that he could do this now because he felt less nervous. Within a month, CG's behavior improved daily and progressed to spending time each day out of Intensive Care. Plans were made to eventually return him to the deaf team.

It was reported that CG responded well to a great deal of structure, was very intelligent and caught on easily to routine. At times, he used his Deafness as an excuse for breaking rules (i.e., "I didn't understand what you said"), and he complained about the Center's lack of staff that signed.

CG had been observed to be antagonistic toward peers who were less intelligent; he easily provoked a group with his behavior. He was not viewed as demanding of staff and generally entertained himself well. There had been one suspected incidence of sexual acting-out with another male resident, which was never founded. CG had required restraint at least monthly, which was often precipitated by not being allowed a home visit.

At this juncture, parental involvement was viewed as difficult. Family counseling was offered but parents did not follow through. Stepfather identified CG as behaving poorly at home, whereas mother was more lenient.

Intake Interview Prior to Art Therapy Treatment

CG and his parents were met for an intake at CG's age 14.9. CG, a Caucasian, curly-haired, well-built youth of medium stature, came dressed in fatigues and a T-shirt. He appeared rather depressed, but was able to respond to questions when asked. The parents were verbal and presented with many questions. Mother expressed concern with CG's previous psychiatric placement (West Seneca Psychiatric Hospital) because of lack of personnel trained in sign language. Both parents expressed that the West Seneca psychiatric staff had been "rough with CG when restraining him," and lodged a formal complaint in the past. They said that there had been a lack of communication regarding such things as visitation and were upset that they have never met with the social worker.

CG admitted to feeling depressed and stated that the hospital had not been "treating (him) right." He identified that the restraints hurt and that he had been ridiculed. When asked if he were ready to attend this new RTF placement, CG signed that he was "somewhat ready" to come.

While CG attended lunch in the RTF cottage, the parents were interviewed individually. Both parents spoke of their anger at New York State, as they felt pressured in the past to have CG placed at Forest Hospital in Illinois. Parents found the distance to be difficult (from their native New

York) and felt helpless when learning that CG had AWOLED. An eventual run resulted in him being picked up by the police, and about a month later, CG returned to live with his parents.

When at home, mother stated that CG may choose which rules to obey– PG (stepfather) expressed that CG had never obeyed him. Mother viewed her husband to be a perfectionist and added that CG has been helping her as of late when home.

At age 14, CG had been home only six weeks when mother reported that he attempted to rape his 12-year-old female cousin. The police were called, but no charges were pressed (although mother wished they were). CG had also been involved in sex play with his younger half-brother, SG, in the past (at CG's age 13). They were unsure how often CG molested SG or the type of sexual activity, even though SG informed them. They experienced SG as a very angry boy and wondered if he questioned why he was victimized. Prior to CG's visits at home, both parents noticed an increase in SG's acting-out. Generally, parents felt that the younger siblings feared CG.

Mother stated that CG had never accepted being Deaf and hated it. She also relayed that CG was very close to his maternal grandfather who died at CG's age 10; this grandfather (MGF) believed that CG would recover or obtain an operation to reverse his Deafness. She reported that CG also believed this idea.

Upon returning from his visit to the RTF Cottage, CG appeared happy and smiling. He acknowledged that he liked what he had seen and enjoyed the game room in the cottage. He felt that he had made a friend while there. When asked how he felt about coming to this RTF placement, CG was quick to say that he was unsure. When encouraged to make a decision, CG felt that he would prefer the RTF over the placement back in Illinois.

Impressions at Intake

CG presented as a saddened, angry youth with low tolerance for frustration. CG has displayed impulsive behavior since an early age, as well as experienced trauma by a hearing loss at age 3. He was subjected to rejection from his natural father and the loss of his maternal grandfather (MGF) with whom he reportedly shared a close relationship. From CG's age 13–15, aggressive and violent outbursts have necessitated psychiatric intervention. CG has been noted to respond to this intense structure over time; however, CG has chosen to AWOL as a means to control the system.

The parents (PG and MG) presented as verbal, concerned parents, who tended to project their behavior onto past agencies and professionals. The stepfather admitted to a strained relationship with CG, as well as past feelings of embarrassment in regard to his behavior. PG (stepfather) appeared to function as the more rigid and punitive parent, whereas MG (mother) minimized the severity of CG's acting-out. Both parents were sensitive toward feelings of blame and have reportedly been inconsistent in following through, although initially committed. The parents expressed positive feelings about the current acceptance into the RTF placement; nonetheless, they will require a firm consistent approach in therapy in order to make any gains.

CG was accepted into the RTF placement in order to address his sexual acting-out, running, poor peer relations, poor response to authority and his unresolved feelings of being Deaf. CG and parents will need to explore permanency issues, as both parents communicated ambivalence regarding a return home.

Psychological Tests Administered

Performance Scale of the Wechsler Intelligence Scale for Children-Revised (WISC-R)
Raven Progressive Matrices
Test of Nonverbal Intelligence (TONI)
Bender Visual-Motor Gestalt
Developmental Test of Visual-Motor Integration (VMI)
Draw A Person
Thematic Apperception Test (TAT)

Background and Observations

CG, age 15, is reported to have a bilateral, profound, sensori-neural hearing loss which followed his being ill with the mumps at age 3. He communicated using a combination of speech and signing. He seemed to understand communication well when speech was used to communicate to him.

CG was currently placed in the RSD/RTF Residential Treatment Facility for the Hearing Impaired. This evaluation was part of the process to officially complete the placement in the RSD educational portion of the RTF. CG's placement at the RTF was on a voluntary basis and began at his age 15.8.

Previous reports indicated that the presenting problems included "numerous runaways, aggressive outbursts toward staff and peers, labile mood, and suicidal ideation." Also another report included "unmanageable at home, and sexually aggressive behavior toward both male and female peers." CG was noted to be nicely dressed and groomed which indicated that he took pride in his appearance. He was slightly stocky in his build. CG wore two hearing aids to the evaluation. He reported that the aids do not help him except when he wants to hear the guitar or drum.

Mental status evaluation indicated clear thought processes and good orientation. He reported no problems with eating and that he frequently tossed and turned while sleeping. He reported that he has frequently been in trouble in the past for drinking, smoking pot, fighting, and stealing.

CG interacted in an open and friendly manner. He seemed to be satisfied by his performance on tests. He confidently produced a full effort. He sustained a good attention span. He performed at an average to fast rate. He demonstrated skilled, planned, logical solutions to tasks. He carefully monitored himself for errors. CG's sustained cooperation for about three hours was excellent (this evaluation followed a morning of audiological evaluation).

Test Results

CG obtained a Performance Scale IQ of 129 on the WISC-R which placed him at the top end of the Superior Range and at the 97th percentile in comparison to his age peers. Subtest performance indicated some variability in cognitive ability with a range from average to superior. On the Test of Nonverbal Intelligence, which measures intelligence as problem solving ability, CG obtained a TONI quotient of 108, which placed him at the 70th percentile. On the Raven, he obtained an IQ equivalent of 110 to 118 and was at the 75th percentile. All tests indicated above average cognitive abilities. Although the TONI and Raven were somewhat lower than the WISC-R Performance Scale, these differences seemed more reflective of areas of varied cognitive ability rather than a true discrepancy in scores.

As noted above, some variability was produced on subtests of the WISC-R. CG was highest on the Object Assembly Subtest, which measures ability to organize parts into an integrated whole dealing with familiar objects, and produced a perfect performance receiving maximum credit for each of the items. CG demonstrated particular speed and skill at completing this subtest and may have benefited from memory of past evaluations. CG was superior on the Picture Completion, Picture Arrangement and Block Design Subtests. CG was able to respond with the correct word for most items on the Picture Completion Subtest and responded quickly. He was very fast and skilled on the Picture Arrangement and Block Design Subtests. CG's lowest score, in the Average Range, occurred on the Coding Subtest, which measures visual-motor dexterity, visual-motor integration, and the ability to learn new information in an associative context. On this subtest he worked at a fast pace, seemed to use memory, but also got stuck toward the end. Possibly as the time pressure increased, CG's anxiety interfered with his concentration.

Visual-motor integration skills as measured by the Bender and the VMI appeared to be at least age-level appropriate. He produced 23 of the 24 VMI designs correctly and the one error was a minimal error. CG produced all Bender designs correctly and was also able to produce 6 of the designs from memory.

The human figure drawing made by CG was quite elaborate. He explained that the person he portrayed was Adolph Hitler. He included the uniform with armband, gloves, hat, gun, ribbons, buttons, and a moustache. When asked about the drawing, he explained that he drew Hitler because he doesn't like him and because he killed Jews and the Deaf.

TAT stories focused on themes of violence, death and sadness. One story also focused on happiness and freedom following an escape from prison. There tended to be an absence of substance to outcomes. For example, in one story a man killed his son for money and was happy about the money, but there was no more elaboration of the outcome. One story with a healthier outcome focused on a woman who attempted to kill herself because her boyfriend had killed himself. The outcome of the story focused on the girl getting help and finding another boyfriend. The stories did not indicate any strong healthy relationships, especially among family members. One of the strongest family-related stories was a lonely boy sitting in the doorway of the home where his family died in a fire and later would grow up with memories of his parents. Family relationships are potentially very confusing for CG. He seemed to be preoccupied with aggressive impulses. While he appeared to express hope for the future, much of his view reflected a vague and meaningless environment.

Psychiatric Evaluation

CG, age 15, was seen for psychiatric evaluation in connection with his admission to the RTF for the hearing impaired. Past evaluations of CG suggested that he was potentially a bright youngster (Performance IQ of 121, alter 129) who had considerable problems accepting his Deafness, suffered from low self-esteem and showed manifestation of a low frustration tolerance, especially with respect to inhibiting sexual impulses. He was thought to do best in a structured environment where he could be kept active. At the Western New York Children's Psychiatric Center he was started on Serentil (Mesoridazine) 25 mg. qid., a neuroleptic which has been continued to the present time.

CG had been attending school on campus, but will be tried at the Rochester School for the Deaf (RSD). Earlier in his stay, CG AWOLED a number of times but seems to have stopped this practice because he considers himself to have "more freedom" since the start of the RTF. However, in recalling where he liked it best in the past, he mentioned the Center for Deaf in Chicago was where "they controlled me better." His home visits have been more peaceable and his younger siblings were said to be less afraid of him now that he does not sexually molest them. CG has a strong interest in go-carts, motorcycles, and mechanical things. His ambition is to be a lumberjack, a bionic engineer, mechanic, or builder of robots. In any event, he prefers working with his hands. In school, he considers himself to be poor in Math, but liking Reading, Social Studies, and Science. As for his past sexual problems, he believes that he has put these behind him since he has sexual involvement with girlfriends when he goes home.

Mental Status

This round-faced adolescent smoked during the initial part of the interview which was conducted with an interpreter. CG was most cooperative and gave the impression of being fairly intelligent. He spoke earnestly of having made a number of improvements and wanting to continue along those lines while in the RTF. He saw himself as being a better listener, trying to obey the rules more, and stopping his AWOL behavior. There were still some indications that he takes umbrage with rules. For example, he expressed dislike of certain staff that followed him and reminded him of the rules. Moreover, there were some contradictions in his speaking of doing best in a very controlled environment while favoring few restrictions. For each of his past offenses, he was quick to state that he had either overcome them or he was well on his way to do so. For example, stealing was no more an issue since he has money. At the same time, he was unaware that he was deceiving his parents when he spoke of having bought motorcycles, which he stored at a friend's house so that his parents would not know about these purchases. The past accident with a motorcycle when he was 11 years old had led to the parents' prohibition about riding such a vehicle. CG also denied having any fears or anxieties, yet, spoke about ghosts which he thought were responsible for the noises he hears at night; for example, of pots and pans being knocked together or believing to hear footsteps behind him. He also described visual images he has of cars racing by when he is daydreaming at night. The youth went on to deny the existence of ghosts and could state that both his auditory and visual hallucinations were imaginary. When he sees certain television programs, particularly about a man who kills girls for sex, he is frightened that he may be killed. Once again, he denied sleep problems or having bad dreams. There were no clinical signs of a pre-psychotic thought disturbance. Although somewhat sober at times, there seemed to be no affective disturbance in this boy. He had the capacity to form relationships; although, he was cautious about involving himself to a point where he might become vulnerable to being rejected. His distrust of adults leads him to test and even provoke to see if he will be rejected. He would benefit from insight-oriented counseling, and creative art therapy (given is propensity for hands-on experiences) in addition to a tightly-run program where expectations and limits are clearly spelled out for him. Consistency and fairness are both necessary for CG to build up his trust in adults and gain in self-confidence.

Diagnosis Upon Admission to RTF Unit

Axis I: Identity Disorder of Adolescence   313.82
Axis II: Borderline Personality Trait
Axis III: Profound Bilateral Sensory Hearing Loss Following Mumps

Abbreviated Art Therapy Diagnostic Assessment

Subject: CG
CA: 15.9
Tests Administered: Kinetic Family Drawing (KFD)
                          House Tree Person (HTP) Chromatic and Achromatic
                          Cognitive Art Therapy Assessment (CATA)
                          Silver Drawing Test (SDT)

HTP Results

CG was administered the House Tree Person Test (HTP). The Chromatic and Achromatic replies yielded similar responses. An overall pattern of need for stability was prevalent in all three of the symbols (house, tree, person). His tree drawing was indicative of his general approach to the battery. Although the tree was initiated at the base (indicating his need for stability) it's blossom depicted disconnection and chaos (Hammer, 1980; Oster & Crone, 2004). The branches were stumped and cut off. CG described the upper branches as "dead." A tiny, stick figure dwarfed by the tree accented CG's view of himself as insignificant and weak. Later, when CG illustrated a person, he delineated Bruce Springsteen, a rock singer. His articulation of a musician underscored the resistance to his handicap and his desire to be a part of the hearing world.

KFD, SDT & CATA Results

The Kinetic Family Drawing (KFD), Silver Drawing Test (SDT), and the Clay Component of the Cognitive Art Therapy Assessment (CATA) were administered in weekly intervals. CG received a total score of thirty-five (35),

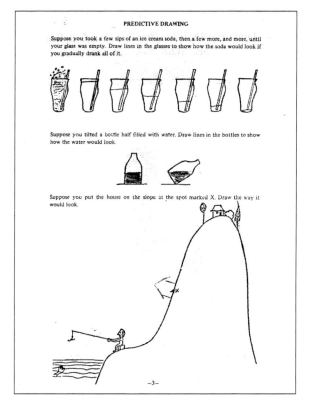

Figure 10–1.

which places him in the sixty-sixth percentile (66%) for grade ten (10). The score appeared to reflect a lower performance than possible due to boredom and general fatigue.

As can be seen by CG's above SDT predictive drawing subtest response, he fails to provide the proper verticality for the house response and instead embeds it into the mountainside. Given his age and ability to predict verticality in the above drawing (that is making the tipped water parallel to the table surface), his response on placing the house perpendicular to the mountain was not only a surprise but typical of a much younger child's ability for conservation and sequencing.

On the next subtest of the SDT, again the response was a surprise: while CG demonstrated to render what was directly in front of him, the transparency of the cylinder on the left as well as far right indicated the response of a much younger child.

Finally, on the final subtest of the SDT, Drawing from Imagination, CG's ability to select, combine, and represent a story from the supplied images rendered a moderate negative theme and reflected CG's identification con-

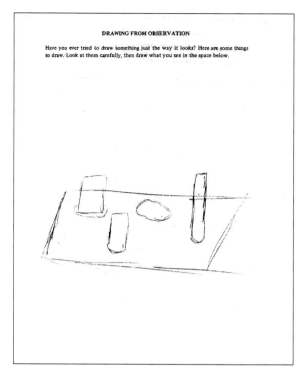

Figure 10–2.

comitant with victim and aggressor.

CG spent most of his time elaborating on the KFD response. Both his mother and stepfather had their backs to CG, indicating his perception of their abandon. Interestingly enough, CG "forgot" to give his half-brother and sisters facial features until this worker pointed out the omission. Again, this underlined CG's unresolved feelings within the family system.

Upon completing the KFD, the CATA unleashed aggressive tendencies connected to the family system. CG chose the clay medium and fashioned a saber. The sword clearly expressed CG's inner hostility and aggressive feelings. Given that he had just completed the KFD, it is quite possible that his aggressive feelings were related to family dynamics.

On the CATA painting response, CG yielded regressive splattering and played with the medium. He described the less chaotic elements as "future life, free of pollutants." The chaotic scrawls he described as "dirty" and "disordered." CG's attempt to reorder his world suggested an inner struggle to realign himself with a hearing world and his family.

CG's drawing on the CATA clearly depicted his resistance and denial of this dilemma. CG drew Captain Hook, with a myriad of handicaps ranging

DRAWING FROM IMAGINATION

On the next two pages are pictures of people, animals, and things. Choose two picture ideas, one from each page, and think of something happening to them.

When you are ready, turn back to this page and draw a picture about what is happening. Don't just copy these pictures. You can change them and draw other things, too.

When you have finished, write a title or name for your picture on the line below.

Title or Story ....

On The street there was a cat
walking Down, met a Dog they started
fighting .

-5-

Figure 10–3.

Figure 10–4.

from his hooked hand to patched eye. Illustrating a handicapped man seemed to personify the ultimate denial of his Deafness. This was also apparent in his verbal associations to the drawing.

SUMMARY AND RECOMMENDATIONS

CG is a bright, personable teenage boy, who is profoundly Deaf and has a serious history of conduct disorder difficulties. Although on the surface he appeared controlled, expression of internal turmoil broke through in his nonverbal and signed/verbalized responses to the artwork. CG has demonstrated the need for placement in a structured mental health setting and has also demonstrated the ability to benefit from the clear, structured guidelines provided by mental health facilities.

Academically, CG has excellent cognitive ability and when motivated and interested, he can sustain performance at a high level as indicated by previous psychological testing and art therapy batteries herein. The educational environment will need to provide an atmosphere that can focus on treatment issues as well as education. (Documented history demonstrates that CG's emotional needs do interfere with obtaining an education–even in a setting designed to meet the needs of his hearing impairment.)

CG is an extremely imaginative teenager and responds well to artistic media for self-expression. Cognitively, he seems to be quite high functioning, falling into the adolescent stage of development (aged 14–17 years), both two and three dimensionally (Lowenfeld and Brittain, 1975). Clearly, CG has a multitude of internal distressors, to which he responds as indicated by his responses on the batteries herein and his verbal and written associates to the artwork. Individual art therapy coupled with family art therapy is highly recommended to offer CG an avenue for ego identification, ego maturation, sublimation of aggressive and sexual impulses, family intervention and acceptance of his Deafness.

Treatment Conference Post-Art Therapy Diagnostic Work-Up

(*Editor's Note:* Prior to the session following the Diagnostic Art Therapy Session, a treatment conference ensued. Below are the highlights from the various clinicians who worked with CG.)

CCW (Primary Child Care Worker for CG)
1. CG expressed a continual need to be like his stepfather (PG) and accepted by him.
2. CG continually denied of sexual (gay) feelings.

Psychiatric Summarization
1. Stepfather objected to CG's friends–stepfather reported conflicts but doing things together at the same time.
2. Displaced covert negative feelings regarding biological father against stepfather; CG has been unable to admit positive feelings toward stepfather.

3. CG has not shown much emotion, yet no sign of oppositional behavior has been present.

Director of RTF Unit

1. CG didn't wait for stepfather at bus stop (met cousin instead during home visit).
2. CG reported weekend conflict with stepfather.
3. CG recognized father's ability to calm down and not escalate during the conflict.

RSD, Educational Therapist Report

1. CG's behavior has been one of positive leadership with his Deaf peers.
2. CG's follow-through with projects has decreased; he is scattered and unable to organize and loses interest quickly–he needs structure to start (Art Therapy is the opposite of this for him, oddly enough).

Social Worker Report

(*Editor's Note:* Social Worker is Deaf, which aids in role-modeling and enhanced communication for this young adolescent.)
1. CG's issues of Deafness increased.
2. Social worker has attempted to focus on impulse control.
3. Social worker's communication with parents–father didn't show up for therapy, but CG handled this well.
4. CG seemed depressed–CG expressed his inability to stay away from trouble.
5. CG and social worker discussed CG's prior sexual activity–contact with boys and girls in the past.

Discussion Amongst Clinical Staff

1. Issue of self-worth seemed ubiquitous (CCW, school, social worker, et cetera).
2. Emotional constricted regarding inappropriate behavior (according to psychiatrist) self-critical, et cetera.
3. Stepfather stopped seeing counselor, mother continued with social worker
   a. Parents need to identify different kinds of feelings.
   b. Parents need to have contact with counselor and follow through with treatment planning.

Significant Sessions

(*Editor's Note:* There were 43 sessions with CG, many including his family. Those below will highlight the significant sessions that led to changes over time.)

Session 2–CG

CG and I discussed his feelings about his parents' impending visit to the residential treatment facility (RTF) and his anxiety regarding the visitation. He admitted feeling tense about the situation. It was explained that it might help bridge the gap between the family system; perhaps advancing communication. Nonetheless, he seemed apprehensive yet willing.

Deflecting from the discussion, CG next glazed his sword (from the CATA response, see Figure 10–4 on p. 197) and then couldn't decide what he wanted to do.

He opted to work with clay after looking at several things in the clay cabinet; he created a creature from "outer space." When asked if he felt like an alien or identified with alien creatures, CG signed, "Yes" with no hesitation and talked about the movie *The Day that Time Stood Still*. CG strongly identified with the movie. Identification with this alien creature could be a stand in for a host of issues: Deafness, feeling dissimilar within the family context and/or hearing world environ, identification with the aggressor (alien), low self-esteem, and identity disorder (Burns & Kaufman, 1972; Hammer, 1980; Henley, 1987; Kramer, 1975; Oster & Crone, 2004; Rubin, 1984).

Figure 10–5.

CG created an air supply and voice box for the alien; these items would aide the alien's ability to "translate into English." I interpreted the similarities between the alien and himself–(e.g., the voice box needed for communication with people and his similar difficulties with hearing people). His appeared crushed and he averted eye contact–clearly pained. When asked if this was difficult for him to accept this, he defended saying, "No," that he would just repeat himself continuously to get across his message. We examined how frustrating this must be for him. He remarked that it was, but maybe in the future "all people would know the language."

Of interest are the other features of the above alien: fanged teeth and a large tongue protrude from the mouth area, suggesting a preoccupation with oral aggressive issues (Burns & Kaufman, 1975; Hammer, 1980; Oster & Crone, 2004). As well, the object appears to be quite phallic in nature, with snakelike features bulging out of the encephalon, cone-head/body and a serpentine tail aback of the creature. While highly imaginative in its depiction, the alien hides a deeper meaning for CG and clearly announces his inner Zeitgeist: by definition, an alien would speak a different language, follow a different culture. All of these factors closely mirrored CG's Deaf world and his attempt to navigate a hearing environment.

Sadly, CG's parents failed to show up later that week, further complicating his treatment and feelings of abandonment so obviated in his above work.

Session 8–Family Art Therapy with Mother, CG and Interpreter

Everyone used clay. Based on the preceding meeting with the RTF director and social worker, this worker recommended (after defining art therapy) that CG and his mother create something about the meeting itself. Some of the discussion revolved around the mother's interaction with CG; they seemed to have a fairly good communication (e.g., his mother was amongst the approximate 12% of the population that in fact used some kind of sign language. While mother's efforts were not great, she did participate in minimal sign language and fingerspelling.).

Figure 10–6.

CG decided to make the cottage and himself as a bird flying away from the cottage, yet attached by an umbilical wire.

At this session, this writer interpreted his attachment to the cottage, even in the face of his desire to "fly away" (of interest was the obvious desire for nurturance and connection as clearly delineated via the wire umbilical cord; Burns & Kaufman, 1972; Hammer, 1980), Mother portrayed herself, PG (stepfather), and CG around the dinner table. Missing was sustenance (a meal, plates and/or utensils for eating) as well as the other family members; this could indicate that MG (mother) sees this struggle between CG, PG, and herself, and not as a family issue. All have outstretched hands—perhaps for communication, yet no one is touching. As well, only one family member (CG) is smiling—both mother and stepfather were depicted with rather solemn expressions. CG reiterated his desire to go home and mother did not respond to this in conversation, leaving CG without affirmation either way.

Figure 10–7.

Session 10–CG and Mother only

I set up and asked CG and Mother what they wanted to do—neither one could decide. I suggested perhaps they think of doing something together. (Of course, they also had an equally difficult time coming up with something together so instead I suggested making Christmas tree ornaments since it was close to the holiday season. Sometimes, the art needs to act as an icebreaker, much like to coffee klatch sessions of yesteryear. Once hands are working, anxiety seems to subside and inhibition falls by the wayside.)

Mother made a Santa Claus ornament (Figure 10–8) and CG made a beautiful plaque (Figure 10–9) that said "Noel" on it. While working together, mother reminisced about having both good and bad memories of CG.

She brought up CG's feats as a child: pulling himself upright at 4 months, walking by 7 months, letting himself out of a latched door using a broom at 3 years, and the hearing loss–the pain; breaking windows in his anger. Of course, CG didn't remember this and I interpreted why. At this juncture, together they created Figure 10–10, an angel (albeit playing a trumpet that CG would not be able to hear).

It is moments like these that remind why I have chosen this field and perhaps why it has chosen me to be its conduit. Mom thanked me at the end. This was an extraordinary moment for both.

Figure 10–8.

Things continued to improve; both stepfather and mother attended regular parenting sessions with the social worker, and more family sessions occurred with both parents. Nevertheless, as I have stated in numerous publications (Horovitz, 1999, 2004, 2005), it is difficult to continue on trajectory towards wellness. The reasons are simpler than one would expect: when one has been in a perpetual state of disease and illness, it is easier to remain "sick"

Figure 10–9.

Figure 10–10.

than move toward wellness.

Thus what happened next was no surprise to me. CG and another resident stole $500 from the RTF office, fled to the airport, managed to buy tickets and flew to Chicago.

If nothing else, I had to marvel at this young man's planning and chutzpah. Nonetheless, upon his return (once found), contracts ensued and CG was on strict 24-hour surveillance by staff.

In a later family meeting, stepfather was able to communicate how much he loved CG and hoped he would avoid a life of crime and jail. Below is a rendition of the work created by stepfather, CG in jail (Figure 10–11).

Figure 10–11.

Sessions 10–13 IP (Identified Patient) Tradeoffs

Of interest is something that commonly occurs in family systems: it seems that someone *always* has to remain ill in order to keep the family in perpetual treatment. As CG became better, OG, his biological brother, deteriorated. OG broke into a car to steal a package of cigarettes. This sibling-switching phenomenon occurs quite readily and, in fact, was something that became quite predictable in terms of treatment issues. Naturally, this resulted in bringing in OG for some much needed family work.

And CG continued to get well, gaining accolades for his artwork (Figure 10–12); below is the newspaper write-up of this award as well as the horse's head that he created in individual art therapy that led to this award.

Daily News / Wednesday

Sculpture Picked For Show

A sculpture by C , 16, son of Mr. and Mrs G of has been selected for the 44th annual Scholastic Art Awards Exhibit at Sibley's in Rochester.

The teen is a junior at the Rochester School for the Deaf.

His sculpture of a horse's head is on display through March 1 at the Sibley's Award Gallery, fourth floor of the department store's downtown Rochester building.

C draws and paints in addition to working with clay, his mother said. "He's a very talented young man. We're proud of him."

Figure 10–12.

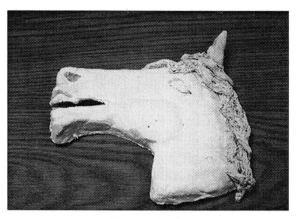

Figure 10–13.

Yet, he couldn't seem to keep up his behavior and switched off with brother OG. We talked about his recent home visitation and how upset he was regarding the visit. Although initially he denied any problems, I told him that I had spoken with his father, who had relayed his anger regarding CG's borrowing his clothing without permission, stealing his hunting gloves, and his socks. (We discussed this while he made a clay mug for his father.) I addressed his obvious sadness regarding the situation with his stepfather. He said that he wasn't able to discuss this with anyone. I empathized with him, saying how sad that was and how lonely he must feel. At first, he denied being sad yet later he admitted that he could talk to his social worker regarding this.

Yet, it was quite clear that talking with the social worker had not resolved the issue. I told him that I hoped that in time he could also talk to me and his parents about these things and that it was okay to use the art time to just work and allow for nonverbal expression. He agreed with sadness and embraced me before he left saying that he felt better. Below are the mugs he created for stepfather during this session

The mugs are quite interesting as obvious stand-ins for CG's desire for unconditional regard and nurturance. Yet the fortressed mug on the left clearly belies the possibility for such avenue–the rim itself with turrets would be near impossible to utilize and the deer mug is adorned with bullet shells, again suggesting concomitant aggression and underlying depression.

Session 31–CG, OG, Mother, Stepfather

OG cried profusely during the session (when the focus lighted on his recent inappropriate behavior–stealing, et cetera) and I asked everybody to

Figure 10–14.

make him something when he threatened to run away from home. CG made him a "Miami Vice Gun." His stepfather made him food. Mother made him a jacket to keep him warm.

Meanwhile, father made CG fishing in a boat; CG joined the stepfather and added an oversized fish to the line (again underscoring CG's need for unconditional regard and nurturance [Figure 10–15]). OG attempted several things but kept nothing suggesting his denial and low self-esteem.

Stepfather told OG that he disliked him as of later and that he was frustrated with him; he told CG that "lately" he was "proud of him and loved him very much."

Shortly after this family session, OG was picked up by the police for another infraction and CG headed towards discharge to home with continued schooling at RSD. While subsequent family art therapy sessions were

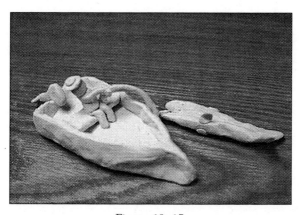

Figure 10–15.

planned post-discharge, the parents failed to comply with treatment and did not bring in CG for continued outpatient care. Therefore, the social worker and I closed the case.

Post-discharge, CG continued to excel in school and actively do artwork. It seemed that the multidisciplinary milieu coupled with individual and family art therapy had provided CG with ample ammunition to resolve some of his family of origin issues, harness ego maturation, increase his self-esteem, and begin to accept his Deafness identification. While clearly, more could have been done, one can only work within the confines that people can handle. In this instance, I can only hope. In the words of Emily Dickinson: *" 'Hope' is the thing with feathers—That perches in the soul—And sings the tune without the words—And never stops—at all. . . ."* (Franklin, 1951).

Case 2: EP

This case involves that of another talented adolescent who struggled with her identification as a Deaf individual. Like most Deaf children, EP was mainstreamed into a hearing world and raised "orally" until approximately age 9, when her hearing impairment deteriorated and she was placed in class for hearing-impaired children.

Complicating matters was her retreat into depression, withdrawing at age 13. This required hospitalization for her Dysthymic Disorder and concomitant rages. This may have been partially due to her mother's alcoholism as well as her own identity confusion with peers and inability to fit into the Deaf or hearing world. (See Genogram and Timeline.)

Psychiatric Evaluation

As described in the timeline below, EP was hospitalized in an inpatient psychiatric hospital (Sheppard and Enoch Pratt) due to social and emotional problems which included: delayed speech, previous bout of hyperactivity (treated with Ritalin until 7 years prior), low frustration tolerance, temper tantrums, poor socialization skills, socially isolated with overdependence on adults, and compensation via imaginary friends and imaginary phone calls to imaginary friends. Family has had difficulty accepting her deafness.

EP viewed her entry into the RTF program as a means of getting away from her mother's alcohol problems and find the means to cope successfully with her "difference" from her peers. EP observed herself as someone who could survive in the hearing world, yet has been increasingly intrigued with the idea of dovetailing with the Deaf world. Moreover, she discerned her parents as "embarrassed" by her. (For example, when she resided at

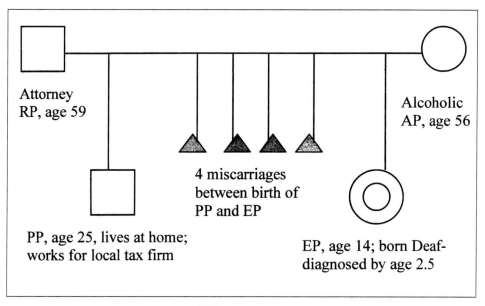

EP's genogram.

Timeline and History:

- Prior to EP's birth, there had been 4 miscarriages with mother losing 30 pounds during the pregnancy with EP. She also had the Asian flu during part of the pregnancy; mother was 40 yo at the time of EG's birth.
- Pregnancy was described as difficult. EP's health at birth was extremely poor; EP's lungs filled with foreign matter prior to birth and it was uncertain whether or not she would live the first 4 days post-birth. EP was transferred to a Neonatal unit and then discharged 10 days later to home.
- EP was bottle-fed and weaned at 6 mos; was slow to eat solid foods.
- Developmentally, EP was somewhat delayed–crawled but did not walk until age 1.5; toilet trained during the day by age 4, but not at night until age 9.
- Hearing loss discovered at age 2.5.
- Age 6, EP hospitalized for minor surgery for a thyroglossal cyst–had tonsillectomy and adenoidectomy at the same time period. She required myringotomies bilaterally due to upper respiratory infection and otitis.
- Siever's disease, involving the heel of her left foot, discovered at her age 12. A plastic heel cup was provided to distribute force equally.
- Allergic to some perfumes and wool; currently on no medication although at 3.5–7 yo, she received Ritalin for hyperactivity. According to the mother, EP is considered to be learning disabled (LD).
- Numerous ear infections from swimming.

- Age 3–5 Elizabeth attended a BOCES program for the Deaf. Yet, she was mainstreamed by kindergarten.
- Ages 6–9, EP was in LD classes; at age 9 her hearing ability decreased and she qualified for a class for the hearing impaired. This was described as a "miserable time" for EP. She did not use signs before age 9 to communicate and all communication was performed orally. EP was encouraged to talk but all her classmates could not talk and, in fact, were quite cruel to her. As a result, EP forged friendships with hearing children.
- At age 13, she was placed at Sheppard and Enoch Pratt hospital for Dysthmic Disorder, Mixed Specific Developmental Disorder and Bilateral Hearing Impairment. As well, it was reported that she was both withdrawn and intermittently explosive. When frustrated she would become destructive, once throwing a rocking chair and resulting to headbanging.
- EP has confusion as to where she fits–she states a preference for operating within the hearing world yet feels "different."

Sheppard and Enoch Pratt Hospital in Maryland, the parents did not let any of the relatives know of EP's whereabouts.) Nevertheless, EP admitted learning much about herself from this previous hospitalization and as a result she has become more openly expressive.

Because EP 's hearing capacity exceeded the other Deaf residents of the RTF, (relying on her oral communication skills) this special status indeed caused a problem and, in fact, counteracted the issues that most plagued her: that is her identification issues.

Diagnosis

Axis I: Identity Disorder   313.82
Axis II: Mixed Specific Developmental Disorder   315.50
          Histrionic Personality Trait
Axis III: Bilateral Hearing Impairment

Abbreviated Results from the Art Therapy Diagnostic Assessment

Tests Administered

Cognitive Art Therapy Assessment (CATA)
Silver Drawing Test (SDT)

Reason for Referral

- Low, self-esteem, poor self-image
- Artistic tendencies

- Denial for art therapy treatment (based on previous agency)
- Hysterical behavior
- Identity issues regarding Deafness

Behavioral Observation and Impressions

Initially, EG voiced her objection regarding attending art therapy. By the end of testing situation, EG engaged readily both verbally and through the art materials.

Silver Drawing Test

Predictive Drawing	8
Drawing from Observation	15
Drawing from Imagination	8

Total Score 31, T Conversion Score 44.46; 44% for Grade 10.

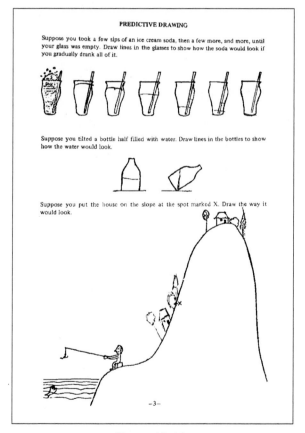

Figure 10–16.

EG's response on the Predicative Drawing subtest of the SDT (Figure 10–16) was quite unexpected. Given her propensity for Drawing from Observation subtest (see Figure 10–17), one would think that her conservation and sequencing abilities would be superlative. Instead, they reflected that of a much younger child. Yet, the second and third subtest (Drawing from Imagination), where EG reconfigured a story from story picture ideas, suggested that she was capable of great cognitive and artistic prowess. Her abilities and attention to detail, as obviated in Figure 10–17, forecasted celebrated artistic inquiry.

Indeed her storyline, "Timid Cat of a Blindmice" (sic) suggested a reference to disability and was perhaps a "stand-in" for some of her own issues regarding her own Deafness and perceived differences.

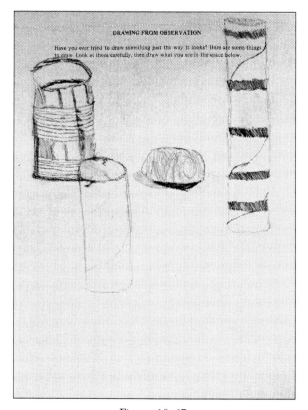

Figure 10–17.

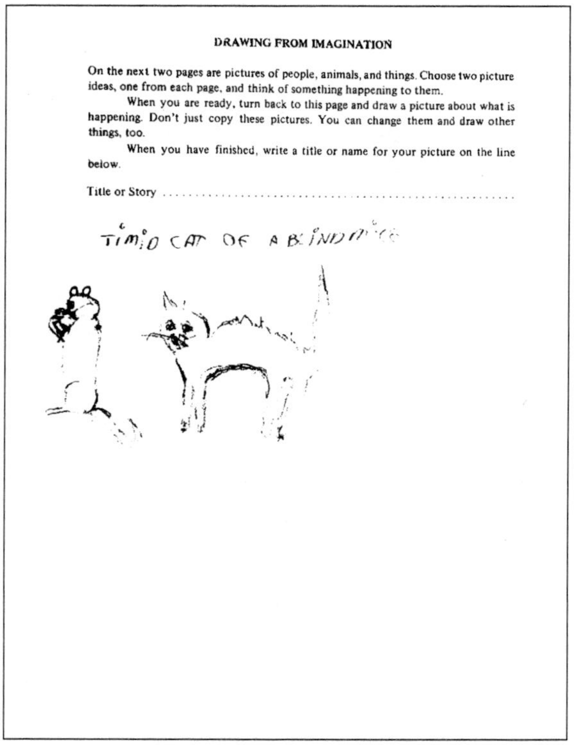
DRAWING FROM IMAGINATION

On the next two pages are pictures of people, animals, and things. Choose two picture ideas, one from each page, and think of something happening to them.

When you are ready, turn back to this page and draw a picture about what is happening. Don't just copy these pictures. You can change them and draw other things, too.

When you have finished, write a title or name for your picture on the line below.

Title or Story . . . .

Figure 10–18.

CATA Results

Developmentally, EP fell into the Adolescent Stage of Development, age 14–17 years, (Lowenfeld & Brittain, 1975). Both her drawing and painting responses yielded much investment and seemed to reflect her need for alienation and isolation from others. However, the clay subtest, a lone seagull, perched atop a dock pots, most aptly mirrored her feelings of alienation, isolation and fragility (see Figure 10–19).

Indeed, during the above session, she reiterated her resistance to art therapy, asking if she would need to come if she "got better." I interpreted her fear of working with me and articulated that if she desired the sessions could be nonverbal. This seemed to lull her inner voice that constantly nagged at her as she made health-related gains in treatment. Offering her control of the direction of the therapy seemed to quell those inner demons.

Figure 10–19.

SUMMATION AND RECOMMENDATION

EG responded well to the art materials and developmentally the test results reflected appropriate cognitive functioning, approximately 14–17 years, (Lowenfeld & Brittain, 1975). Overall, the results revealed EG's feelings of inadequacy and low self-esteem. Although she attempted to mask her fragility, her protests reflected her inner fears.

In the final testing session, EG expressed her desire to continue individual treatment and engage her mother (specifically) in family art therapy sessions. While individual art therapy appointments (twice weekly) and eventual monthly family art therapy sessions were recommended, there were 42 individual art therapy sessions and no family sessions since the parents never followed through for treatment. Objectives included forming a therapeutic alliance and utilizing the art materials to express feelings of inferiority, isolation and low, self-esteem. As well, since EG claimed to have a nonexistent twin sister, it was hoped that cognitive, behaviorally-oriented sessions could eliminate the need for the alter-ego, enhance her sense of self, and allow for greater ego maturation and gratification vis a vis the art materials.

Significant Sessions

Of interest is what happens when allowing for therapeutic self-management. In this case, it enabled EG to discuss the very feelings that she protested against during the preceding diagnostic assessment. By offering EG the space *not* to divulge her feelings, a dike was released. In the next few weeks that followed, EG was a watershed of discourse: she talked about her emotional descent, which led to the Sheppard-Pratt hospitalization. EG was depressed over many things at the time: her mother's alcoholism, father's denial of mother's problems and retreat into work, her brother's failure at law school, her struggle with weight gain and her inability to cope with all of these factors. This pronouncement flooded the well stream of therapy, like a cascading waterfall. While it was positive for her to release these pent-up feelings, it was abundantly clear that my armament would need to include therapeutic- kit gloves, donned and ready for the approach-avoidant posture that was sure to follow. Therapy is like a dance sometimes. For every step forward, there seems to be a two-step retreat backward. Getting better and change is very hard work. Her resulting artwork for this time was as clear a metaphor as one can get in this field of ours that by-steps the collective unconscious.

Figure 10–20.

In this drawing of a fragile white rabbit, EG divulged the parts that she related to: like the White Rabbit in Carroll's tale *Alice in Wonderland*, EG always felt like she, too, was racing. (For sure, her mind was.) She described the flip side as a red dragon, which was angry and trying to get her to slow down. The mixed metaphors were fairly interesting but what was really fascinating was her inner recognition and identification with her more "manic" qualities (the racing rabbit), which left her clearly in the seat of concomitant depression and rage in the form of the angry red-dragon. For the next few sessions, she worked nonverbally albeit entering wanting to her "spill her guts" yet being unable to "talk."

Yet in the next few weeks, her discourse was emotionally-laden, continuous and bordered on hysterical, histrionic patter. Topics included her fixation on anorexia nervosa, projections of other family members' "issues" (as opposed to her own), continuous fantasies about her twin sister and being discharged from treatment. Since she benefited from art therapy, her sessions were increased to three times a week after the first 13 sessions. This was just the medicinal ticket she needed.

EG was finally able to accept her inability to change the familial patterns of behavior. Within the next month her work blossomed and I secured a scholarship for her to attend Memorial Art Gallery classes on Saturday and she began to make active plans to work toward acceptance at NTID or Gallaudet as an art student. As well, she entered a contest and won an Honorable Mention for her fabulous piece below.

And once again, there was the two-step that followed. She retreated into denial around her Deafness. With this onslaught came her prattle about "being able to take care of herself" (while simultaneously admitting that her parents were not able to caretake her) and her refusal to wear her hearing aids so she could pass as "normal." While chipping away at these issues, she worked on a clay hearing aid. Nonetheless, she destroyed and made a "baby seal" in its place. According to EG, the baby seal "always gets killed." Oddly enough, for all of her insight, she was unable to make the metaphoric connection between that baby seal, her familial situation and herself.

Within time, EG was able to accept that while she continuously longed for unconditional regard from her parents (specifically from her mother), this was not about to happen. She finally accepted her parents' steadfast refusal to come to family art therapy sessions (or any family sessions for that matter). No matter how fabulous her art nor how wonderful a gift she could give them (Figure 10–21), it would never be enough. She was Deaf. By default, she was not like them. This acceptance was painful yet, in time, she accepted her self, despite her Deafness. Once this occurred, she flourished, was discharged and did indeed attend NTID.

Figure 10–21.

Figure 10–22.

CONCLUSIONS

While I have no idea what happened to EG after our work together, I felt great comfort knowing that her ability to transition from residential treatment into college was due to the gains she made while in residential care. The combined efforts of the entire interdisciplinary team led to EG's maturation, improvement, emotional, behavioral and cognitive gain. The art therapy allowed for sufficient subliminal and verbal discharge, maximized her potential for emotive resolve and aided her release of artistic talent. And perhaps this is really enough.

REFERENCES

Burns, R., & Kaufman, S. (1972). *Actions, styles and symbols in kinetic family drawings (K-F-D): An interpretive manual.* New York: Brunner/Mazel.

Franklin, R. W. (Ed.). (1951). *The poems of Emily Dickinson.* Cambridge, MA: Harvard College: Presidents and fellows of Harvard College.

Hammer, E. F. (1980). *The clinical application of projective drawings.* Springfield, IL: Charles C Thomas.

Henley, D. (1987). Art therapy with the special needs hearing impaired child. *American Journal of Art Therapy, 25* (3), 81–89.

Horovitz, E. G. (1999). *A Leap of faith: The call to art.* Springfield, IL: Charles C Thomas.

Horovitz, E. G. (2004). *Spiritual art therapy: An alternate path.* (Second Edition complete with new CD-ROM), Springfield, IL: Charles C Thomas.

Horovitz, E. G. (2005). *Art therapy as witness: A sacred guide.* Springfield, IL: Charles C Thomas.

Horovitz-Darby, E. G. (1988). Art therapy assessment of a minimally language skilled deaf child. Proceedings from the 1988 University of California's Center on Deafness Conference: *Mental Health Assessment of Deaf Clients: Special Conditions.* Little Rock, Arkansas: ADARA.

http://kidshealth.org/parent/medical/digestive/pyloric_stenosis

Kramer, E. (1975). *Art as therapy with children.* New York, NY: Schocken Books.

Lowenfeld, V., & Brittain, W. L. (1975). *Creative and mental growth* (6th edition). New York, NY: Macmillan.

Oster, D. G., & Crone, P. C. (2004). *Using drawings I assessment and therapy* (2nd ed.). New York & Britain: Brunner-Routledge.

Rubin, J. A. (1984). *The art of art therapy.* Levittown, PA: Taylor & Francis.

Silver, R. (2002). *Three art assessments.* New York, NY: Brunner-Routledge.

AUTHOR INDEX

A

A. G. Bell Associates, 139, 146
Ainsworth, M. D. S., 97, 109
Allen, P., 158, 161
Altshuler, K. Z., 11, 14, 22, 58, 60, 61, 81, 82
American Psychologist, 144, 146
Anderson, F., 165, 180
Annual Survey of Hearing Impaired Children and Youth, 9, 22
Arnos, K. S., 9, 23
Atkinson, J. M., vii, xxiii, 5, 83, 84, 95, 97, 99
Axline, V., 167, 169, 180

B

Bahan, B., 8, 9, 10, 22
Bailey, J., 156, 161
Barbe, W. B., xx
Baroff, G. S., 11, 22
Beaulaurier, R. L., 144, 146
Bell, J., 165, 180
Bender, L., 159, 161
Bettelheim, B., 114, 129
Bienvenu, M. J., 138, 146
Bowen, M., 41, 57
Brannigan, G. C., 47, 57
Brauer, B. A., 7, 11, 23, 60, 63, 81, 163
Brittain, W. L., 47, 51, 57, 81, 198, 213, 214, 218
Brucker, M. A., vii, xxiii, 5, 59
Buck, J. N., 47, 57
Bull, T. H., 83, 109
Burch, S., 136, 137, 146
Burns, R. C., 47, 49, 57, 89, 90, 109, 200, 201, 202, 218
Buss, D., 151, 152, 161

C

Caccamise, F., 45, 57
Calderon, R., 132, 139, 146
Canter, D. S., 155, 161
Carretero, M., 149, 161
Casterline, D., 11, 23
Chomsky, N., 149, 161
Cooper, A. F., 78, 81
Corbett, C. A., 23
Corsini, R., 18, 22
Critchley, E. M. R., 78, 81
Crone, P., 94, 96, 109, 200, 201, 218
Croneberg, C., 11, 23
Crystal, D., 150, 161

D

Decker, S. L., 47, 57
Delk, M. T., 42, 58, 82, 97, 109, 150, 162
Deming, W. E., 81
Dirst, R., 45, 57
Dissanayake, E., 151, 161
Dobbs, D., 152, 161
Duchesneau, S. M., vii, viii, xxiii, 5, 7

F

Fletcher, P., 150, 161
Forquer, S., 164, 180
Fourcin, A. J., 149, 161
Franklin, R. W., 208, 218
Friedemann, V., 173, 180
Frost, J. L., 145, 146
Fusfeld, I. S., 25, 39

SUBJECT INDEX

A

abandonment, 73, 97, 183, 201
abuse, viii, 66, 82, 172, 178, 180, 182
abusive, 21, 187
adenoidectomy, 209
adolescent(s), xxiv, 24, 82, 84, 164, 166, 170,
    179, 180, 182, 183, 185, 187, 189, 191,
    193, 195, 197, 198, 199, 201, 203, 205,
    207, 208, 209, 211, 213, 215, 217
adult(s), vii, viii, xiv, xxiii, 5, 21, 22, 23, 26,
    28, 39, 59, 60, 61, 63, 67, 69, 71, 73, 75,
    77, 79, 81, 83, 102, 118, 122, 128, 145,
    173, 178, 183, 184, 187, 193, 194, 208
aggression, 20, 65, 87, 101, 114, 167, 171, 172,
    173, 176, 206
Alexander Graham Bell Association for Deaf
    and Hard of Hearing, 139
ALLALO, 154
All-Russian Organization for the Deaf
    (VOG), 137
American Art Therapy Association (AATA),
    ii, viii, ix, 39, 109
American Sign Language (ASL), 8, 10, 11, 12,
    14, 15, 16, 17, 18, 20, 21, 23, 43, 44, 51,
    65, 66, 72, 73, 81, 82, 112, 132, 138,
    139, 149, 155, 166
Americans with Disabilities Act, 12, 23, 138
Ameslan, 42, 43, 149, 150, 153
amplification devices, 8, 9
anger, xiv, 43, 44, 51, 52, 56, 73, 77, 85, 167,
    171, 173, 176, 177, 178, 188, 203, 206
anxiety, 15, 68, 86, 96, 113, 114, 116, 129,
    145, 163, 166, 191, 200, 202
Asia, 140, 144
Asian and Pacific Decade of Disabled
    Persons, 144

Asian, 144, 147, 209
auditory, xx, 3, 5, 19, 20, 65, 78, 83, 112, 193
autistic savant, 128, 129
autistic, viii, 11, 65, 111, 113, 114, 116, 117,
    119, 124, 125, 129, 130
AWOL, 182, 189, 192, 193

B

behavioral disturbances, 61, 65
Bender Visual-Motor Test, 159, 190
Bender-Gestalt Visual Motor Test II, 47
bilingual, 43, 135, 139, 150
body image, 66, 96, 116, 176
borderline, 72, 194
Britain, 134, 135
British Sign Language (BSL), 135

C

Caucasian, 9, 13, 186
chronic fatigue syndrome, 15
cochlear implants, 8, 9, 139
CODA's (Children Of Deaf Adults), 42, 83,
    97, 100, 150
Cognitive Art Therapy Assessment (CATA),
    39, 46, 49, 85, 86, 89, 112, 194, 196,
    200, 210, 213
collective consciousness, 144
collective unconscious, 215
Computer Assisted Learning (CAL), 149,
    155, 156, 157, 158, 159, 160, 161
Conduct Disorder, 187, 198
confidentiality, 18, 63, 174, 175
countertransference, 18, 73
cross-cultural, 17, 33, 150
Cytomegalovirus infection, 15